Hilary Matfess
Putting Women in their Place

Women, Peace and Security

Edited by
Sara E. Davies and Jacqui True

Volume 7

Hilary Matfess

Putting Women in their Place

Gender, Power, and World Politics

DE GRUYTER

ISBN (Paperback) 978-3-11-165948-0
ISBN (Hardcover) 978-3-11-166442-2
e-ISBN (PDF) 978-3-11-166288-6
e-ISBN (EPUB) 978-3-11-166361-6
ISSN 2941-2110

Library of Congress Control Number: 2025943850

Bibliographic information published by the Deutsche Nationalbibliothek
The Deutsche Nationalbibliothek lists this publication in the Deutsche Nationalbibliografie;
detailed bibliographic data are available on the Internet at http://dnb.dnb.de.

www.degruyterbrill.com
Questions about General Product Safety Regulation:
productsafety@degruyterbrill.com

For Lily, for being the best part of my day.

Acknowledgments

I am so profoundly grateful to all of the people that have worked so hard to make this book possible. I am deeply indebted to all of the people that have spoken to me for my research over the years, from Nigeria to Ethiopia, to Colombia, to Uganda, and elsewhere. I can only hope to do your stories justice. I am also grateful to the editorial team I've had the pleasure of working with. From our first conversation—underneath dueling pistols at Denver's Brown Palace—Ze'ev Sudry has been an incredible wall to bounce ideas off of and a cheerleader for this project. Thank you for your support and your friendship. Thank you also to Jacqui True and Sara Davies for believing in this project, letting it have a home in the Women, Peace and Security series, and for your pioneering work as feminist scholars and community builders. Thank you as well to Judah Grunstein for helping me refine my authorial voice and for showing me that there is a need for accessible, feminist analysis of world events. Thank you to my small but mighty team of research assistants: Linda Egbubine, Mattie Embry, Clara Normand, and Jonathan Rockford. Your help was invaluable! Thank you as well to the local cafés that have let me camp out for hours at a time writing: Bivouac Coffee in Evergreen and Corvus Coffee in Littleton.

Finally, I would not have been able to do this work without the unfailing support of my friends and family. Thank you to Kait Sims, for all of the feedback you provided on this project and for being the most thoughtful, funny, and supportive friend I could ask for. Thank you to my mom and dad for being incredible grandparents to Lily — and for taking her for hours at a time so I could do some deep thinking and writing. Thank you to my husband, Dan, for making the coffee in the morning, understanding my inability to work at a clean desk, and sharing his life with me. Thank you to my dogs, Dolos and Nyx, who are steadfast albeit incompetent research assistants. Finally, I owe a great deal of gratitude to my daughter, Lily. She is a chaos muppet, an unrelenting source of joy, and the greatest thing to ever happen to me.

https://doi.org/10.1515/9783111662886-001

Contents

Acknowledgments —— VII

Prologue and the Scope of the Book —— 1

Chapter 1
Introduction —— 4
    Learning the Lingo —— **5**
    Sex, Gender, and Gender Norms —— **5**
    Masculinity, Femininity, and the Gender Hierarchy —— **7**
    Intersectionality and the Gender Hierarchy —— **11**
    Gender Hierarchy as an Analytical Framework —— **13**
    Contributions and Aims of this Book —— **14**

Section I: Politics and Gender Hierarchy

Chapter 2
Gender Hierarchy and Everyday Politics —— 19
    What Women (and Men) Want (Politically): Political Preference and
    Participation Gaps —— **21**
    Gender Hierarchy and Socialization in the Home —— **25**
    Parents as the First Example of Political Engagement —— **27**
    Motherhood and Gendered Political Socialization —— **28**
    Fatherhood and Political Socialization —— **30**
    When Private Matters become Public Concerns —— **31**
    Conclusion —— **34**

Chapter 3
Gender Hierarchy and Behavior of Political Elites —— 36
    Party People: Political Parties and Gender Hierarchy —— **37**
    How Female Political Elites Behave —— **40**
    Women on the Campaign Trail —— **40**
    Women in Office —— **42**
    Substantive and Descriptive Representation: Do Women Represent Other
    Women in Office? —— **44**
    How Male Political Elites Behave —— **45**
    On the Campaign Trail —— **45**

How Male Elites Behave in Office —— **48**
Substantive and Descriptive Representation: Do Men Represent Other Men? —— **51**
Conclusion —— **53**

Section II: **Economics and Gender Hierarchy**

Chapter 4
Gender Hierarchy in the Household Economy —— 57
The Household as an Economy —— **58**
The Gendered Consequences of Household Economics —— **59**
Historical Roots of Gendered Labor —— **63**
Breadwinners and Homemakers: Gender Norms that Govern the Household Economy —— **64**
Renegotiating the Household Bargain —— **67**
Conclusion —— **71**

Chapter 5
Gender Hierarchy and National Economies —— 73
Gender Hierarchy, Government Regulations, and Taxation —— **74**
Who Can Have—or be—Property —— **75**
When Labor is Legal and When it is Exploitative —— **78**
Tax Policies —— **80**
Gender Hierarchy and Government Spending —— **82**
Welfare Programs —— **82**
Childcare Programs —— **84**
Development and Industrial Policies —— **86**
Optimism and Caveats about Economic Policies and Gender Hierarchy —— **88**
Conclusion —— **89**

Chapter 6
Gender Hierarchy and International Economics —— 91
Gender and International Trade —— **92**
Gender and International Austerity Programs and Liberalization —— **97**
Gender Hierarchy and International Economic Sanctions —— **99**
Conclusion —— **103**

Section III: **Security and Gender Hierarchy**

Chapter 7
Gender Hierarchy and Justifying War — 107
 Why do We Go to War? — 108
 Masculinity and Warfighting — 108
 Femininity and Recruitment into Armed Groups — 113
 Conclusions — 120

Chapter 8
Gender Hierarchy and War — 121
 Gender Hierarchy and Socialization in Armed Groups — 122
 Men's Socialization in Armed Groups — 124
 Women's Socialization in Armed Groups — 127
 Gender Hierarchy and Patterns of Violence in War — 130
 The Legacies of Wartime Socialization under Gender Hierarchy — 134
 Gender Hierarchy and the Socialization of Civilians in War Zones — 137
 Conclusion — 138

Chapter 9
Gender Hierarchy and International Security — 140
 Gender Hierarchy and Likelihood of War — 142
 The Women, Peace, and Security Agenda, Feminist Foreign Policy, and
 State Security — 142
 The State as a Masculine Protector — 147
 Masculine Protectors Abroad — 147
 Masculine Protectors at Home — 150
 Conclusions — 154

Section IV: **The Fight Ahead**

Chapter 10
Gender Hierarchy and Backlash — 157
 Backlash: What is it and Where Does it Come From? — 159
 The Precarity of Masculinity and Backlash Politics — 160
 "Good Girls" and Backlash — 162
 How and Where Backlash Manifests — 163
 The International Community and Backlash — 163

Backlash at the National Level —— **164**
Backlash at the Individual Level —— **169**
Conclusions —— **170**

Chapter 11
Conclusions and the Way Forward —— 172
Way Forward: —— **173**
Eroding Gender Hierarchy —— **173**
In Our Personal Lives, We Can: —— **174**
In National Politics, We Can: —— **175**
We Can Also Push for Change in the International System: —— **178**
Being a Feminist in Public —— **179**
Closing on a Note of Hope —— **181**

Works Cited —— 182

Index —— 212

Prologue and the Scope of the Book

I never intended to study the world by looking at the lives of women. My whole career as a scholar and a feminist and a feminist scholar has basically been a se- ries of accidents and strokes of good luck. When I was a graduate student, I was working with my advisor on a project tracking the Boko Haram insurgency in Northeast Nigeria. I begged my advisor to fund a trip to Nigeria. I like to think that I put together a compelling case that it was difficult to understand the nu- ances of an insurgency in a country I had never even set foot in, but in all likeli- hood, he probably figured that it would be worth the money to buy me a ticket just to get me to stop bugging him.

Ahead of my first trip, I had grand and—in hindsight—ridiculous expecta- tions. I wanted to understand the rebellion that had upended life in North East Nigeria. I assumed that meant I had to speak to the young men that had taken up arms and joined Boko Haram. I had grandiose ideas about that first trip. Em- barrassingly, I pictured myself stepping off the plane and stepping into the shoes of reporters like Christiane Amanpour, getting the story from battle-hardened men barely younger than myself.

Upon arriving in Nigeria, my bubble burst. It became clear almost as soon as I stepped off of the plane in Abuja that I would not have the opportunity to sit down with the folks I thought were at the heart of the war. It turns out that in- surgents in an on-going war are rarely so bad at operational security that a wet behind the ears academic would be able to find them. I wasn't some super spy, I was a 20-something graduate student with some notebooks and a knack for writ- ing.

Frustrated, I set up the interviews that I could get: conversations with women whose lives had been radically disturbed by the war. In retrospect, I'm embar- rassed about how dismissive I was at first. My attitude was basically "fine, I sup- pose I'll talk to the women while I figure out a way to get the real story." I was surprised when these conversations revealed compelling—and unreported—con- flict dynamics alongside stories of profound human courage.

Over the course of subsequent trips to Nigeria, my attitude shifted. These con- versations were no longer a consolation prize but rather fascinating and precious insights into a poorly understood war. The stories that these women told me have stuck with me over the years. For example, Aisha, one of the women I spoke to during a 2016 trip, told me that she had placed her elderly mother in a wheelbar- row and fled her home to Maiduguri, where we met on the grounds of a mosque that had given some land to displaced people to settle amidst the war. She ex- plained to me that she had fled in defiance of the insurgents: "Boko Haram told

https://doi.org/10.1515/9783111662886-002

me to leave my mother behind to come with them to do the work of God. But I told them I could not leave her, and if I did, I would never stop thinking of her." She was now trying to rebuild her life in a new place, living with the threat of another Boko Haram attack hanging over her head—now paired with the daily question of how she and her mother would get enough to eat.

With each trip I took, I became more and more convinced that there was no way that we could understand the war in North East Nigeria without looking at the lives of women. I became furious that women's experiences were rarely considered relevant in the hypermasculine study of "security." Later, diving into feminist security scholarship, I underlined and highlighted with glee and relief V. Spike Peterson's (1992) assertion, "The assumption of men's (more specifically, elite men's) experience as representative of human experience emerged as a systemic bias of codified knowledge and cultural ideologies. Deconstructing the errors of androcentric scholarship revealed — and continues to reveal — patterned distortion of truth claims about 'social reality'" (p 7). But in those early days, I felt frustrated that women were not a part of mainstream security studies.

I wrote my first book, *Women and the War on Boko Haram*, in order to show that taking women's lives "seriously"[1] resulted in a more clear-eyed understanding of how the war was fought, why it began, and what life would be like when it ended. I pursued a PhD in order to investigate these questions even more deeply and to build relationships with other feminist scholars of security (and because it didn't seem likely that I would land a good job in Washington, DC following the election of Donald Trump in 2016).

I'm writing this book now—roughly a decade after I first visited Nigeria and began my career in earnest—for the next generation of researchers, activists, and policy makers. I'm writing this book for everyone that finds themselves curious about or frustrated by how gender shapes the world around them. This is the book I've been drafting in my mind in nearly every conversation I've had with friends and family about the work I do and why it matters.

This book provides an approachable and actionable framework for understanding how women's lives—and the gender inequality that shapes them—are at the center of world politics, global economics, and international security. In the chapters that follow, we consider how gender inequality is important for understanding what causes changes in international politics, economics, and secur-

---

1 Enloe, C. (2013). Investigating crashes and crises as if women mattered. University of California Press.

ity, and how these changes are experienced by men and women.[2] This book illustrates how the lopsided distribution of power between men and women has far-reaching implications for politics, economics, and security.

2 There is important scholarship being done showcasing the perspectives and significance of queer, non-binary, and trans people; however, such work lies beyond the remit of this book.

Chapter 1
Introduction

"No two countries run by women would ever go to war," declared Sheryl Sandberg, apparently in celebration of 2022's International Women's Day. Sandberg made a name for herself both in her role as Chief Operating Officer of Meta (Facebook and Instagram's parent company) and for her 2013 book *Lean In: Women, Work, and the Will to Lead.* As a successful, vocal, and filthy rich white woman, Sandberg became a visible manifestation of #girlboss feminism. The goal of that particular brand of feminism was not necessarily a total overhaul of the political system and economy aimed at a more egalitarian future but rather securing for a certain subset of elite women the same privileges elite men enjoy. At the same time that Sandberg was telling women to lean in and change the world for the better, she was at the helm of an organization radically reshaping the world. Not always for the better.

Sandberg was in charge at Meta when the social media platform served as a springboard for genocidal violence in Myanmar, helped spread Russian misinformation in the run-up to the 2016 American Presidential elections, and was linked to mental health problems in young women (Ghaffary, 2022). That means that by 2022, Sandberg should have known better than to say that the key to world peace was female leaders. As a powerful woman she personally greenlit bad behavior that led to human suffering and instability around the world. Having a woman at the head of the company did not stop bad behavior at Meta.

Saying that the recipe for world peace isn't as simple as "add women and stir" does not mean that women are irrelevant to world politics (Langdon, 2019). Far from it: women's subordination to men (often referred to as "gender hierarchy" or "patriarchy") is one of the most influential forces in world politics. This book considers how gender inequality shapes world politics, economics, and security.

Box 1.1 Defining Gender Hierarchy and Intersectionality

Gender hierarchy is a system of power that affects both men and women. Gender hierarchy doesn't just prioritize men over women (a system called "patriarchy"), it also privileges certain types of men over other men and certain women over other women. Gender hierarchy relies on the idea of a "hegemonic masculinity" that sits atop the hierarchy (Connell and Messerschmidt, 2005).

This chapter will also consider how gender hierarchy intersects with other systems of power, including racial, ethnic, and religious hierarchies. In academic and activist circles, this is referred to as "intersectionality." The Center for Intersectional Justice defines intersectionality as "the ways in which systems of inequality based on gender, race, ethnicity, sexual orientation, gender identity, disability, class and other forms of discrimination "intersect" to create unique dynamics and effects." They emphasize, "All forms of inequality are mutually reinforcing and must therefore be analyzed and addressed simultaneously to prevent one form of inequality from reinforcing another."

The gender hierarchy can explain why Myanmar's military has raped and sexually assaulted women and girls in their campaign against the Rohingya—and why it can be so hard for Rohingya women to report these assaults and get the help they deserve. The hierarchy can explain why young women would join the Islamic State and why young men are so susceptible to radical right-wing and "incel" propaganda in the United States. In short, this book gives readers the tools to understand how women's subjugation is at the heart of world affairs. It gives readers a framework for understanding how gender hierarchy affects world affairs.

But before we can understand the world in a new way, we have to familiarize ourselves with some new vocabulary. This introductory chapter guides readers through a discussion of some key terms in this book, like gender, masculinities, and femininities. This discussion will help readers understand the difference between looking at women and analyzing gender dynamics.

Then, this chapter will introduce a framework for understanding how gender hierarchy sits at the heart of world affairs.

Learning the Lingo

Sex, Gender, and Gender Norms

Drag queen and television star RuPaul sang: "We're all born naked and the rest is drag." What does that mean though? RuPaul's bubbly, foot-stomping song (and whole career, really) highlights that there can be profound differences between our biological sex and our performance of gender (Butler, 1990). In other words, sex refers to "biological male or femaleness," but gender encompasses "the personality traits and conceptions of self that we expect people to have on the basis of their sex" (Sjoberg and Tickner, 2013).

The term gender norms refers to the expectations that we foist upon people on the basis of their biological sex. Some people abide by gender essentialism, or "the belief that males and females are born with distinctively different natures, determined biologically rather than culturally. This involves an equation of gender and sex" (Chandler and Munday, 2011). Others recognize how our behavior and presentation are guided by what is expected of us in our families and communities.

Men and women are judged by different standards. In other words, there are different gender norms for men and women. Although no critical feminist theorist herself, even Sheryl Sandberg (2013) identified the pernicious effects of this hierarchy, writing that "Men are continually applauded for being ambitious and powerful and successful, but women who display these same traits often pay a social penalty" (n.p.). These different standards shape how we perform our gender. A 2017 survey of Americans, for example, found that the most valued traits in men were related to honesty and morality, followed by professional success. For women "physical attractiveness" and empathy topped the list (Parker, Horowitz, and Stepler, 2017). Similarly, a survey of Nigerians revealed four social norms surrounding gender and marriage. The survey identified the influence of ideas like "A respectable woman marries early"; "a respectable woman is submissive to male authority"; "a suitable woman is not promiscuous" and; "a woman is worth more as a wife than as a daughter" (van Veen et al., 2018, p. 3). In both cases, we see pressure for men are to be strong and powerful, while women are expected to be pretty and nice. Those that transgress those expectations are subject to social sanction. In Nigeria, that included "peer pressure, condemnation, exclusion and force" (Van Veen et al., 2018, p. 3).

These expectations and value systems translate into how men and women behave in their homes, communities, and workplaces. That same survey of Americans found that 57% of men said they faced "a lot" or "some" pressure to "be willing to throw a punch if provoked." (Parker, Menasce, and Stepler, 2017, n.p.). Four in 10 reported "a lot" or "some" pressure to "have many sexual partners" (Parker, Menasce, and Stepler, 2017, n.p.). These expectations can also shed light on why American women spend significantly more on keeping up their physical appearances than men (Olya, 2024). The Oxfam survey of gender norms in Nigeria linked the prevalence of those expectations to rates of early marriage and female genital cutting (Van Veen et al., 2018).

But gender norms are not iron-clad. As RuPaul's lyrics (and reams of feminist and queer theory) suggest: gender is a performance. You can transgress the gender expectations that you face or play into them. RuPaul was born biologically male but has become famous around the world for his ability to transform into a statuesque female singer and performer as a drag queen. We might be born with a specific set of genitals, but we make choices about the clothes we wear, the way we carry ourselves, and the hobbies we pursue. Those choices may not be as glamorous as drag queens' gowns and make up, but they can still be seen as a performance of gender—even a form of drag.

It's not only those that play with gender expectations like RuPaul that are performing gender. Think about how professional male athletes' pre-game warm-ups are often designed to make them feel more powerful or masculine. Mitch Marner, a professional ice hockey player from Canada, described one of his favorite warm-ups to Red Bull: "We hammer soccer balls at each other, chirp each other, and try to get into each others [sic] heads early on" (Spriggs, 2021, n.p.). It's not just about loosening up their muscles by kicking around a ball, it's also about riling themselves up with "chirps" (the hockey slang for insults). Insulting others and being insulted is a way of performing the sort of rough-and-tumble masculinity associated with grinning, gap-toothed hockey players. These men are also performing gender.

Women can play up their femininity or defy gender norms by behaving in "masculine" ways. Recent years have seen a surge of "TradWife" (a portmanteau of traditional and wife) content on the internet, in which women play into gender-essentialist tropes and conservative ideals of womanhood (we will discuss this phenomenon more in Chapter 10). These women project an image of domestic bliss, making elaborate meals from scratch in a full face of make-up and flattering (but modest) clothes. They are performing their femininity—when they make an apple pie from scratch in an A-line dress and with their hair down, they are not dressing for efficiency in the kitchen. Just compare their outfits to what professional pastry chefs wear. They are putting on a costume in order to play a part. Tradwives often traffic in the idea that they are meant to behave this way because they are women. This is a classic example of gender-essentialist thinking.

Other women have challenged the predominant conceptualization of femininity. Consider Ilona Maher, the professional American rugby player, who told CBS, "I feel that I can be a beast and can play this very physical, aggressive sport while also keeping my femininity while I do it" (Yuccas and Novak, 2024). Her signature look on the field is a striking red lip, which she told *New York Magazine* is Maybelline Super Stay Matte Ink (LaMantia, 2024). Her incredible mix of powerful physicality and femininity subverts expectations—and has made her an icon for athletic girls and women everywhere, myself included. Ilona, if you are reading this, thank you—and can we please hang out?

Masculinity, Femininity, and the Gender Hierarchy

Gender is both a social construct and a system of ranking, so different genders are not afforded the same status (Kilman, 2013). Gender hierarchy refers to the relative ranking of men and masculinity with respect to women and femininity. In practice, gender hierarchy almost always refers to the subordination of women and femininity to men and masculinity. This situation is often referred to as the "patriarchy," though using the p word often attracts more eye rolls than interest. But gender hierarchy is not as simple as valuing men over women—it's also about ranking certain types of masculinity over others. The notion of gender hierarchy allows us to investigate which types of masculinity and femininity are valued, in a way that the term "patriarchy" does not always lend itself to.

Masculinity under Gender Hierarchy

At the pinnacle of most gender hierarchies is hegemonic masculinity, which is "the currently most honored way of being a man" (Connell and Messerschmidt, 2005, p. 832). It's not enough to be a man—you have to be the right type of man. Boys and men are exposed to powerful incentives to act like "real men"—that is, to embody the characteristics associated with hegemonic masculinity.

Box 1.2: Boys Don't Cry

As a cis woman (meaning someone who was born biologically female and who identifies as a woman), I've only been a spectator of the policing of masculinity that men and boys face. But from my vantage point, it seems exhausting. In the America I came of age in, the ideal man oozed confidence, excelled in work and school, boasted six-pack abs, and pursued an endless stream of physically attractive (female) sexual partners. Insecurity and vulnerability were anathema—which led to a lot of over-compensation.

These expectations are foisted upon even little boys. When I was 9 years old, I played on a "Fall Ball" little league baseball team where I was the only girl. One day at practice, I got hit with a baseball (because I was not especially good at baseball). My eyes welled with tears and my dad (inexplicably an assistant coach) asked me if I was okay. I nodded and ran up to the dugout to give him a hug. After a few seconds of being held and reassured that everything was alright, I happily trotted back onto the field. Just a few minutes later, another player got hit with a ball (our team, as a whole, was not very good at baseball). His eyes started to fill with tears and his dad (also an assistant coach) asked him if he was okay. The little boy angrily wiped at his face and insisted he was fine, rebuffing his dad's outstretched arms. At 9 years of age he knew what type of man he was supposed to be. It wasn't a man that cried and it certainly wasn't a man that hugged. He was going to be a tough guy, a "real man." His dad, dejected and a little embarrassed, retreated into the dugout. Ideas about how "tough" guys should be robbed this little boy of the opportunity to be comforted and his father of the opportunity to hug his son and give comfort.

Because masculinity is associated with prestige, it is something that men want to maintain. However, masculinity is "precarious" and requires vigilant maintenance (DiMuccio and Knowles, 2020). That's where the idea of fragile masculinity comes from: men must constantly work to ensure that their masculinity is pristine, lest they lose their privilege. As academics Sarah DiMuccio and Eric Knowles (2020) note, "a man's failure to adhere to masculine expectations is especially threatening because it can lead, not only to ostracism or a loss of esteem in the eyes of peers, but to the revocation of his very membership in the high-status 'man' category" (n.p.). Academic jargon can make fragile masculinity seem abstract; anyone that has been on a playground, however, knows that it's insulting to tell a boy he "runs like a girl." Boys will run footraces over and over and over on the playground to prove that they don't and to try to reclaim their wounded manhood. If only all responses to emasculation were so harmless.

A *Harvard Business Review* study found that when men felt emasculated at work, they responded with a variety of anti-social behaviors, "including withholding help, mistreating coworkers, stealing company property, and lying for personal gain" (Kouchaki et al., 2023). When men feel emasculated politically, "backlash" against women's empowerment often mounts. This can range from the resurgence of traditional gender norms and conservative politics to outright violence against women. Academics Jelena Cupać and Irem Ebetürk note that backlash politics "commonly blame women's progress for causing 'female burnout', 'infertility epidemics', 'emasculation', 'neglected children', and 'moral collapse'" (Cupać and Ebetürk, 2020, n.p.).

Backlash, as we will see in Chapter 10, is a global phenomenon. With Marie Berry and Roudabeh Kishi, I conducted a study examining the relationship between women's representation in parliament and violence targeting women in Kenya. We found that as women's formal representation climbed, so too did the threats they faced while engaged in public life. Even in Sweden—which typically tops the charts of most gender-egalitarian countries—one study found that when women out-earned their partners, they were more likely to go to the hospital for domestic-assault related injuries (Bergvall, 2024).

The worldwide prevalence—and vehemence—of backlash makes more sense when you think about gender inequality as an unequal distribution of power. Women's subordination is not accidental. It is the result of a systematic prioritizing of men and masculinity over women and femininity. And when men see their privilege ebbing, they react swiftly to restore their position atop the hierarchy.

Femininity under Gender Hierarchy

Women, too, are expected to perform their gender and are inundated with messages about what it means to be a "good woman" from a young age. Here I have first-hand experience. As a mildly rebellious pre-teen growing up in suburban Georgia, nearly every day was an opportunity for someone to point out how I strayed from "ladylike" behavior. This included, in one case, a neighbor calling my parents to complain that I was running in just a sports bra and shorts. In 100 degree heat. When I was 12 years old and had no functional need for a bra of any kind.

My parents, eager for me to fit in, enrolled me in a ballroom dance and etiquette class in middle school. I was expected to trade in my t-shirts and jeans for high heels, a knee-length skirt or dress, and white gloves once a week. This wasn't just about enforcing a dress code, it was also about setting standards of how young ladies and gentlemen behaved. This went over with me about as well as you'd expect. Once, when my (mandatory, and mandatorily opposite-sex) partner Tyler was practicing introducing me, the lead instructor told me that my handshake was "emasculating" and that it would be a problem for my partners in the future. Tyler was supposed to be confident; I was supposed to be demure. Tyler eventually got a better handshake, but I never quite figured out the key to lady-like behavior.

Like many tomboys, I've worn my inadequate femininity as a badge of pride. My ability to do so with only minor social censure, however, reflects the gender hierarchy (and my privilege as a well-off white woman from a progressive family). Psychological studies have found that femininity is not subject to the same precarity as masculinity. One study found that when women were given feedback suggesting that they looked less feminine than average, they exhibited higher levels of anxiety and lower self-esteem. However, when they were told that their personalities were not especially feminine, their anxiety did not spike, nor did their self-esteem take a big hit. This is in contrast to men in the study, who had more consistently negative responses to both types of feedback (Wittlin et al., 2024). In short, this study affirms something that so many women have experienced: the incentives to look like a (beautiful) woman but act like a man.

Because femininity is afforded less status than masculinity, some women have sought to improve their status by taking on certain masculine features or by proving they can act like a man. I was struck in my conversations with female veterans of the Tigray People's Liberation Front (TPLF), a rebel group that fought for control of Ethiopia from the mid 1970s to 1991, that many of the women recalled spending much of their early training trying to prove that they were just as strong as their male counterparts, lugging around heavy equipment and never showing fatigue. These women felt tremendous pressure to prove themselves, even though they were members of an organization that abided by a radically gender-egalitarian ideology. One female veteran of the TPLF explained to me: "In the beginning [of the war] when the [political] consciousness was less, we wanted to prove ourselves physically. This was wrong." It took years of fighting for the TPLF and serving as a leader among female TPLF members for her to arrive at this hard-won revelation that she shouldn't have had to act "like a man" to enjoy equal rights. Interviews with women in state-affiliated militaries around the world suggest that this is hardly an isolated experience for women in armed groups. For example, a woman in the British army told researchers: "I can remember being pleased when I'd been classed as 'an honorary bloke'. The term 'bloke(s)' is used even by women to refer to those you work with" (King, 2015, n.p.).

Though masculinity enjoys a privileged position atop the gender hierarchy, there are certain forms of femininity that are more prestigious than others. Mirroring the relationship between hegemonic masculinity and other masculinities, hegemonic femininity sits atop all of the other femininities. As academic Mimi Schippers observed, "Hegemonic femininity consists of the characteristics defined as womanly that establish and legitimate a hierarchical and complementary relationship to hegemonic masculinity and that, by doing so, guarantee the dominant position of men and the subordination of women" (2007). While hegemonic femininity changes over time and manifests differently in different communities, it often centers on "compliance, empathy, and nurturance" (Bose, Tanupriya, and Singh, 2024).

Other studies have confirmed what anyone that has lived through girlhood already knows: hegemonic femininity often involves the performance of such attributes in a manner that upholds their power (Paechter, 2018). The 2004 movie *Mean Girls* captures this dynamic perfectly. Regina George, the high school "queen bee" tells a classmate: "Oh my God, I love your skirt! Where did you get it?" The girl replies that it was her mother's in the 1980s and walks away pleased with herself. Once she has gone, Regina turns to her friend and says "That is the ugliest f-ing skirt I've ever seen" (Mean Girls, 2004). In public, Regina comes across as kind and thoughtful—but she uses her fake compliments to create in-groups and out-groups that cement her position atop the social hierarchy.

Performing femininity can also be a means of self-preservation. Turkish academic Deniz Kandiyoti used the term "patriarchal bargain" to describe such behavior. The deals that women have struck with the patriarchy have changed over time and according to the cultural context that they find themselves in. Across time and space, however, she observes, "women's strategies are always played out in the context of identifiable patriarchal bargains that act as implicit scripts that define, limit, and inflect their market and domestic options" (Kandiyoti, 1988). Women that abide by the requirements of the patriarchy receive protection from that system. Women that defy the patriarchy are left to fend for themselves. Women bargain with the patriarchy to make the best of the crappy hand that they are dealt.

Intersectionality and the Gender Hierarchy

The gender hierarchy is just one way in which power is stratified. It overlaps with other forms of discrimination and domination in any given society. The term "intersectionality" was first coined by activist and legal scholar Kimberlé Crenshaw to describe how each facet of an individual's identity—including their race, class, gender, etc.—intersected to produce unique forms of discrimination and privilege (Crenshaw 1989; for a more digestible explainer see Coaston, 2019). Intersectional analysis considers how various social hierarchies interact to condition communities' and individuals' experiences and opportunities.

Take for example, the notion of hegemonic masculinity and femininity. In many Western cultures, these ideal types are racially coded. The characteristics that might be seen as desirable in a white man could be deemed suspect when exhibited by a black man. An "aggressive" White man in America might be seen as a confident go-getter, whereas an "aggressive" Black man could be interpreted as a threat.

Or consider how in many places in the Global North "white, affluent, heterosexual women are typically best positioned to collect a femininity premium" (Hamilton et al., 2019). A femininity premium is not the cherry on top of the sundae—it is often a matter of physical safety and equal rights under law. A group of academics asserted that:

> Successful performance of hegemonic femininities entitles (white) women to protection. Their purity and respectability are to be defended, which often involves invoking the violence of white men, the police, or other authorities... Notably, many of the gains of white feminism, including protections against domestic violence, increase state involvement in family life in ways that may benefit white women but have disproportionately negative effects on people of color and undocumented immigrants. Rather than the pedestal of the past, white women performing hegemonic femininities are offered a platform—provided they stay on script. They can be cruel, nasty, rude, or simply inconsiderate and then use their tears or discomfort to silence the objections of those in less powerful positions (Hamilton et al., 2019).

In the American south, lynchings of black men were justified on the basis of protecting "vulnerable" white women (Messerschmidt, 2007). But really, such violence was a way to uphold raced, classed, and gendered hierarchies that benefitted elite white men. We've seen a similar dynamic crop up in Europe in recent years as immigrants from the Middle East and North Africa have sought refuge within the Schengen Zone, in which some people have supported xenophobic and discriminatory policies in the name of "protecting" women. Italian academic Sara R. Farris (2017) dubbed this dynamic "femonationalism." As she explained to a journalist, "If you look at how often they [right-wing European politicians] talk about gender issues, it is always to promulgate their anti-immigration and anti-Islam policy" (Stacey, 2024, n.p.).

Others have described how hegemonic masculinity can sometimes depend on the appearance of defending "good" women. In the foundational essay "Can the Subaltern Speak?," Gayatri Chakravorty Spivak critically examined the idea,

"White men are saving brown women from brown men" (Spivak, 1988, n.p.). Often coupled with the efforts to "save" brown women are endeavors to make them more like white women. This is particularly clear when you look at colonial "civilizing" missions. Christian missionaries and European authorities in Africa[1] often put forth a narrative that these women needed "protection" from their own societies (Jeater, 2006). These protections, however, were tied to expectations that African women abide by European moral codes and sensibilities. We'll explore these dynamics in greater detail in Chapter 9 when we discuss the role of the state as a "masculine protector" (Young, 2003).

Gender Hierarchy as an Analytical Framework

In this book, I provide you, the reader, with a framework for understanding the world around you, allowing you to look for how gender hierarchy affects global politics, economics, and security and how men and women experience these phenomena differently. Understanding the wide-reaching implications of gender inequality for international relations is like looking at Claude Monet's famous paintings of water lilies. A pioneering Impressionist painter, Monet used visible brush strokes that, when viewed up close, are beautiful but disconnected. It is only when stepping back to look at the bigger picture that the full landscape and beautiful flowers come into focus. This framework is the step back, which transforms individual studies into a portrait of gender hierarchy's impacts, from the kitchen table to the United Nations General Assembly.

This framework is simple and consists of two parts: First, gender hierarchy drives changes in international politics, economics, and security. Second, gender hierarchy conditions how these changes are experienced by men, women, and non-binary folks (though much of this book focuses just on men and women). This book illustrates how the lopsided distribution of power between men and women has far-reaching implications for politics, economics, and security.

---

1 Some have gone so far as to suggest that gender itself is a colonial imposition. Writing on the Yoruba in southwest Nigeria, Oyèrónkẹ́ Oyěwùmí asserts, "From a Yoruba stance, the body appears to have an exaggerated presence in Western thought and social practice, including feminist theories. In the Yoruba world, particularly in pre-nineteenth century Oyo culture, society was conceived to be inhabited by people in relation to one another. That is, the 'physicality' of maleness or femaleness did not have social antecedents and therefore did not constitute social categories. Social hierarchy was determined by social relations" (Oyěwùmí, 1997, n.p.). Others suggest that interaction with colonial authorities and the slave trade altered gender relations by creating incentives for different performances of masculinity and femininity (Mbah, 2019).

Contributions and Aims of this Book

The book is written to be accessible for the non-expert and, importantly, engaging to a lay audience. This book believes that feminism and feminist international relations are "for everybody" (hooks, 2000). I've written this book with my non-academic friends and family members in mind. Reading about feminist international relations should not feel like a joyless chore. Many of the articles and books that take a feminist perspective on international relations can be dense, full of jargon, and written for other academics. While this work has value (or at least, as an academic that has written those sorts of articles, I hope it does), it is critical to bring these ideas to a broader public around the world.

This book reflects (and, in many places, conveys) my own experiences navigating and understanding the gender hierarchy as a white, American woman. I've included my own experiences for several reasons—because I believe that storytelling is a powerful pedagogical tool, because I think it is a helpful way of illustrating the connection between the personal and the political, and to provide context for how I approach the question of gender hierarchy in world politics. My education (getting my undergraduate and master's degrees at Johns Hopkins University before pursuing a PhD at Yale University) and my professional experiences (working adjacent to the U.S. government in a range of research positions at places like the National Defense University and the Institute for Defense Analyses before taking up a position as a professor at a policy school) were focused on empirical approaches to policy-relevant questions.

This book adopts a liberal framework, which distinguishes between public and private spheres, politics and economics, and domestic and international policy. This book reflects that approach and way of looking at the world. These realms, in reality, often bleed into one another—so much so that a number of academics would argue that these distinctions are not defensible. My adoption of the liberal framework in this book both reflects my own education and my belief that these distinctions are helpful for newcomers to the field.

This book offers several corrections and contributions to the current literature on women, gender, and world politics. First, this book is a response to the flattering, but ultimately untrue, belief that the key to world peace and prosperity is getting women into positions of power. Across a number of government policies, corporate agendas, and political campaigns, we've seen the same theme repeated time and again: if we simply give women a seat at the table, good things will follow. This position has produced policies like quotas for women in a variety of leadership roles and calls for gender-integration of the military. Yet, women have the capacity to be just as cruel, violent, short-sighted, retributive, and competitive as men.

As such, this book is not a "girl power" polemic. While women's accomplishments on the world stage and in their individual lives are worth celebrating, it is ridiculous to consider all women angels. It details how, in many cases, women are complicit in their own subordination and in the oppression of others. Women have been willing to support violence and uphold discriminatory systems when they benefit—even partially—from them. In fact, women in positions of power often adopt especially belligerent and masculine characteristics in order to deflect any criticism from political opponents who might accuse them of being "soft.' For example, simply watch a video of Theranos' Elizabeth Holmes affecting an unnaturally deep voice and dressing to evoke male tech CEOs like Bill Gates. For a less ridiculous example, consider how the Falklands War helped the first female British Prime Minister maintain her position and her reputation as an "Iron Lady" (Kennedy, 2019).

Second, this book puts politics and power back into the conversation about women's oppression. This book critically examines the popular notion that getting women a seat at the table will fix global economics and politics can make gender hierarchy seem like an easily rectified accident of fate. It is not. Gender inequality is a distribution of power which reflects deeply held beliefs about the proper roles for men and women. This book emphasizes that women's oppression is a tricky, persistent, and insidious political phenomenon. Efforts to promote actual equality between men and women are often met with fierce resistance because this equality entails taking power away from men.

Third and finally, this book shows that gender hierarchy is central to the conduct of world affairs. For decades, feminist international relations has been relegated to the sidelines of international relations scholarship. Yet women and gender inequality are critically important to the topics this field of study investigates. By providing a framework for understanding how gender hierarchy affects every facet of international relations, this book makes feminist scholarship approachable and a part of everyday political conversations.

To that end, this book is divided into four parts:

Part I: Gender Hierarchy and Politics from Local to Global: This section will explain how gender hierarchy affects political decision making from the kitchen table, all the way to the highest echelons of politics. This section is broken into three chapters. In Chapter 2, we will dig into the idea, "the personal is political" by examining how gender hierarchy can lead men and women to adopt different political preferences and relationships to politics. In Chapter 3, we consider how those same dynamics are at play in the campaigns and policies adopted by politicians and political elites. Through these chapters, we'll walk through the ways that gender norms and gender hierarchy condition political decision-making everywhere from the kitchen table to the UN Security Council—and take a closer look at how the system defends itself from challenges to the status quo.

Part II: Gender Hierarchy and Global Economics: This section will explore how gender hierarchy affects the global economy. This section is divided into three chapters. Chapter 4 introduces us to the concept of the "household economy," and considers how gender hierarchy shapes how we divide responsibilities in our homes—and how these decisions can then reinforce the patriarchal order. In Chapter 5, we examine the gender dynamics and implications of domestic (meaning national- or state-level) economic policies. Finally, in Chapter 6 we explore the link between gender hierarchy and international economic policies. Through these three chapters, we can see how gender hierarchy influences economic decisions ranging from who makes the kids' lunches to policies protecting domestic steel industries from foreign competitors.

Part III: Gender Hierarchy and International Security: This section will explore how gender hierarchy affects international security. This section is divided into three chapters. In Chapter 7, we consider how gender hierarchy influences individuals' decisions to go to war. In Chapter 8, we then consider how armed groups leverage norms about masculinity and femininity to train recruits into their new identities. Finally, in Chapter 9, we look at how these dynamics manifest at the state level, influencing why states go to war and how they behave during conflicts. This chapter also includes a discussion of the Women, Peace, and Security (WPS) agenda.

Part IV: The Fight Ahead: This section considers what we can do to resist gender hierarchy and explores the forces that conspire to reinforce it. In Chapter 10, we examine the backlash that crops up in response to challenges to the gender hierarchy. It unpacks how backlash can occur within our personal lives, in national politics, and on the international stage. It also considers how backlash can result from political, economic, and security-related challenges to the gender-hierarchy. In Chapter 11, we talk through the steps we can take in our personal lives and through our engagement in politics, economics, and security matters to create a more egalitarian future.

Section I: **Politics and Gender Hierarchy**

Chapter 2
Gender Hierarchy and Everyday Politics

It was a sweltering day in Maiduguri, the capital of Borno State in North East Nigeria. My lower back was slick with sweat and my cheeks were stinging with the beginnings of a light sunburn. I had spent hours talking to young women who had joined Boko Haram, a Salafi-jihadist rebel group that had plunged the region into violent instability. These women had generally joined voluntarily but had been captured by the military and placed into a rehabilitation program, which is where we met. We sat on woven mats on the grounds of their "safe house" and talked about their lives. Our conversations were wide-ranging, but we spent much time talking about their families and relationships, tracing their lives before and during their time in Boko Haram.

Interviewing can feel extractive and intrusive—imagine peppering someone you just met with a one-sided battery of questions. To avoid making interviews feel transactional and alienating, I try to be an open book about my own life. I showed these young women photos of my family and told them about where I grew up. Since we had talked so much about how they lived and their families, I also showed them photos of my parents, my friends, and my apartment in Washington, D.C. It was a "cozy" (meaning unrenovated and small) two-bedroom I shared with a roommate I found through a Craigslist ad. We got a discount on rent because the walls were noticeably pitched inward. It was the first time I had been able to afford an place above ground. I loved that apartment.

I was shocked when these young women laughed at the photos I showed them. Peering at my phone screen, one told me flatly that I needed to "find a richer husband." Another laughed that they wouldn't live there—it was too small! Their judgment stung, and my face flushed with embarrassment (masked helpfully by the budding sunburn).

There was also a surreal element to their criticisms. After all, we had just spent all day talking in a minimally furnished compound, just yards away from armed guards preventing them from leaving, near the steps of the building where they piled in next to one another to sleep.

I've spent a lot of time thinking about this exchange. It may seem like a minor thing, but both my pride in my apartment and their dismissal of it as a suitable living arrangement speaks to our different expectations of what life at home should be like—and who is responsible for providing that lifestyle. These young women expected their husbands to go out into the world and earn enough money to give them a comfortable life; their responsibility would be to manage the home and raise their children. They were raised to expect this household di-

https://doi.org/10.1515/9783111662886-004

vision of labor—and even to aspire to it—as a woman working outside of the home could reflect poorly on her husband.

In contrast, I had been raised with the expectation that I would need to support myself financially as an adult. I did not expect to ever get married—so I would have to bring home the bacon and fry it up. Our expectations reflected how gender hierarchy operated in our respective communities. And our respective expectations about what it meant to be a woman, wife, and daughter colored how we approached the world.

In this chapter, we explore the relationship between the gender hierarchy and everyday politics. Many of you have probably heard the phrase "the personal is political." Though associated with the second wave of feminism in the United States, it has been adopted by a range of political movements. Here we use it to help guide our thinking about everyday politics.

The phrase "the personal is political" captures two critical dynamics for understanding how gender hierarchy affects everyday politics and decision-making among regular people. Firstly, it speaks to a connection between relationships within the home and the conduct of politics outside of the home. Indeed, how "private" matters are handled in our personal lives and our homes ripple out to the broader community and even into international politics (Hudson, Bowen, and Nielsen, 2020). As Cynthia Enloe emphasized, "the personal is international" (Enloe, 1991, p. 343).

Secondly, it underscores how the home has often, wrongly, been seen as an apolitical space. This is because gender hierarchy devalues women's interests and domains; thus, family life and the home have been considered distinct from—and far less important than—public political life.

To unpack the politics of the personal, the remainder of this chapter is organized as follows: first, we discuss the gender political preference gap—or the propensity for men and women to have different political priorities. Then, we consider the sources and prospects for closing this gap. We then discuss how the socialization of children, mothers, and fathers within the home has profound political implications.

The chapter then changes tact a bit, to consider state intervention into domestic matters. Together, we consider how the boundary between the "personal" and the "political" has never been especially clear, even as the overlap has been underplayed. Furthermore, this section will highlight how the gender hierarchy conditions the effect of these political interventions into personal life.

Throughout, this chapter highlights how the gender hierarchy, which privileges men over women, works to discount the importance of "women's issues" and shapes how women and men identify their political interests. These individual processes aggregate to produce domestic and international politics. We finish the chapter with a summary of its main points.

What Women (and Men) Want (Politically): Political Preference and Participation Gaps

Men and women tend to value different types of political initiatives and government services. This gender gap does not emerge from differences in how men and women's brains are "wired;" it is a function of the different roles, responsibilities, and characteristics assigned to men and women in and by their communities. In other words, it is a function of how men and women are socialized under gender hierarchy.

Using a political economy approach, Torben Iversen and Frances Rosenbluth assert that the political preference gap is a function of gender norms under patriarchy—and argue that a greater demand for women's work outside of the home can loosen those norms. They characterize the gap in men's and women's political preferences as "a feisty dissatisfaction with the status quo" (Iversen and Rosenbluth, 2010, p. 130). While some would have us think, "men are from Mars, women are from Venus," the reality is that we share one world, and our preferences reflect our roles in it.

Consider, for example, the types of things that women value relative to men in their communities. In American politics, "women are more likely than men to support gun control measures, access to abortion, and increases in spending on social welfare after programs" (Gothreau, 2021, n.p.). These preferences reflect women's lived experiences, everyday struggles, and the roles that they have been socialized to take up. More than 4 million American women have been threatened by their intimate partner with a gun (Everytown, 2024). One in four American women have an abortion in their lives (Guttmacher Institute, 2024). Protecting themselves from violence and maintaining their ability to make choices about their bodies, health, and families are not some abstract political ideals for American women. They are matters of life and death.

Similarly, a wide variety of studies in developing countries—like India, Indonesia, and a variety of countries in Sub-Saharan Africa—suggest that women place a greater premium on water-related projects than their male counterparts (Chattopadhyay and Duflo, 2004; Olken, 2010; Gottlieb, Grossman and Robinson, 2018). In India and elsewhere, this preference reflects their disproportionate responsibility for things like cooking, cleaning, and their family's health — all things that require them to have access to clear water.

Men's political preferences also reflect their socialization under gender hierarchy. For example, men are more likely than women to support war or military action—which speaks to the connection between masculinity and warfare (something that we will unpack in greater detail in section three of this book) (Clements, 2012). There is some evidence that men are more supportive of hierarchical systems in general. One study posited, "we see men's greater support of racism, conservatism, militarism, and violence as being symptomatic of their greater social dominance orientation, or general preference for group inequality, and we see women's greater support of social welfare programs and extending rights to disenfranchised groups as being symptomatic of their lower levels of social dominance orientation" (Brown, 1997, p.50). In other words, because men have benefitted from their dominant position in the gender hierarchy, they have a vested interest in maintaining many forms of inequality. This preference for inequality means that men often support policies that end up harming them—poor men that vote against redistribution policies and a more robust safety net, for example, are picking their own pockets.

Yet, gender hierarchy does not just produce differences in what men and women value—it also results in women discounting their own priorities or curtailing their participation in politics. Academic Sarah Khan investigated women's priorities relative to men's in Pakistan. She asked women to describe what goods and services would do the most to improve women's lives; she then asked them what their own political preferences were. Strikingly, she found, "when asked about their personal preferences, women seem to prioritize the goods and services that directly impact household members other than themselves" (Khan, 2017, p. 47). Khan's work highlights how women construct their political preferences: not just with their individual identity as a woman in mind but also taking into account their family's broader needs.

Khan also found that women were not comfortable expressing their political preferences to the relevant political authority—even anonymously. Khan found that more than three-quarters of women "forego the opportunity to make their own preferences known, and instead choose to pass on their spouse's preferences" (Khan, 2020, p. 13). She further observes, "Men behave in exactly the opposite way: under the same conditions of anonymity and no cost, 88% choose to communicate their own preferences over their spouse's" (Khan, 2020, p. 13). She attributes this profound difference to entrenched gender inequality within the home. Women did not feel empowered to express their political demands, since they have been socialized to believe that politics is not their place.

Similarly, in her study of the gendered participation gap in India, academic Soledad Artiz Prillaman found that, while men and women tend to vote at similar rates, men were much more active in other forms of political participation. She suggests that this is because political decision-making is done at the household level, where male authority reins. She asserts, "Women are expected to be subjects of their household, not citizens of their village" (Prillaman, 2023, p. 91). When women vote in line with their husbands' wishes, it bolsters male authority, "while their more general political participation threatens male authority without reaping rewards for men" (Prillaman, 2023, p. 8). Khan and Prillaman's work both point to the ways in which intra-household power dynamics constrain women's participation in politics—with implications for women's well-being throughout the country and the maintenance of gender inequality.

Several cross-national studies confirm the widespread prevalence of the "participation gap" between men and women. This chasm looks different in different places; the specific characteristics and the depth of the participation gap reflects the construction of gender hierarchy in that specific community. A cross-national study of 13 countries in Asia finds negligible differences in the rate at which men and women vote but found important differences in their rates of campaigning, participation in collective action, and attendance at protests (Liu, 2022). In contrast, a study on 18 countries in Sub-Saharan Africa, for example, found that women were more likely than men to organize collectively, which the study classified as things like "attending a community meeting" and "joining others to raise an issue" (Coffe and Bolzendahl, 2010, p. 251). This pattern reflects gendered political socialization that gives women the responsibility for matters close to home. Furthermore, women's rates of participation in collective organizing might speak to the ways that they seek safety in numbers when articulating their political concerns.

Other studies find that women's responsibilities in the home can present formidable obstacles to participating in political life—regardless of what form such participation takes. One study of German politics, for example, found that women had difficulty attending political party meetings because these meetings conflicted with women's responsibilities in the home (Davidson-Schmich, 2016). Louise Davidson-Schmich (2016) writes "German women spend more hours on household chores than do German men. Given that there are a finite number of hours in a day, these two findings are likely highly correlated: German women simply have less time on average than German men to devote to voluntary activities such as party membership" (p. 81).

The "preference gap" and the "participation gap" are siblings—both born of gender hierarchy but with their own characteristics. Though persistent, the gender gaps in preferences and participation are not immutable.

Let's first consider the political dynamics within matrilineal societies, or those in which the family line is drawn through the mother rather than the father. One study in India found that the traditional gender gap in political preferences was inverted among women in matrilineal communities in India, where women generally inherit generational wealth and have greater decision-making authority over money matters (Brulé and Gaikwad, 2021). Similarly, a study comparing patrilineal and matrilineal communities across Sub-Saharan Africa found that the progressive gender norms in matrilineal societies resulted in smaller gaps between men and women's participation in political life. They observe, "the success of matrilineality in improving women's prospects, we argue, is that it gives women access to social and material resources in a way that creates common expectations of greater female influence and can thus sustain more progressive gender roles" (Robinson and Gottlieb, 2021, p. 70). The authors clearly tie their findings to socialization under gender hierarchy, writing, "decisions about whether to participate in civic and political life cannot be fully described using a cost–benefit analysis. Whether or not an individual is *expected* to participate also conditions that decision. Societies promote different beliefs about which individuals are welcome in the public sphere, and women are frequently thought to be unwelcome participants" (Robinson and Gottlieb, 2021, p. 69).

Or let's consider what happens when women take up traditionally "male" tasks. One study conducted across more than two dozen countries in sub-Saharan Africa found that as women took jobs outside of their homes, the gap between men and women's preferences on investment in infrastructure and access to clean water shrank (Gottlieb, Grossman and Robinson, 2018). When men and women play the same roles in society—in the home and on the job—their political preferences move closer to one another's. Similar experiences and socialization can produce similar preferences.

Here it's worth emphasizing that academic studies on the dynamics of the political preference and participation gaps are imperfect. Studies examining the gender gap in political participation and political preferences often rely on quantitative methods and try to "control" for things like socioeconomic status and political interest. "Controlling" for something means including the variable in the model in order to see whether it affects the main relationship of interest—between gender and political engagement in this instance. When these controls are included, gendered gaps in participation are sometimes attenuated or disappear entirely for some forms of participation. Yet, we should be wary about what we are "controlling" for with these measures. As this chapter will show, women are often discouraged from engaging in political life—which would be reflected in how they report their interest in politics. The next section of the book will address the relationship between gender hierarchy and economics but suffice to say here that women are often shunted into lower-paying, less prestigious work. There are a lot of reasons that academic studies try to "control for" these variables, but doing so can obscure the effects of gender hierarchy.

Furthermore, differences within countries and even within communities can be papered over in traditional political science and international relations studies. When we talk about political preference and participation gaps at the national level, it obscures how different identities can intersect and interact with an individual's gender identity, making them more or less affected by the factors that drive those gaps. Intersectional analysis, which takes these identities and factors into account, is critical for understanding these dynamics that underlie the national average.

Before we dive into gendered socialization in the home, it is worth emphasizing again that this is not the only process of socialization that exerts an influence on how individuals learn what is expected of them in the world. Hierarchies of race, class, and religion all come with different processes of socialization. Consider, for example, the different socialization that an Amish woman who is barred from using modern technology in Lancaster, Pennsylvania and an economically-privileged, secular, and chronically-online woman in Los Angeles are exposed to. They are both taught what it means to be a "good" woman but in radically different ways because of the different norms and expectations that their religious communities, position in the class structure, and geographic locations impart. This book focuses primarily on the implications of gender hierarchy for world politics—but it would be foolish to think that this is the only social order that matters. Gender hierarchy and associated gender socialization intersect with racial, class, religious, and other hierarchies and the socialization processes attached to them.

Understanding the political preference and participation gaps between men and women—how they make everyday political decisions and advocate for their preferences—thus requires that we investigate what it means to be a "man" or "woman" and how responsibilities are divided according to gender. And that requires taking a closer look at what goes on in the home, where we get some of our first and most consequential lessons in what is expected of us as men and women, sons and daughters, fathers and mothers.

Gender Hierarchy and Socialization in the Home

Maya Angelou, the celebrated author and poet, once wrote, "I believe that one can never leave home. I believe that one carries the shadows, the dreams, the fears and the dragons of home under one's skin, at the extreme corners of one's eyes and possibly in the gristle of the earlobe" (Angelou, 2008, p. 3). What does it mean to carry home with you wherever you go, to quite literally embody your home long after you close the door behind you?

This process is (less poetically) described as "socialization." The process by which members learn what is expected of them is referred to as "socialization." Jeffrey T. Checkel (2017) characterizes it as "... a process whose intended result is not simple behavioural adaptation, but a deeper change in an actor's sense of self" (p. 594). Socialization is a process of identity transformation. Socialization in the home includes things like whether boys and girls are extended different opportunities or burdened with different expectations. This is the process of gender socialization.

One of the clearest, earliest, and most impactful forms of gender socialization is what we are expected to contribute to the household. Early on, a heavier burden of household duties are placed on daughters' shoulders, setting the stage for a lifetime marked by that unequal division of labor. Though families might believe that they are assigning their sons and daughters the same amount of chores, time diaries reveal that daughters end up spending more time on household chores than sons (Tucker, McHale, and Crouter, 2003; Bianchi and Robinson, 1997; Gager and Sanchez, 2004). Furthermore, sons and daughters are often responsible for different types of chores. As sociologists Sara Raley and Suzanne Bianchi note, "Girls do more feminine chores (e.g., cooking and cleaning) than boys and boys do more masculine chores (e.g., household repairs, outdoor work) than girls" (Raley and Bianchi, 2006, p. 407). They also note, with seeming compassion, "Parents may start out with gender egalitarian intentions by assigning equal household workloads to their sons and daughters but fall short of this goal by ultimately sex-typing the types of chores that are done by sons and daughters" (Raley and Bianchi, 2006, p. 407). This early assignment of what we are responsible for and how much time we should be dedicating to such tasks has long-lasting effects on our political preferences and engagement, as we will see throughout this chapter.

Gendered socialization also comes from how we see the upkeep of the home divided between male and female family members, not just the tasks we are assigned. One study found that children start to take note of what chores are "for girls" or "for boys" by age 4 (PNAS, 2024). This means that toddlers are already internalizing gender roles when they are still learning to button and unbutton their coats (CDC, 2024). We will further interrogate the economic consequences of this socialization in later chapters. Suffice to say now: while social science has not probed whether socialization is stored in the corners of our eyes or in the gristle of our ear lobe, it has found that gender socialization begins early and has lifelong effects. Gender socialization, particularly in the home, is a key way in which the gender hierarchy is perpetuated. It also offers suggestions about how we can challenge gender hierarchy by changing how we socialize our children into gender roles.

Parents as the First Example of Political Engagement

Expanding on the significance of the home as a place where we learn what is expected of us and what we can expect from the world, a group of academics put forward the idea of "gendered political socialization" as the process by which "children infer that politics is for men and girls infer that political roles conflict with their defined gender roles" (Bos et al., 2022, p. 484). The authors find, "all children turn away from politics as they get older but that for girls this change is more dramatic," because of gendered political socialization into the idea that politics is a "man's world" (Bos et al., 2022, p. 496).

Parents are an important part of their children's gendered political socialization. One study of Canadian women, for example, found that having a politically active mother was an important predictor of whether women had engaged in both formal politics (like membership in a political party) and informal politics (like signing a petition or participating in a demonstration) (Gidengil, O'Neill and Young, 2010). Mothers are powerful role models for their daughters; a politically active mother can help imbue girls with the idea that women should engage in politics. Indeed, one study found that the "role model" effect of women running for office was not driven by the example that these candidates set but rather by the kitchen-table conversations about women and politics that their campaigns sparked (Campbell and Wolbrecht, 2006). If parents do engage their daughters in political conversations, these exchanges can drive young women's interest in the political world (Campbell and Wolbrecht, 2006). By engaging their children in conversations about politics, parents are implicitly teaching them that their opinions and engagement with politics matter.

Of course, the gendered political socialization we undergo at our parents' knees can also uphold the gender hierarchy. Consider the literature suggesting that parents are more likely to talk about politics with their sons than their daughters (Campbell and Wolbrecht, 2006). When parents engage their sons in political conversations more than their daughters, they are teaching both that politics is for men and that the girls shouldn't worry their pretty little heads.

While much of the socialization literature focuses on how parents socialize their children, there is compelling evidence that parents are also socialized by their children. Indeed, the very act of becoming a parent can be a radical identity transformation that reshapes how one defines their political interests and engages with the political world.

Motherhood and Gendered Political Socialization

Becoming a mother radicalized me and changed my approach to politics—and I was already a pretty political person. I am not alone; reading accounts from other moms and talking to them about their process of matrescence (or becoming a mother), I've been struck by what a politically influential process it is. The identity transformation that becoming a mother entails can be as dramatic as the physical effects of pregnancy.

Becoming a mother provides a new perspective on how the gender hierarchy operates in our communities. Pregnant women and new mothers can find themselves overwhelmed and frustrated by what is expected of them and disheartened by what little support they would receive in that endeavor. Under gender hierarchy, women are expected to be "naturally" excellent mothers—if they are struggling, they are conditioned to believe it is their fault, not a sign of a desperately inadequate system.

Becoming a mother can shine a light on the absurdities of life under gender hierarchy that we have become inured to over the years. Consider author Jazmina Barrera's reflection on being gifted multiple breastfeeding covers while expecting her first child:

> What is it with all these shawls and aprons? What's the message? That breastfeeding in public is indecent, polemical, risky? Apparently it's not obvious that the primary function of breasts is to feed babies; that hungry children can't wait; that women shouldn't have to hide what they are doing. I think all that, but then it occurs to me that the shawls aren't so bad, and might protect me from the unsettling stares of strangers or people I don't trust (Barrera, 2022, p. 63).

She eloquently bristles against the constraints of living under gender hierarchy—but also recognizes that a failure to conform (here by covering up while breastfeeding) could be even worse.

Adrienne Rich, a pioneering feminist author, distinguished between motherhood as a patriarchal "institution," which leaves women feeling lonely and bearing tremendous guilt about being inadequate mothers, and motherhood as an "experience," which was often filled with joy and meaning. She also described being a mother to her sons as a process which imbued her with a new sense of political urgency about how we teach our children to move about in the world:

> What do we want for our sons? Women who have begun to challenge the values of patriarchy are haunted by this question. We want them to remain, in the deepest sense, sons of the mother, yet also to grow into themselves, to discover new ways of being men even as we are discovering new ways of being women. We could wish that there were more fa-

thers — not one, but many — to whom they could also be sons, fathers with the sensitivity and commitment to help them into manhood in which they would not perceive women as the sole sources of nourishment and solace... Until men are ready to share the responsibilities of full-time, universal child-care as a social priority, their sons and ours will be without any coherent vision of what nonpatriarchal manhood might be. The pain, floundering, and ambivalence our male children experience is not to be laid at the doors of mothers who are strong, nontraditional women; it is the traditional fathers who — even when they live under the same roof — have deserted their children hourly and daily (Rich, 2021, pp. 213–214).

Rich's personal experience as a mother, raising sons in a world of patriarchal order, made her all the more certain that we needed to eradicate the gender hierarchy and push for more humane politics.

Becoming a mother can also offer women an on-ramp into political engagement that may not have been previously available to them. A woman advocating for her own political interests might be regarded as selfish or overly ambitious, a woman advocating on behalf of her children is often afforded an air of nobility and given greater leeway to engage in politics. When women engage in political activity under the banner of "mothers," they successfully bridge the divide between public life and home life.

Box 2.1: Motherhood as a Political Identity

Motherhood has been used as a means of mobilizing political support around the world, for a wide variety of different causes. In the United States, one of the largest civil society groups promoting gun control is "Moms Demand Action." The organization was started by Shannon Watts, a mother of five children who was shaken by the Sandy Hook school shooting in which twenty children and six adults were massacred.

Or consider the demonstrations of wives and mothers in front of the Russian Defense Ministry, in response to the widespread military mobilization of men to facilitate the invasion of Ukraine. These women stood up to a brutal autocracy to demand time limits for the military service of their husbands and sons, knowing well that previous movements had been decried as "foreign agents" and suppressed by the government (Radio Free Europe/ Radio Liberty, 2024).

Or consider the *Mothers of Plaza de Mayo* in Argentina. These women began silent marches in the Plaza de Mayo in response to the disappearances of their children undertaken by a brutal military dictatorship. The mothers wore white head scarfs, which they explained were not only a way to identify one another but symbolic of diapers and doves. Though these women deliberately invoked the idea of women as peaceful and nurturers, they were also taking on a huge personal risk by engaging in these protests. They faced derision from people who called them crazy, the police breaking up their demonstrations with dogs and tear gas, and arrests. One of the women brushed off these pervasive threats, asking rhetorically "What can be worse than their taking my child?" (Southern Poverty Law Center Learning for Justice, n.d., n.p.).

Motherhood has also been used to justify conservative political movements. Indeed, mothers played an important role in the post-war conservative movement in America, using their position in the home to mobilize against things like school integration and in support of the anti-communist movement (Nickerson, 2014).

The range of political and civil society movements that use the "mother" moniker speaks both to how becoming a mother can alter women's self-defined political interests and engagement. The process of becoming a mom can shift how women think about politics and offer them a platform to make their voices heard by dint of their new social role.

Fatherhood and Political Socialization

Becoming a father also shifts how men engage with politics. In particular, having a daughter can bring about changes in how men think about the world around them. Some studies find that having a daughter can nudge businessmen towards hiring more women and running more socially responsible corporations (Cronqvist and Yu, 2017). These findings suggest that the prospect and process of raising a woman makes men more keen on reducing discriminatory barriers and systems.

Fatherhood can make men confront aspects of the gender hierarchy that they had not noticed, or had taken for granted because they benefited from them. One study found that when a father's first child was female, they become more supportive of policies promoting gender equality (Sharrow et al., 2018). The authors opine,

> it may be that the initial entry into fatherhood with a daughter marks a pivotal moment when men, regardless of their age, awaken to gender inequalities in society, making them newly receptive to political messages that identify such issues and provide measures to combat them... However, for men whose entry into fatherhood (with a son) did not orient them toward gender inequality in the same way, subsequent daughters may not have the same impact on their policy preferences (Sharrow et al., 2018, p. 499).

Strikingly, the study did not find a similar effect of first daughters on mothers' preferences for gender-egalitarian policies (Sharrow et al., 2018). This may well be because these women are already well-versed in the consequences of patriarchal gender hierarchy and already had a vested interest in policies that undermine it. In contrast, the harms of patriarchal systems might not become concrete to men until they have flesh and blood negatively affected by it.

Other research suggests that having a daughter can polarize their father's political positions (Singal, 2017). This means that becoming a father doesn't change their mind but rather hardens their pre-existing political stances (Signal, 2017). Whether fathers shift their political preferences or double down on their already-held positions, it appears that having a daughter makes them more invested in bringing about a better world—however defined.

Though fatherhood might prompt men to reconsider the world around them, men do not seem especially likely to rally politically under the title of "concerned fathers." In 2023, Rob Okun wrote for *Ms.* magazine: "Moms Rising, Moms Demand Action and Mothers Out Front are among the most well-known groups, but there are countless other mother-led organizations across the country. Where are Dads Rising, Dads Demand Action, Dads Out Front? I don't care where Waldo is; I want to know 'Where's Dad-o?'" (Okun, 2023, n.p.). The relative paucity of such dad-centered civil society groups could reflect the fact that politics has always been a man's world under patriarchal gender hierarchy. They do not need to use their relationship to their children to justify their engagement in politics.

One of the few civil society movements in which men have adopted the "dad" title to justify their activities is in the fathers' rights movement. While the variety of organizations that comprise this movement have different tactics and objectives, they are broadly united by a frustration with family laws that frequently default to giving mothers primary custody of their children during divorce proceedings. It is telling that these men invoke their fatherhood when pressing for changes that reflect gender hierarchy's emphasis on women's place in the home and men's place in the public sphere. The difficulty that many divorced fathers face while navigating custody arrangements is one of the ways that gender hierarchy ends up hurting men—prompting them to work against it and invoke the importance of their role as fathers.

When Private Matters become Public Concerns

Hopefully by this point in the chapter, I've convinced you that what happens in the home is political. But home is not just the first place where we learn gender roles and what is expected of us as men and women—expectations that then shape our political preferences and participation. It is also the focus of a variety of state interventions. Personal issues—especially things related to fertility and family—become critically important political divides and matters of state intervention. And the ways that states intervene into these matters frequently means expanding government control over women's bodies.

Think about the process of getting married. In most contexts, people cannot simply turn to one another and say "I'd like to spend forever with you," and be married. There are a wide variety of forms to fill out to inform the state of your new status (to say nothing of the social expectations surrounding a wedding). A government can also simply refuse marriage licenses for marriages that it does not approve of—in some contexts that has meant barring interracial or same-sex marriages.

Box 2.2: The US Government's Regulation of Marriage

The United States has a long history of discriminatory legislation regarding marriage. It was only in 1967 that the Supreme Court ruled in *Loving vs Virginia* that restrictions on interracial marriages were unconstitutional (Archie, 2022), Or consider that it was only in 2015 that same-sex marriage was legalized nationally in the Supreme Court case *Obergerfell v Hodges*.[1] The bans on interracial and same-sex marriage did not only deny such couples recognition of their loving relationship—it also prevented them from enjoying the legal privileges that accompany marriage (NYCLU, 2024). Both of these rulings found that the restrictions on marriage were in violation of the 14th Amendment, which guarantees equal protection under law. Of course, the 14th Amendment was ratified in 1868, meaning that the protections that this amendment provided for interracial couples and same-sex couples went unrecognized for nearly a century and nearly 150 years, respectively.

Governments also frequently concern themselves with the fecundity of the marriages they sanction. They have often intervened to promote the "ideal" family size. Whether they are encouraging families to have more children or to maintain small families, these programs have run into profound obstacles and have frequently threatened women's autonomy.

Box 2.3: Increasing Birth Rates in Hungary

Hungarian Prime Minister Victor Orbán has been at the forefront of the modern movement panicking about low birth rates in the West. Orbán's rhetoric pairs concerns about women having fewer children (or no children at all) with racism and xenophobia; in practice, this means government policy that disparages immigrants (Skujins and AP, 2024), and that tries to nudge Hungarian women to have more children. He once stated that: "Part of the picture of the decade of war facing us will be recurring waves of suicidal policy in the Western world. One such suicide attempt that I see is the great European population replacement program, which seeks to replace the missing European Christian children with migrants, with adults arriving from other civilizations" (Beauchamp, 2022, n.p.).

Hungary spends an estimated 5% of its national gross domestic product (GDP) on programs to encourage women to have children. These incentives range from exempting mothers of four or more children from paying taxes for the rest of their lives to "upfront loans of $36,000, which get written off for couples that have at least three children... And there are even government-owned fertility clinics" (Martuscelli, 2023).

---

1 Obergerfell v Hodges.

Though expensive and wide-ranging, the results of these programs are underwhelming. Hungary's birth rate has barely crept up over the past decade (Martuscelli, 2023). Hungary's experience is reflective of the overall inefficacy of efforts to increase fertility. One 2024 study examined the effect of things like "child care subsidies, extended parental leave and tax incentives" aimed at increasing the birth rate. It found that none of these interventions increased the live births per woman by more than 0.2—meaning none of them were especially effective at increasing the number of children women had, even if they had other positive impacts on the well-being of families (Cheng, 2024).

Under patriarchy, it is all too easy to value the birth rate over women's autonomy and rights. Writing on the recent panic over low birth rates, a researcher told CNN: "There is a real threat in some governments trying to pressure women to have more children. It's very easy to go from encouraging women to have more children to being a little bit more coercive" (Cheng, 2024, n.p.). We know that this threat is real because we've seen such government interventions before. Just consider the real-life regulations demanding that women have four children under Ceaușescu in Romania or conservatives' opposition to "birth control and voluntary sterilization" that inspired Margaret Atwood to write the dystopian novel *The Handmaid's Tale*, in which a class of fertile women (handmaids) are ritually raped and forced to have children for the elites. In a 2019 interview, Atwood explained that the book was not drawn from thin air: "As I've said about a million times, I didn't make it up. This is the proof – everything in these boxes" where she kept clippings of relevant news stories (Atwood, 2019).

Box 2.4: The One Child Policy in China

As a result of concerns about China's birth rate threatening the country's economic development, the government adopted the One-Child Policy in 1980. As the name suggests, this policy limited families to just one child. The policy was unpopular and required strict enforcement, which often involved invasive and coercive medical procedures. According to one report, in 1983 there were 21 million children born in China (Feng, Gu and Cai, 2016). In comparison there were more than 14 million abortions and more than 20 million sterilizations performed, many of which were involuntary (Feng, Gu and Cai, 2016).

Though some sought to circumvent the regulations or bore the weight of the associated fines, many families were limited to having just one child. Because of prevailing gender norms, many families preferred to have sons. Boys were preferred to girls, as they carry on the family name, inherit family property, and care for their parents in their old age (Pletcher, 2025). Families resorted to extreme actions to ensure that their one allotted child was male. Some estimate there are tens of millions of missing women in China today because of sex-selective abortions, infanticide of daughters, the abandonment of baby girls, and a failure to report the births of daughters (Jozuka, 2016). An ostensibly gender-neutral policy, which limited the size of families in order to promote economic development for the country as a whole, had a devastating impact on a generation of women because of the gender hierarchy's privileging of men over women.

Even though the Chinese government rescinded the policy, today the country is struggling with the implications of the country's skewed ratio of men to women. Because men outnumber women, the marriage market in the country has become profoundly skewed (Textor, 2025). Young, unmarried men are referred to as "bare branches," because they mark an end to their family trees (Nicholson, 2017; Hudson and Den Boer, 2004). In China, marriage is understood as an important part of the transition to adulthood (Jin et al., 2013). Those young men who cannot get married and start a family struggle to perform the masculinity expected of them. Some are concerned that these young men's frustration will boil over into criminality and violence (Nicholson, 2017).

In order to help their sons transition into adulthood, start a family, and become a "real man," some families are going into debt in order to finance exorbitant wedding costs. According to a study on the marriage market in rural China, "the shortage of marriageable women leads to an increase in marriage expenses for men, and families with sons must face heavy financial burdens. Since the 1980s, rural men's marriage expenses, including a new house, new furniture, bride price, and wedding, have increased rapidly" (Jin et al., 2013, pp. 3–4). The study's authors note, "in some villages, the cost of a son's marriage is *8–20 times the annual household income*" (emphasis added) (Jin et al., 2013). For comparison's sake, in the United States, a wedding that cost eight times the average household income in 2022 would be nearly $600,000. The government's intervention into personal matters has created successive waves of crises, affecting men and women alike.

Conclusion

In this chapter, we've explored how the maxim "the personal is political" plays out in everyday political life. As a young woman at the Safe House in Maiduguri, I was not just talking to women about their time in Boko Haram, but also how their socialization into the gender hierarchy pushed them towards that group. Those young women had made decisions—including, in many cases, the decision to join Boko Haram—as a result of how they were socialized about the role of men and women in their community. I too had made decisions that led me to the Safe House, which reflected my own socialization and my expectation that I would have to forge my own way as a professional woman.

Despite the clear differences in our expectations and opportunities, we still found ways to bond. After our conversations, some of the young women braided my hair and gave me intricate henna tattoos that snaked up my hands. I remember thinking that, despite the unrelenting heat and the armed guards at the entrance of the compound, it felt like I was at a sleepover. We were all doing the best that we thought we could with the information we had and the norms that were instilled in us as children.

In this chapter, we have considered how the personal is political by digging into the differences between how men and women think about their political interests and engage in public life. We've traced these differences to differences in their socialization under gender hierarchy. This discussion detailed that, though the home is often discounted as a political space because of its association with women and femininity, it is the site of profound political socialization for children, as well as their parents. We then considered how seemingly "domestic" or "private" matters often involve profound state or societal intervention. Across a variety of contexts, governments have regulated family matters and swept in to ensure that their citizenry was composed of the "right type" of people.

So what can we take from all of this? Firstly, gender socialization is a powerful driver of individuals' political interests and participation. Socialization under the gender hierarchy teaches us to elevate men and the masculine over women and femininity and to divide the world into gendered categories. The chasm between men and women's political preferences and willingness to engage in politics can be explained by such socialization. Secondly, the "gender gap" in politics is not immutable. In fact, there is compelling evidence that as men and women take on similar responsibilities and roles in their communities, the political preference and participation gap shrinks. In other words, socialization that challenges the gender hierarchy can reduce the gender gap.

Thirdly, we cannot ignore the home as the site of gender socialization. Not only do parents raise their children with expectations of how "good" men and women behave, but the experience of becoming a parent can produce profound shifts in how individuals engage with politics. Socialization in the home can uphold or challenge the gender hierarchy (and often does both, helping cement some aspects of the gender hierarchy while critiquing others).

Fourthly, "feminine" subjects like home and family are often marginalized or considered "unserious," even as states have frequently concerned themselves with these matters. Both the motivations for state interventions into things like marriage and child-rearing and how these policies are implemented are influenced by the gender hierarchy. These interventions often come at the expense of women's well-being. We pick up this thread in the following chapter, where we investigate how gender hierarchy influences the decision-making of political elites.

Chapter 3
Gender Hierarchy and Behavior of Political Elites

The previous chapter looked at how gender hierarchy affects everyday politics and ordinary people. This chapter looks at how gender hierarchy affects how the political elite act. They may have more money and influence than regular citizens do, but that doesn't make them any less susceptible to gendered expectations. In fact, all that time in the public eye can mean intense pressure to put on gendered performances. As we will see in this chapter, gender hierarchy and gender norms influence how government officials around the world behave on the campaign trail and in office.

Take for example, Indira Gandhi. The former Indian Prime Minister was a trailblazer for women in politics in India and around the globe. Yet, Gandhi distanced herself from the F word, stating "I'm not a feminist. Till I was 12 years old I hardly knew the difference between being a boy or a girl. I was brought up amongst boy cousins climbing trees, flying kites and playing marbles." She considered herself a "biform human being"—someone for whom the categories of man and woman did not apply (Ghose, 2017).

Her contemporaries took notice of Gandhi's approach to leadership. Henry Kissinger, among the most powerful men in American foreign policy deliberations, described her as an "Iron Lady," referencing her steely fortitude (of course, he also called her a "bitch" in a conversation with then-President Richard Nixon, perhaps for that very same characteristic) (Ramesh, 2005). Gandhi, juggling military confrontations with China, Pakistan, and Sikh separatists, clearly had political incentives to avoid being thought of as soft, pliable, and womanly. Indira Gandhi carved out and cast aside those parts of herself that were considered too feminine in order to gain respect and cultivate political credibility.

Of course, male political elites also operate within the gender hierarchy. This chapter considers how male leaders perform masculinity and how gender expectations influence their policies in office. Compare the boyish, yoga-practicing, enlightened masculinity that former Canadian Prime Minister Justin Trudeau embodies (Paling, 2016), the flashy, brash, and toxic masculinity practiced by current American President Donald Trump (Becker, 2021), and the eccentric and militarized image of former Libyan leader Muammar Gaddafi (Porter and Davidson, 2009). How each of these leaders interpret what it means to be a "real man" has implications for how they cultivate voters and the policies they champion in office.

Before getting into the experiences and strategies of individual political elites, however, this chapter opens with a discussion of political parties. In nearly every

https://doi.org/10.1515/9783111662886-005

country, parties are critical political players because they decide who gets to run for office. I consider how parties' electoral and reputational concerns—developed within the context of gender hierarchy—influence the gender composition of a country's political elite. These organizations are designed to win elections. They have incentives to be aware of how gender hierarchy shapes voters' concerns. The chapter then considers female and male political elites' behavior in the context of gender hierarchy. It closes with a summary of how gender hierarchy affects the behavior of political elites.

Party People: Political Parties and Gender Hierarchy

Political elites are not bestowed upon a country by some powerful, superhuman force. In nearly every country, political parties act as aggregators of individuals' political interests and gatekeepers selecting who can represent the party. Political parties' bylaws and electoral strategies both play an important role in determining the gender composition of elected representatives.

Identifying candidates to run for office is a process of winnowing, generally run by political parties. In theory, anyone that meets the citizenship, residency, party membership, and age requirements can run for office—meaning that we start off with a huge pool of potential representatives. But just because you are eligible to do something doesn't mean that you want to do that thing. For example, I am eligible to go skydiving, but I find myself firmly rooted on the ground because I have no interest in freefalling.

The next step of winnowing is to shift from the eligibles to the aspirants—those who are interested in seeking elected office. Parties act as gatekeepers, carefully tending to the egos of aspirants and seeking out eligible folks that might not yet see themselves as possible political representatives yet. This process is at work behind the scenes, resulting in the slate of candidates that we cast our votes for on election day.

Throughout this process of winnowing and selection—even before a single vote has been cast—the gender hierarchy dampens women's opportunities. Around the world, women's disproportionate share of responsibilities in the home and providing care work can prevent them from engaging in politics. Davidson-Schmich's study of German politics revealed, for example, that the care work that falls disproportionately on women's shoulders crowds out time that might be spent on politics (Davidson-Schmich, 2016, p. 81). Everyone has the same 24 hours in a day—but women with children generally have fewer leisure hours in that 24-hour span than others. Because women have less time to spend at party meetings, they struggle to meet the party membership requirements for being an eligible candidate or to capture the attention of party power-brokers.

Even when women are politically active and eligible to run for office, norms about who is a political leader can prevent women from thinking about themselves as potential candidates. In one survey in Germany, for example, 11% of men and 2% of women surveyed stated that they aspired to hold political office (Davidson-Schmich, 2016). Because politics is generally understood to be a "man's world"—even in a relatively gender-egalitarian country like Germany—women are less likely to think of themselves as potential political leaders. Similarly, one study from the United States even found that when women were the breadwinners—meaning that they are responsible for earning the majority of their family's income—they were less interested in running for office than men. The study found this was especially true for mothers, whose free time is further eaten up by the notoriously time-intensive process of raising children (Bernhard, Shames and Teele, 2021).

Gender quotas have emerged as a popular response to the persistent underrepresentation of women in politics. Half the countries in the world have some form of a gender quota and a wide variety of political parties have adopted their own (non-legally binding) quotas, affecting the decision-making processes of political parties (International Institute for Democracy and Electoral Assistance, n.d.). Gender quotas provide a mandate for cultivating female political talent and they have achieved their objective of increasing the number of women in office worldwide. As of 2023, for example, more than a quarter of legislative positions around the world were held by women (Congressional Research Service, 2024).

But gender quotas are not a silver bullet for the problem of women's underrepresentation in politics. In many cases the adoption of a gender quota and other measures to increase women's representation are motivated by gender essentialist reasoning and the norms developed under gender hierarchy. Anyone that has ever played in a mixed-gender sports league that mandates a minimum number of "women on the field" knows how often wives, sisters, and girlfriends are dragged out to the game and then merely tolerated by their "teammates." Quotas can become box-ticking exercises, rather than transformational policies.

Quotas are often adopted and implemented in a way that helps cement the gender hierarchy in general and men's authority within the party in particular. Melody Valdini, a political scientist, argues that (generally male) party elites engage in an "inclusion calculation" and accept more women into elite roles when it makes electoral sense for them to do so and when women's presence does not threaten their own power (Valdini, 2019). Her research finds that parties typically bring women in to clean up messes; specifically, she argues corruption scandals and government crackdowns on human rights are likely to produce more women in office, as the party seeks to polish its image. Gender norms that portray women as more honest and compassionate allow parties to improve their public image by feminizing themselves (Valdini, 2019). Indeed, one cross-national study of political parties in 35 countries between 1976 and 2016 found that female-led parties were seen as more moderate than male-led parties (O'Brien, 2019).

Box 3.1 Gender Quotas in Rwanda:

Rwanda has often been lauded for having the highest proportion of women in parliament in the world. At the time of writing, nearly 64% of the seats in the Chamber of Deputies are held by women, as are more than 50% of the seats in the Senate (Parliament of Rwanda, 2024). This surge in representation followed the adoption of a quota in 2003 that dictated that 30% of all elected seats must be held by women.

Though strikingly egalitarian on paper, Rwanda is not a feminist utopia. The country is a brutal dictatorship. The country's President, Paul Kagame, has been in power since 1994 and has cemented his political party's (the Rwandan Patriotic Front or RPF) hegemony through intimidation, violence, and repression. Much of the power in the country is concentrated in the executive's hands, meaning that despite the legislature's gender egalitarian composition, there are clear limits on how much change it can enact. In 2024, Freedom House observed that

> Government policy is largely set and implemented by the executive branch, with the security and intelligence services playing a powerful role. The president is not freely elected. Parliament generally lacks the independence to serve as a check on executive authority, and tends to merely endorse presidential initiatives, especially on political and security matters. It can play an oversight role on issues that are less politically sensitive, such as women's rights, education, and public health (Freedom House, 2024, n.p.).

Rwanda's gender quota underscores the importance of looking not just at the number of women in office but also turning a critical eye to the characteristics of the system they operate within and the actual degree of power that they wield.

Women are not the only group whose political participation is impeded by structural marginalization. In general, elected officials are generally richer, better educated, and paler than the general population. As this chapter will discuss in greater detail, the numerical domination of men in office has not meant that all men are well-represented. In every society, there are multiple hierarchies of domination and subordination that intersect with one another to make it more or less possible for folks to seek political office.

In summary, the men and women that hold elected office or who act as political elites are not a random sample of the population. They have all navigated the gauntlet of eligibility, aspiration, and party politics in the context of gender hierarchy and other systems of domination and oppression. This whole process also has implications for how men and women behave on the campaign trail and in positions of political power.

How Female Political Elites Behave

Women on the Campaign Trail

When women do overcome the formidable barriers in the way of running for office, their campaigns have to grapple with gendered stereotypes. Gender essentialist assumptions that women are the weaker sex or not cut out for the rough-and-tumble world politics present hurdles to women seeking office.

We've all likely seen female candidates grappling with gendered stereotypes on the campaign trail, even if we did not recognize their gendered performances for what they are. Think about how frequently women running for office try to signal that they are tough enough for the job. Then-US Vice Presidential candidate Sarah Palin's quip "Do you know they say, the difference between a hockey mom and a pit bull? Lipstick!" went viral during the US 2008 Presidential campaign in the United States (Henig, 2008). The message was effective because it played up important parts of Palin's femininity—that she's a mom that wears makeup—while also emphasizing that she's strong and aggressive enough to get the job done.

Or let's consider the public image cultivated by Marine Le Pen, a far-right politician in France. Part of the reason for Le Pen's success, according to one account, is that her charisma is masculine-coded and inspires "the belief that she is a woman who can perform exceptional feats" (Geva, 2020, p. 27). Academic Dorit Geva notes that balancing this, Le Pen's supporters also saw her "as a caring, feminine figure who represented caritas, a feminine capacity for care and love" (Geva, 2020, p. 27). Le Pen's political career depends upon her proving that she can do what a man can—but in heels. Or think back to Indira Gandhi's careful attempts to navigate her identity and her unwillingness to call herself a feminist.

In some circumstances, gender essentialist stereotypes about women can work to female candidates' benefit—meaning that they can "lean into" gender norms about women being nurturing and kind. Let's consider the political strategy adopted by Catherine Samba-Panza. She leveraged gender norms to shore up her support as the Central African Republic's first female head of state, who came to power amidst a devastating civil war. In one of her speeches, Samba-Panza took up the mantle of the nation's mother, stating "I call on my children, especially the anti-balaka [one of the warring factions], to put down their arms and stop all the fighting. The same goes for the ex-Séléka [another warring faction] – they should not have fear. I don't want to hear any more talk of murders and killings"; she further stated that "Starting today, I am the president of all Central Africans, without exclusion" (BBC, 2014, n.p.). By referring to the militia members as her "children," she was able to put herself in a position of moral authority over them in which she could welcome them back home and rehabilitate them—just as a mother cares for a wayward child.

Gender essentialist campaigns can rely on the positive characteristics associated with femininity to draw support for female candidates. Examining the 2006 election in the United States, academics Kim L. Fridkin and Patrick J. Kenney found that female senators "were viewed as more honest and more caring than male senators" (Fridkin and Kenney, 2009, p. 316). This was associated with a higher level of trust in female senators to handle healthcare issues, which loomed large in that election cycle (Fridkin and Kenney, 2009). The association between women and care worked to female politicians' benefit here—but still left them constrained by gender essentialist expectations. Similarly, a review of more than 100 political parties across 18 Latin American countries found that parties were more likely to nominate women when there was widespread mistrust of the legislature and when the legislature was perceived as being corrupt (Funk et al., 2021). These parties relied on the gender-essentialist association between women and trust-worthiness to try to bolster their chances at the ballot box. The study authors note the difficult position this puts female politicians in, writing, "the glass cliff analogy—that women are promoted during difficult times but ultimately positioned for failure—suggests that, if discontent were to become extreme, more women could obtain political power but with the deck stacked against them" (Funk et al., 2021, p. 474).

While politicians on the campaign trail design stump speeches and campaign ads to convince voters that they are up to the task, their opponents try to poke holes in those claims. Negative campaigning, which relies on reducing support for your opponent rather than cultivating support for your candidate, sometimes relies on gender stereotypes. For example, "In the Philippines, President Rodrigo Duterte described Senator Leila de Lima as "immoral" and an 'adulterer' when she challenged his leadership, actions that female colleagues condemned as 'slut-shaming,'" and which relied upon gendered norms of propriety to undermine her suitability for office (Krook and Restrepo Sanín, 2020, p. 745). One study found that attacks that centered on the ways in which a candidate violated expectations associated with their gender or political party were especially effective against Democratic women (Cassese and Holman, 2018). Put another way, women running for office in the United States as Democrats, the more socially progressive party, were particularly vulnerable to attacks that suggested that they were not sufficiently feminine. We've also seem these sorts of attacks in France, where one conservative politician "repeatedly addressed the president of the National Assembly as Madame le Président (using the masculine form of "president"), despite her telling him multiple times to use Madame la Présidente, the feminine form" (Krook and Restrepo Sanín, 2019, p. 745). His refusal to refer to her as *Madame la Présidente* was a way of undermining her femininity and reinforcing the idea that political leadership is a man's job.

Right now you're probably thinking: "Wait, didn't we just establish that women running for office often try to prove that they are *masculine* enough? Why would they do that if attacks on their *femininity* are especially damaging to their electoral prospects?" You're right—and herein lies one of the especially thorny issues that women seeking office face: they must be masculine enough to be considered competent but not so masculine that it compromises their femininity. Further, their party affiliation can make this even more fraught. It is a tricky double-bind for women with political ambitions.

It is also not the only catch-22 that women seeking office face. One study, focusing on American politics, revealed that voters preferred candidates that were married and had children. On the face of it, that should not limit women's ability to hold elected office (indeed, women are a pretty important process by which families have children). Yet because women with children are often saddled with additional childcare responsibilities, they are less likely to have the time to run for office. The study authors conclude,

> Ultimately, the single and childless women available to serve as politicians are not favored by voters and political elites, whereas women who are married with children may be less interested in the job, or required to work extra hours because of gender-unequal family burdens. Thus voters' and political elites' avowed preference for female candidates in the abstract is potentially offset by their preference for candidates who are wives and mothers (Teele, Kalla and Rosenbluth, 2018, p. 534).

What voters want is Wonder Woman—someone unbound by the constraints of time, biology, and physics.

Women in Office

Despite formidable obstacles to getting on the ballot and winning office, women do hold elite political positions around the world. Women serve not only as roughly a quarter of elected representatives worldwide but also as high-ranking political appointees in a number of countries. In 2024, 23 % of Ministerial positions around the world were held by women and 26 countries had a female head of state (UN Women, 2024). Even though women remain under-represented in politics, their numbers have skyrocketed in recent decades. Yet, even once women have risen to the ranks of the political elite, the gender hierarchy is still at work, conditioning the scope of their authority and how they behave in office.

Consider, for example, the committees and ministries that women in office are often assigned. Mona Lena Krook and Diana Z. O'Brien, examining female cabinet ministers around the world, note that women have often been locked out of the most powerful positions (Krook and O'Brien, 2012). Women are often assigned portfolios dealing with family issues, women's issues, and health; it is rare to see a female Minister of Defense or Secretary of the Treasury (Krook and O'Brien, 2012). Female political elites are often relegated to the "pink ghetto" of politics, where they are shunted into lower-prestige work.

When women do wield influence over "masculine" portfolios, there's compelling evidence that they adopt masculine personas and aggressive footings. For example, one study found that women heads of states in democracies were more likely than male leaders to initiate conflict (Schramm and Stark, 2020). Women have good reason to act this way—another study suggests that their resolve is doubted by their counterparts during crisis bargaining, meaning that their threats are taken less seriously than those levied by their male counterparts (Post and Sen, 2020). When women have access to the resources of the state, they can use these capabilities to help shore up their reputations as credible, strong leaders in response to gendered assumptions that they are less aggressive and tough than their male counterparts. Perversely, expecting women in power to be less aggressive than men can backfire spectacularly.

Box 3.2: Margaret Thatcher and the Falklands War

Let's consider how Margaret Thatcher, the first female Prime Minister of the UK, managed gendered political expectations. Though she is now memorialized as an effective (albeit often ruthless) conservative Prime Minister, ahead of the war her political career was in a precarious position. One commenter noted that, before the war, "...Thatcher appeared a weak, broken leader with little support even within her party" (Jenkins, 2013, n.p.). On April 2, 1982, Argentina invaded the Falklands Islands, a British overseas territory. In response, Thatcher sent naval forces to reclaim the islands, which they did in fewer than 75 days (Kennedy, 2019, n.p.). A columnist for *The Guardian* argued, "Previously, she had little public profile at home or abroad. The war had shown her a dominant presence. Her language, her decisiveness, her determination were its watchwords. Afterwards, she was a world celebrity and a changed leader" (Jenkins, 2012, n.p.). Thatcher didn't just reclaim the territory, she also realized the power in projecting masculinity and toughness to pursue her political agenda.[1] From there, Thatcher used her newfound image to pursue radical cuts to the welfare state, a series of reforms that is now known as "Thatcherism."

Substantive and Descriptive Representation: Do Women Represent Other Women in Office?

As a part of efforts to end women's underrepresentation in politics around the world, advocates have often relied on the idea that women in power will be effective representatives of women's interests in general. In political science jargon, they argue that descriptive representation (the number of women in office) will facilitate substantive representation (improvements in policies for women in general).[2] But does this expectation bear out?

The evidence generally points to a weak link between descriptive and substantive representation. Reviews generally find a "mixed" or "complicated" relationship between descriptive and substantive representation (Field, 2021; Childs, 2006). In some cases, female political elites have been stalwart proponents of women's issues or have effectively delivered on matters important to their female constituents. Indeed, when India adopted a randomized political reservation system to increase the number of women serving as Village Council (Gram Panchayats or GPs) heads, one study found that female village heads were more responsive to the needs of female constituents. The study author assert that the reservation system

> ...affects policy decisions in ways that seem to better reflect women's preferences. The gender preferences of men and women are proxied by the types of formal requests brought to the GP by each gender. In West Bengal, women complain more often than men about drinking water and roads, and there are more investments in drinking water and roads in GPs reserved for women. In Rajasthan, women complain more often than men about drinking water but less often about roads, and there are more investments in water and less investment in roads in GPs reserved for women (Chattopadhyay and Duflo, 2004, p. 1411).

In other cases, however, women have advocated for profoundly regressive policies that end up hurting women's rights and wellbeing. Consider, for example, Amer-

---

1 I actually learned about this from a student of mine. Thank you Sam, for your hard work on your term paper on this subject!

2 This has also been described as "standing for" versus "acting for" in Piktin's seminal *The Concept of Representation.*

ican activist Phyllis Schlafly, who is most famous for her campaign against the Equal Rights Amendment, which would have codified gender equality into the U.S. Constitution (Johnson, n.d.). Her presence in the halls of power actually prevented women from securing Constitutionally-guaranteed equal protection in the United States.

Amina Mama, a Nigerian-British activist and academic, underscores the dangers of assuming that female representatives and even ministries dedicated to women's issues will bring about positive changes for women in general. She describes the rise of "femocracies," which she describes as "a feminine autocracy running in parallel to the patriarchal oligarchy upon which it relies for its authority, and which it supports completely." Femocracies benefit "...the interests of a small female elite, and in the long-term undermining women's interests by upholding the patriarchal status quo" (Mama, 1995, p. 41). Similarly, academic Sarah Childs (2006) concludes, "...the elision between women's bodies and feminist minds should also be rejected" (p. 17).

How women get access to political office matters for how they behave in office —including whether they support pro-woman policies. When women come to power with an expectation that they will represent women, they have more leeway to promote such policies. For example, there is some compelling evidence that women that are put in power through a quota sometimes behave differently than their non-quota counterparts. In Taiwan, for example, quota women were more likely to spearhead bills regarding health, education, and welfare issues than non-quota women (Wang, 2023). This may suggest that the quota system does not only increase the number of women in office but also imbues them with a sense of responsibility to act on behalf of women generally. In other contexts, women that are elected through quota systems are denigrated as being party puppets that are unwilling to work across party lines to advance women's rights. Given the profound ways that women in power are influenced by gender expectations, how does the gender hierarchy influence men in office?

How Male Political Elites Behave

On the Campaign Trail

The gendered associations between men and leadership can sometimes make it hard to clock how men on the campaign trail also grapple with gender stereotypes. But male candidates also perform their masculinity for voters; as Jessica Smith put it, they "play the man card" (2021, p. 451). The way that men play this card depends on the hand that they were dealt—meaning that their other identity characteristics and associated expectations influence how they perform their masculinity.

Box 3.3: Joe Manchin's All-American Manhood

Let's consider the American politician Joe Manchin, who occupied an interesting and sometimes even paradoxical place in American politics during his time representing West Virginia. Because he was a member of the more liberal American political party, while also representing a generally conservative state, Manchin had to work hard to cultivate an electable public persona. That included telegraphing to voters that he was not some effete Washington elite; he was a down-home, rough and tumble West Virginian *man*.

In 2010, while running for the U.S. Senate Manchin released a campaign ad titled "Dead Aim." In it, he told viewers that he would protect their access to firearms, "defend West Virginians" and "take on... this Administration" (never mind the fact that the administration he was so staunchly against was from his own political party). But Manchin was not only talking tough—the ad also featured him loading a hunting rifle and shooting a hole in the middle of the Cap and Trade bill, a piece of environmental legislation that was unpopular among coal miners in his state.

The ad was designed not only to explain to voters what Manchin would do if elected to office but also to show them the type of man he is. "Dead Aim" kicked off a new trend in America campaign ads, which tapped into the association between (white) masculinity and American gun culture.[3] One study found that nearly 50 candidates running for state or federal office had released an ad with them carrying a gun between 2010 and 2019. Nearly three-quarters of those candidates were men, 70% were members of the Republican party, and "all but three were White or White-passing" (Neville-Shepard and Kelly, 2020, p. 467). Black politicians might not be able to telegraph dependability, strength, or credibility by whipping out a gun, reflecting the racist double standards in American political life.

Elections around the world have served not just as a choice between candidates but also as a referendum on different performances of masculinity. The 2019 General Election in the United Kingdom also included fierce competition on the basis of who was a "real man." Both Boris Johnson, the Conservative Party leader and incumbent, and Jeremy Corbin, the Labour Party leader, sought to telegraph that they were the right type of man to lead the country. As a part of their bids, they often relied on masculine imagery to prove to voters that they were "man enough" for the job. One academic study observed that

---

3 As academics Neville-Shepard and Kelly argue, "...the trend of candidates bearing arms in political ads represents the enactment of White masculinity through a theater of violence that capitalizes on the spectacular qualities of networked media environments to spread and legitimize a recuperative White male politics. This politics entails White men standing up to perceived threats to hegemonic masculinity with arresting public displays of paramilitary violence, including the open carry of firearms" (2020, p. 467).

Johnson demonstrated elements of 'hypermasculinity' showing his strength and dominance in the form of traditional, working class masculinity and exaggerated displays of toughness. He was pictured on building sites and in factories sporting hard hats and high-vis jackets. Despite calls for more compassionate, read stereotypically feminine, politics, Corbyn's campaign was still located in masculine imagery through consistent displays of agency, addressing rallies of supporters (Smith, 2021, p. 451).

Even in countries without free and fair elections, would-be political elites often work hard to prove their masculinity to the public to shore up their support. Vladimir Putin, the intelligence officer turned Russian President, also cultivated support early in his political career by performing a particularly potent hyper-masculinity. His public persona in this period centered on his promise to restore Russia to its previous strength and prestige on the world stage, following the humiliating collapse of the Soviet Union and the chaos that followed. Putin's public persona has also embraced a visceral, rough-around-the-edges masculinity that is described as "street masculinity;" this performance is characterized by "taboo references to sweat, snot, bodily fluids, blood, and more" (Ashwin and Utrata, 2020, p. 19). Academics Sarah Ashwin and Jennifer Utrata observe that "... Putin was at first welcomed by many Russians as a force for order and sobriety, the kind of strong ruler that Russia needed given how unpredictable and challenging it had become to just survive in the post-Soviet period" (2020, p. 19).

China's Xi Jinping, the President of China, has also marketed himself as a masculine reformer. For Xi, however, his performance centers less on physical aggression and strength and more on ideological purity. As Kevin Rudd, the former Prime Minister of Australia, observed, "He is a true believer in Marxism-Leninism; his rise represents the return to the world stage of Ideological Man" (Rudd, 2022, n.p.). This sort of masculinity does not require shirtless photos of Xi riding horses or braggadocious accounts of his sexual conquests—but it is no less meaningful for the conduct of politics in China and the country's foreign relations.

These different forms of masculinity reflect not only each man's politics, identity characteristics, and life experiences but also a different promise to voters about what type of leader they will be. In each press event, campaign ad, rally, and summit, these men offer competing narratives of whether modern male leadership should be compassionate and empathetic or authoritative and headstrong. These competing visions underscore the ways in which the gender hierarchy also entails intra-male competition; not every man has the ability to perform conventionally desirable masculinity. As Smith observed, "...to say that 'politics is masculine' does not mean that all men will inevitably benefit. The male advantage in politics may only be reserved for 'masculine' men, and/or the most masculine candidate. In this way, the gender politics amongst men is laid bare" (Smith, 2021, p. 453). The political playing field is not the same for all men—that's why male politicians expend so much energy proving that they are the right type of man. This performance of masculinity continues once men are in political office, with profound implications for the policies they adopt.

How Male Elites Behave in Office

Male politicians and political leaders have frequently depended upon performances of masculinity to implement their policy agenda and bolster their legitimacy. This can manifest in how these politicians relate to one another and how they govern. Consider, for example, the relationship between the American President Franklin Delano Roosevelt and the British Prime Minister Winston Churchill. In his inaugural address in 1933, FDR boomed, "there is nothing to fear but fear itself." But when confronted with a nude Prime Minister of the United Kingdom holding a cigar in one hand and a drink in the other, FDR was clearly shaken. In response to FDR's offers to leave, Churchill stated "You see, Mr President, I have nothing to hide" (The Economist, 2024, n.p.). Churchill's stunt kicked off a one-hour meeting between the two heads of state, just weeks after the Japanese attack on Pearl Harbor, which acted as a turning point for America's involvement in World War II. Churchill's naked political tactics (pun intended) speak to the ways that male politicians' performance of masculinity seep into their policies and behavior as representatives of the people. This interaction further underscores that male politicians perform their version of masculinity not only for their countrymen in a bid to gain support but also to jockey for position among their fellow powerbrokers.

Box 3.4: Erdoğan and Masculinity in Turkish Politics

Turkish President Tayyip Erdoğan has been both criticized and admired for his "arrogant, brash, and stubborn" approach to politics (Korkman and Aciksoz, 2013, n.p.). At the 2009 World Economic Forum, for example, he confronted Israel's President about the country's military activities in Gaza, saying "When it comes to killing, you know well how to kill children on beaches" (Eksi and Wood, 2019, n.p.). He then "stormed out" of the meeting (ibid). This confrontation was framed not as an emotional outburst but as a way in which Türkiye as a country could reclaim its pride on the international stage.

Betul Eksi and Elizabeth A. Wood (2019) observe that Erdoğan's outburst bolstered his domestic support, writing, "Almost a decade later, shortly before the presidential election in summer 2018, supporters of Erdoğan were still referring to this Davos performance as a marker of Erdoğan's great qualities of leadership and state and his abilities as the only man who could protect and defend the country from its enemies, including the corrupt, humiliating West" (n.p.).

Erdoğan has also relied on crass performances of masculinity in response to domestic political challenges. In response to the Gezi Park Protests in 2013, for example, Erdoğan refused to compromise with the protestors. Instead, at a party meeting amidst the protests, "he asserted, 'Now, they say the Prime Minister is so tough. What do you expect? Am I supposed to bend over [emphasis ours] before a couple of wanderers and ask them kindly to quit protesting? If you think that I am tough, sorry, but Tayyip Erdoğan won't change!'" (Korkman and Aciksoz, 2013, n.p.).This exchange emphasizes that Erdoğan relies on his image as tough, unyielding, and masculine in order to justify his political decision-making.

Furthermore, Erdoğan sought to delegitimize the protestors by spreading rumors about gender transgression within the protests. Zeynep Kurtulus Korkman and Salih Can Aciksoz (2013) argue that this is reflective about his broader approach to politics, writing that

> Erdoğan has been intensifying his exercise of power through performing this masculinity as the very instrument of his governance. He repeatedly recommended that women of Turkey have three children, recently supported a prohibition on the retail sale of alcohol after ten pm, and reported that girls were sitting on men's laps in Gezi Park to delegitimize the resistance movement. Put differently, he enacts the role of a husband who wants three kids, a father who forbids drinking at night, a brother who snitches on his sister for socializing with men (n.p.).

Thus Erdoğan's approach to politics is one that ties his legitimacy to his populist, conservative masculinity. These gendered performances matter not just for how he maintains electoral support but also for the policies that he adopts in office.

Or consider Ugandan President Yoweri Museveni, who has depended upon his identity as a veteran of the country's liberation movement to justify his decades-long rule. Museveni led the National Resistance Army (NRA) as it overthrew the Ugandan government and took power in 1986; he has remained atop the organization as it transformed into the National Resistance Movement (NRM), the country's dominant political party.

Throughout this process, Museveni has carefully managed his public image to underscore that he is the right man to lead Uganda. In his autobiography, *Sowing the Mustard Seed: The Struggle for Freedom and Democracy in Uganda*, published in 1997, Museveni "carefully constructs his identity as a revolutionary leader who is also an intellectual and who, upon assumption of political power, pursues a transformative and development-oriented agenda" (Mutie, 2018, p. 26). He portrayed himself simultaneously as a war-hardened veteran, as well as an adept farmer, capable of fostering growth in Uganda through his careful process of tending and weeding. Museveni has often referred to himself as "freedom fighter number one" (Reuss and Titeca, 2017, p. 1), and Ugandan politics in general includes frequent references to the liberation war. In recent years, as the memory of the liberation war has faded and Museveni has aged, he has doubled down on his performance of veteran masculinity. In the face of younger challengers, the 80 year-old Museveni relies upon his physical "stamina" and the legacies of the liberation war to justify his continued rule (Chitando and Mlambo, 2024).

Museveni's public image is deeply connected to how he governs. One can trace his tightening grip on political space in Uganda to his military and agrarian styles of leadership, both of which center on top-down decision-making processes. Museveni's performance of masculinity is reflected in his intolerance for dissent and coercive governance tactics. In general, leaders' interpretations of masculinity affect how they govern—with implications for their countries and for the world in general.

Box 3.5: Masculinity, the Cold War, and the American Presidency: A Toxic Trifecta

A cursory review of American politics during the Cold War shows how performances of masculinity are connected to policy-making. Consider American President John F. Kennedy. After eking out a narrow victory over Richard Nixon in 1960, Kennedy was the youngest elected president in American history. Kennedy's campaign had benefited from the fact that he was young, handsome, and charismatic—but in the throes of the Cold War, JFK worried that he would not be taken seriously on the international stage (Engelbrecht, 2020). As Englebrecht observed, Kennedy came into office "...determined to fight the Cold War with a new 'toughness' and masculinity not seen by the previous administration" (Engelbrecht, 2020, p.62).

Kennedy's vim, vigor, and self-consciousness about his bona fides as a sufficiently masculine world leader resulted in him fast-tracking the "Bay of Pigs" invasion, which his predecessor, Dwight D. Eisenhower had initiated. The operation involved providing support to a group of 1,400 Cuban exiles, who would invade the island and overthrow Fidel Castro, Cuba's communist leader. Englebrecht asserts that Communist Cuba was a particularly appealing proving ground for masculinity for three reasons: its geographical proximity to the United States, (just 90 miles off the coast of Florida); its value in proving his capacity to conduct foreign policy quickly' and because "...he wanted to assert his dominance over Fidel Castro, the man described as the epitome of masculinity" (Engelbrecht, 2020, p. 62).

Instead of providing Kennedy with a quick victory and proof of his capabilities as head of state, the Bay of Pigs was a disaster and humiliation for the United States. The US-backed invaders were crushed by Cuban armed forces in just two days. In the aftermath of the failed invasion, Castro's public image as a strong leader, both in Cuba and on the world stage, was bolstered. Furthermore, the botched military operation provided more fodder to those who believed Kennedy to be too weak or inexperienced for the job—a group which included Soviet leader Nikita Khrushchev.

Just a few weeks after the failed invasion, Khrushchev and Kennedy met at the Vienna Summit. As David Reynolds notes "each man thought if he 'played it tough, the other man would come around'" (2007, 198). Kennedy was flustered during the summit, allowing himself to be drawn into conversations about the merits and nuances of Communist ideology, where Khrushchev shone. Furthermore, Kennedy was shaken by Khruschev's stoney resolve; Kennedy told a *Time* magazine reporter, "[I] talked about how a nuclear exchange would kill 70 million people in 10 minutes, and he just looked at me as if to say, 'So what?'" (Little, 2021, n.p.; Morgan, 2023). Kennedy would later describe the meeting as the "worst thing in my life," because the Soviet leader "savaged" him in the discussions (Little, 2021). The Soviet leader may have felt emboldened, as the botched invasion of Cuba affirmed Khrushchev's assumption that Kennedy was in over his head—and fed his suspicion that Kennedy might also try to instigate a regime change in the Soviet Union.

The Kennedy administration provided a cautionary tale to any future American statesmen about the perils of making foreign policy decisions based on what seems the most manly. However, Kennedy's Vice President and successor Lyndon B. Johnson seemed impervious to this lesson.

Indeed, even before he took office as Vice President, Johnson had earned a reputation for his brash displays of physical intimidation. He was known to get his way politically by subjecting anyone that stood in his way with the "Johnson Treatment," described by one journalist as "an incredible, potent mixture of persuasion, badgering, flattery, threats, reminders of past favors and future advantages" (Smithsonian National Portrait Gallery, 2024, n.p.). This haranguing was often delivered in close proximity, with Johnson's 6'4" frame towering over his opponent. Johnson was also infamous for frequently showing his penis, which he nicknamed "Jumbo," to colleagues and subordinates in a show of domination (Van Hooker, 2022).

Johnson took over the Presidency on November 22, 1963, after JFK's assassination in Dallas. Johnson inherited both the Vietnam war and an assumption that the American President best served the American people by being the toughest guy in the room. The latter influenced the conduct of the former, dragging the US even deeper into a failed military effort.

Some assert that Johnson was not convinced of the strategic value of Vietnam but, "the potential psychological effects of 'softness' worried him deeply" (Young and Buzzanco, 2008, p. 374). Withdrawing from Vietnam, he believed, could embolden the Communists and weaken American standing in the world. Indeed, Dean underscores how torn Johnson was, "...simultaneously endorsing caution [in Vietnam] and disparaging the unmanly weakness of those who urged it" (Young and Buzzanco, 2008, p. 374).

Johnson's justifications for the war and explanations of military maneuvers often employed crude metaphors and "locker room talk." According to one account, when pressed about the Vietnam war by reporters, Johnson "unzipped his fly, drew out his substantial organ and declared, 'This is why!'"(Van Hooker, 2024, n.p.). In Johnson's eyes, Vietnam was a test of American strength, virility, and masculinity.

Both Kennedy and Johnson made disastrous foreign policy decisions in no small part because of their concerns about not appearing sufficiently masculine. Even though these men performed their masculinity in profoundly different ways, both interpretations of masculinity ultimately weakened America's position in the world.

Substantive and Descriptive Representation: Do Men Represent Other Men?

While academics and policymakers have spent considerable time debating whether and when female political elites will adopt pro-woman policies, much less effort has been put into assessing the degree of substantive representation male representatives provide for their male constituents.

Part of this is because politics has been, for so long and so frequently, a "man's game." With just a cursory glance at who exercises political power, it may seem ridiculous to suggest that we need to "empower" men to engage in politics. However, an intersectional lens—which considers not just gender but how that one identity intersects with race, class, religion, and ethnicity—reveals that it is only a narrow set of men that have been able to exercise power. Indeed, Rainbow Murray observes, "...the men in politics are disproportionately white, able-bodied and socially privileged, and less diverse than their female counterparts" (2024, p. 5). These are often the men that rest atop the intra-male gender hierarchy—the "real men" in that community. As such "...while men as a group are heavily over-represented, this advantage does not carry through to all men; many disadvantaged men also get left behind" (Murray, 2024, p. 5).

Viewed through that lens, the question of the substantive representation of men becomes a pressing concern for anyone interested in egalitarian politics. As Murray asserts, "expanding the study of substantive representation to include men does not undermine the important focus on women; indeed, it provides a useful, arguably necessary, complement to such work" (Murray, 2024, p. 2). The relative absence of women and most types of men is a function of the gender hierarchy, which subordinates everyone to the most elite sliver of men. As such, "challenging the dominance of the most privileged men offers a more inclusive model of men's representation while also breaking down some of the barriers that women face" (Murray, 2024, p. 2).

Examining the substantive representation of men can also help us understand how men behave in office—and why. Murray notes, "... cultures of masculinity are so deeply engrained that they are easily mistaken for the cultures of political institutions themselves" (2024, p.7). Not only is politics dominated by the most elite of men—once in office they face incentives to perform exaggerated versions of masculinity.

The dominance of elite men in political positions has implications for the conduct of politics in general. In India, male representatives from lower social classes were some of the most adamant opponents of a gender quota. This may be surprising, given their stark under-representation relative to elite men and the ways that they would benefit from reforms to make the political system more representative in general. However, academics Sarah Childs and Melanie Hughes (2018) assert that the less elite men may see women as a threat to the narrow hold on power they have achieved, rather than a threat to the lop-sided distribution of power in general. This study highlights how male elites are the assumed "default" political representatives; representatives "with adjectives" (e.g. female representatives, quota representatives, ethnic, racial or caste representatives) are then in competition with one another to fill the alternative political space, rather than united in the fight against the over-representation of the elite.

Conclusion

Indira Gandhi once said that her father Jawaharlal Nehru, a leader of the Indian nationalist movement who served as Prime Minister from 1947 to 1964, "was a statesman, I am a political woman. My father was a saint. I am not" (Fallaci, 1975, n.p.). Gandhi's observation speaks not only to their different personalities but also how differently they were received. As the Republic of India's first Prime Minister and a leader of the non-aligned movement, Nehru was revered at home and abroad. Nehru slots easily into the "great man of history" narrative—in which charismatic male leaders are responsible for shepherding their constituents into a golden age. Gandhi, as the first female Prime Minister of India, did not benefit from pre-existing narratives; at every stage she faced friction from prevailing expectations about women and politics. Nehru could be a saint in the eyes of many, but Gandhi would always be viewed with suspicion.

This chapter helps us understand why that is. From this chapter, we can take away that gendered norms and expectations shape the behavior of the political elites—with important consequences for national and international politics. In this chapter, we considered how the decision-making process by political parties reflects the system of gender hierarchy that we are operating within. Their process of identifying and running candidates both reflects the gender hierarchy and has meaningful consequences for the gendered composition of the ruling class.

These dynamics affect men and women alike in positions of power. In this chapter, we explored how politicians often compete on the basis of who is performing a more desirable form of masculinity. Furthermore, we also considered how performances of masculinity have varied across different politicians over time and around the world, with implications for the policies that they pursue while in office. Women in politics must also grapple with how they perform masculinity and femininity. This chapter unpacks the double bind that so many female politicians face, in which they are expected to be able to go beat for beat with their male opponents without appearing too masculine. Female politicians walk a tightrope between being appropriately masculine and conventionally feminine, with their electoral prospects hanging in the balance.

These gendered performances affect more than political appointments and electoral outcomes. They also influence the policies these political elites adopt. In this chapter, we've considered how female political elites often face particular pressure to promote "women's interests," as well as how male political elites' concerns about being appropriately masculine have driven their foreign policy and domestic policies.

So what can we take from this? Firstly, political parties are not neutral actors. They are powerful gatekeepers, who determine what their party stands for and who can represent them in office. These parties are also influenced by gender hierarchy—and take gender norms into account when constructing their electoral strategies. Secondly, gender hierarchy can provide incentives for politicians to perform masculinity. These incentives shape the behavior of male and female political elites on the campaign trail and in office. Thirdly, we cannot assume a linear relationship between descriptive and substantive representation. Gender hierarchy will not be undone merely by putting more female butts in seats of power.

This chapter and the previous one considered how gender hierarchy affects political decision-making among ordinary civilians and among the political elites. These chapters have also considered how women have risen to power. The next chapter will consider what happens when women's inclusion in politics and public life is interpreted as a threat to the gendered status quo.

Section II: **Economics and Gender Hierarchy**

Chapter 4
Gender Hierarchy in the Household Economy

Meryl Streep, an iconic actress, won her first leading role Academy Award for her portrayal of Sophie Zawistowska in the 1982 film *Sophie's Choice*. In the movie's pivotal scene, Streep stands in line with her two children for processing at the Nazi concentration camp at Auschwitz. When a Nazi officer learns she is a Catholic Polish woman, he presents her with an impossible decision: she can choose whether they send her daughter or her son to the gas chamber. If she does not choose, both of them will die.

To say the scene is gut-wrenching is putting it mildly. Streep clutches her children, frantic and sobbing, repeating that she cannot choose. As Nazis grab both of her children, she makes an impossible decision: she sends her daughter to a certain death so that her son might have a shot at life.

The movie's mainstream and critical success transformed the film's title into shorthand for unthinkable choices. Urban Dictionary, an online lexicon of popular slang, defines a "Sophie's Choice" as "...an impossibly difficult choice, especially when forced onto someone. The choice is between two unbearable options, and it's essentially a no-win situation" (Urban Dictionary, 2009). Sophie's titular choice to save her son or her daughter meant that no matter what decision she made, she would live with crushing grief and guilt for the rest of her life.

Decisions about whether to prioritize sons or daughters—our own personal Sophie's choices—are made every day. And while most of our lives will never approach the harrowing choices Streep's Sophie had to make in a World War II concentration camp, in small ways and large, we all can see how these decisions usually favor boys.

In this chapter, we investigate how gender hierarchy is intertwined with the economic decisions we make in our homes and families. To do so, this chapter introduces readers to the concepts of the "household economy" and "household economics." Leveraging the tools of household economics, this chapter helps us explore how reasonable efforts to maximize welfare in the household as a whole can often come at the expense of individual members—specifically, daughters, mothers, and sisters. Families frequently prioritize men and boys over women and girls, because the family as a unit is more likely to see a "return on investment" from the labor, education, and health of sons, fathers, and brothers. We then consider the constraints on women's ability to "opt out" of this inegalitarian household distribution of labor. In this section of the book, we trace how the gender division of labor that families practice in their home ends up impacting the structure and characteristics of the international economy.

https://doi.org/10.1515/9783111662886-006

The Household as an Economy

Let's start out with a quick thought exercise. When you were growing up, who was responsible for taking out the trash? For doing the laundry? For mowing the lawn? For cooking dinner? How were these decisions made? Did you have a weekly chart that rotated chores in a more or less equal fashion? Or were certain people responsible for certain tasks most of the time? For many of us, our parents and siblings all had specific roles about who did the grocery shopping and who cleaned and who walked the dog. Because we are raised seeing this division, it can seem normal or even natural. But, as we will see in this chapter, the creation of "women's chores," "men's chores," and the distribution of tasks between family members all result from bargaining within the household under the conditions of gender hierarchy. This bargaining process has implications for women's equality far beyond their front door.

A subset of economics, called household economics, considers how families make decisions and divide responsibilities in order to maximize the whole household's well-being. Using the same tools that economists use to study companies' and countries' economic decisions, household economists put forth the idea, "... couples engage in a division of labor to take advantage of gains from trade" (Iversen and Rosenbluth, 2010, p. 56). Members of a household specialize in certain tasks—chores, paid work, emotional labor—where they have a comparative advantage (Becker, 1986, p. 4).

Box 4.1: Specialization, Comparative Advantage, and Rationality in Economics

This section of the book uses some economic jargon out of necessity.

Specialization is a term economists use to mean "focusing on a narrow area of knowledge or skill or activity" in order to become more efficient in that area.

Comparative advantage is an economic term describing "the ability of one economic actor (an individual, a household, a firm, a country, etc.) to produce some particular good or service at a lower opportunity cost than other economic actors can" (Johnson, 1994, n.p.).

Rational Actor/Rationality is an assumption in economics "that people behave in rational ways and consider options and decisions within logical structures of thought, as opposed to involving emotional, moral, or psychological elements" (DiRita, 2014).

This division isn't inherently a "bad" thing—in fact, it can be incredibly rational, as the economists would say. One of the foundational figures in the development of household economics is the academic Gary Becker. He writes that:

A substantial division of labour is to be expected in families, not only because altruism reduces the incentive to shirk and cheat... but also because of increasing returns from investments in specific human capital, such as skills that are especially useful in child-rearing or in market activities... a family is more efficient when members devote their time to different activities, and each invests mainly in the capital specific to his or her activities (Becker, 1986, p. 9).

This specialization in the home mirrors how factory workers on an assembly line are tasked with screwing on a single piece of the produce, rather than putting together a machine from soup to nuts. Or how a country might specialize in making certain goods, like how Bangladesh and Taiwan become an export powerhouse for garments and semiconductors, respectively. Specialization—in the household, in a factory, or in the global economy—is all done in the name of increasing productivity.

While equating the warmth of family life to the hard-nosed operations of a company might seem alien—I certainly hope that my daughter does not primarily associate me with the idea of "household productivity" but rather has fond memories of the decidedly unproductive time we've spent cuddling and dancing— much of our home lives are governed by contracts and rules similar to those that bind employers and employees. Consider, for example, the marriage vow that many partnered couples take to stay faithful to one another "for better, for worse; for richer, for poorer; in sickness, and in health."[1] In making these vows to each other, spouses are, in effect, pledging to insure each other against the vagaries of the world. Marriage comes with its own job description and benefits package. As hinted at in Becker's emphasis on the role of altruism in the household, we could expect families to be more closely bonded because they are held together by the ties of affection rather than a cold contract exchanging work for wages.

The Gendered Consequences of Household Economics

However, specialization in the home has generally produced crappy working conditions for women. One of the ways this manifests is by assigning women a set of repetitive and time-intensive tasks. Time-use surveys from around the world suggest that women are more likely to be responsible for childcare and other care work in the home than men are. In the United States, women were more than

---

1 Thank you, Kait Sims for bringing this to my attention (and for all the support you have provided me in this project and others)!

twice as likely to do things like "cleaning or laundry" than men were (48%, compared to 22%). A 2019 Pew Research Center study found that women were much more likely than men to report being in charge of grocery shopping and meal prepping. In contrast, men reported being responsible for things like "...home and car repairs, lawn care and one-and-done type tasks like putting together furniture or installing a new appliance" (Borresen, 2023).

But, it's not just that women are responsible for certain kinds of household tasks; they also spend more time taking care of the home—doing the cooking, cleaning, housework, childcare, and scheduling that keeps the household going. Oxfam International estimates that women (and girls) are responsible for 75% of the unpaid care work done globally, amounting to 12.5 billion hours each day (n.d.). One study of adults in Peru found that this gap between men and women spent on household tasks peaked in their thirties, which the researchers connect to the time intensive demands of mothering that typically materialize in those years (Avolio et al., 2024). The authors observe "an inverted U-shape pattern, in which the gender gap is maximized during motherhood and decreases in later life stages" (Avolio et al., 2024, p. 18).

Box 4.2 Unpaid Care Work in the Global Economy

If women had to be paid as tutors for the homework help they give, or as chefs for the meals that they cook, or as nurses for the scraped knees they tend to, their pay would be roughly three times the size of the global tech industry. According to Oxfam (n.d.), "when valued at minimum wage this would represent a contribution to the global economy of at least $10.8 trillion a year." Women are responsible for a disproportionate share of unpaid care work in developed and developing countries alike. The 2024 American Time Use Survey found that in 2023, the average woman spent an average of 2.7 hours on housework a day—compared to 2.1 hours for men (U.S. Bureau of Labor Statistics, 2024).

You might be thinking, alright, maybe care work offsets the paid employment men do outside the home. This could be an even trade—women pick up the burden inside the home, and everyone ends up working roughly the same amount regardless of if it's for pay or not. But in the modern economy, many women balance both paid employment outside of the home and care work in the home, starting a "second shift" of care work and cleaning when they step through their front door (Hochschild and Machung, 2012). The situation is even more dire for moms. Kids are, famously, a lot of work—and women are often the "primary parent," taking up the bulk of childcare tasks. At times, this can be rational—it might make sense for a breastfeeding parent to spend more time handling baby's mealtimes. But even once there are no biological incentives for women to specialize in caretaking, women still take on more work taking care of children.

Furthermore, women with children are also often subject to the "motherhood penalty" in the office—meaning that their paycheck usually takes a hit once they become moms (American Association of University Women, n.d.). Women's earning potential declines at the exact time that they experience a sharp increase in expenses and demands on their time. In short: women who become mothers take on even more work and earn even less. A supportive partner can help, but, when we're thinking about heterosexual couples, broader social norms conspire to make motherhood a more costly proposition than fatherhood. Even when men report that they want to engage in more care work at home, they also report formidable barriers from their employers and the social expectations placed on them "as men" (Stryżyńska, 2023).

Why has this pattern of specialization—with women taking up more labor at home and men taking up the responsibility for earning wages outside of the home—emerged? Becker asserts that

> ...the gain from specialised investments implies that the traditional sexual division of labour if women have a comparative advantage in childbearing and child-rearing, or if women suffer discrimination in market activities.... even small differences in comparative advantage, or small amounts of discrimination against women, can induce a sharp sexual division of labour (Becker 1986, pp. 9–10).

Becker is highlighting here how discrimination outside of the home contributes to internal household decision-making.

Just because this is the way households tend to divide labor doesn't mean it's the only way we can specialize and share the load. Under a Marxist approach to household labor, the household would divide its chores between its different members such that the most gets done while taking the least amount of work. This kind of division (while perhaps unpopular given its namesake) is actually the most "efficient" way of splitting tasks. Using this approach, we would expect the children to go to school (since their labor probably doesn't earn much money, especially in contexts where child labor is illegal and can therefore cost the household if they're caught breaking the law) and the parents to work for pay in the labor force. We can expect a division of chores to follow similar lines—if one parent is particularly handy, they would be responsible for household repairs while the other takes on cognitive labor tasks like planning meals. Of course, even the Marxist model can fall into the patriarchal patterns; for example if boys are taught how to be handy and girls are taught how to cook. Broader gender social norms and expectations, again, condition how we are raised and make decisions within the household. Gender hierarchy is the proverbial water that fish swim in, affecting the decisions we make so thoroughly that we sometimes fail to recognize that it's all around us.

Some academics have taken aim at the assumptions underpinning household economics. For example, the foundational studies in household economics assumed that the household operates as a unitary actor,[2] with its governing principle being to maximize productivity for the family unit. That means that if one

---

2 See Hobson (1990) for a particularly interesting critique.

member of the family is harmed by a decision, but the household as a whole benefits, then the household should still make that decision. A range of critiques have been levied at the unitary model of the household. Primary among them is that members of a household might have different preferences from one another—or might protest decisions that are made for the family's "greater good." Researchers and academics such as Claudia Goldin, Nancy Folbre, Jessica Calarco, and Janice Peterson have investigated the consequences of gendered specialization in household activities for women, interrogating how different actors in the home benefit from or bear the cost of decisions that are made "in the family's best interest." Indeed, academic Barbara Hobson (1990) argues that there is much to be gained by setting aside the unitary model in favor of a "...view [of] the family as a bargaining unit where negotiations can cover a wide range of decisions involving the allocation of money, time and the division of market and domestic work" (p. 237). She asserts, "Once we accept the premise that the family consists of individuals who often have different goals and expectations and compete for resources (both time and money), then an individual's bargaining position becomes essential to the analysis, and the question of power and dependency comes into play" (p. 237). Later in this chapter, we will consider what determines individual members of the family's bargaining positions.

Furthermore, feminist interrogation of the household economy reveals how gender hierarchy affects how resources—like food or parents' time—are distributed within the home. We have compelling evidence that when families face limited resources—something that affects everyone at different times and in different ways—they often prioritize the men and boys in the home. These decisions are characterized by economists as "rational" because the family is more likely to see a "return on investment" on boys than they are girls. Gender hierarchy is at play in this decision-making process: when men have a higher earning potential and social status, it makes economic sense to dedicate more resources to them (Becker 1995). In some cases, families' decisions about the gendered distribution of household resources are matters of life and death. The World Food Programme (WFP), for example, observed, "In countries facing conflict and hunger, women often eat last and least." While the WFP suggests that these women are "sacrificing for their families," it is perhaps more accurate to say that they are being sacrificed (n.d.). These quotidian Sophie's Choices rarely capture the attention of Hollywood bigwigs, yet their impacts are felt every day around the world.

Prioritizing boys over girls creates a self-fulfilling prophecy of gender inequality: when households focus their energy (and time and money and food) on boys, we see gaps in girls' education and healthcare that have lifelong ramifications for girls' own lifetime employment, earnings, and well-being. These society-wide gaps make it even more rational for families to invest in their men and boys, which then reinforces women and girls' disadvantages. There is a self-reinforcing cycle, in which one family's rational decision to invest in men and boys makes it more rational for other families to do the same. Household economic decisions are made under the conditions of gender hierarchy—which has the subjugation of women to men baked in. Anyone that has been in the ocean before knows that it is easier to go with the flow than swim against the tide.

Historical Roots of Gendered Labor

It seems profoundly unlikely that women are somehow biologically "hardwired" to be more enthusiastic and skilled grocery shoppers, cooks, and caretakers than men. So how are we to understand the persistence and popularity of such a division of labor?

Part of the answer, according to historical economic analysis, is the technology we've developed to make us more productive. For an example of this, Alberto Alesina, Paola Giuliano, and Nathan Nunn (2013) point us to the humble plow.[3] They argue that the introduction of this technology not only radically changed agricultural practices but also proved instrumental in the rise of modern gender roles. They observe, "unlike shifting cultivation, which is labor intensive and uses handheld tools like the hoe and digging stick, plough agriculture requires significant upper body strength, needed to either pull the plough or control the animal that pulls it" (p. 470). Thus, the plow puts a premium on upper body strength to move the equipment across a field. Because men have greater upper body strength, on average, than women, the plow made it more efficient for men to dedicate more time to agricultural work (Conger, 2012). In economic terms, men began to "specialize" in the kind of work that produced food for the household to eat and, potentially, sell at the market.

Yet, work inside the home still had to get done—the cooking and cleaning and mending that made the small-scale farm run. This meant that women faced complementary incentives to "specialize" in activities inside of the home. This set us on a course in which gendered rules of thumb were developed, based on this type of gendered division of labor.

Subsequent technological developments have alternatively strengthened and challenged gendered divisions of labor. Let's consider the Industrial Revolution. This period marked a shift from agriculture and cottage industry to machine-manufacturing and industrialization. According to academic Louise A. Tilly (1994),

---

3 These authors are testing an idea first put forth by Danish economist Ester Boserup.

"With the coming of the Industrial Revolution, men's higher wages earned outside the household undergirded their stronger bargaining power early on, while women's increasingly incommensurate contribution was most often ignored and discounted" (p. 113). She also observes that the Industrial Revolution brought about "...a set of newly rigidified household division of labor (with the primacy of the male provider over the female domestic specialist) and workplace arrangements (the limitation of women to a narrow range of jobs with uniformly lower wages and strictly limited access to advancement) that again institutionalized gender inequality" (pp. 133–134).

Mechanization of production decreased, to some degree, the physical advantage that men enjoyed by substituting machinery for pure physical brawn. However, women who left their homes to seek paid employment still found themselves at a disadvantage relative to men. Women working in factories often find themselves facing unsafe working conditions for lower pay than their male counterparts (Seguino, 2020). Gendered assumptions about and the socialization of young female employees means that they're perceived as less likely to make demands of their employers and will be easier to control than their male counterparts.

Still, some suggest that the opportunity to work outside of the home facilitated challenges to patriarchal norms. Iversen and Rosenbluth (2010) paint a portrait of economic development and the weakening of patriarchal norms going hand-in-hand, arguing, "...agrarian societies have the most discernibly patriarchal values, and they put pressure on girls to play to the marriage market rather than to acquire market-relevant skills on their own. Patriarchal values begin to attenuate in industrial societies, but they tend to be far weaker in postindustrial societies" (p. 18). While their argument has been contested, the broader point stands: patriarchal norms and economic production play off of one another to produce norms about who should do what work. In the following section, we take a closer look at how these norms function.

Breadwinners and Homemakers: Gender Norms that Govern the Household Economy

Understanding the durability of gender inequality requires understanding how norms constrain our behavior—even when the persistence of gender inequality defies economic reason and our personal preferences. The norms that accompany gender hierarchy compel women to be altruistic caretakers of the family, while men are encouraged to be hard-charging breadwinners. Rather than understanding women's empathy and men's competitiveness as innate characteristics, we should be cognizant of how the performance of these roles is rewarded under gender hierarchy. Iversen and Rosenbluth (2010) put it bluntly, arguing that patriarchy has survived for so long not because "...men have tricked women into subservience," but because "patriarchal norms have tracked economically efficient uses of human resources, creating a bigger economic pie than in their absence" (p. 18). Though there are competing accounts to explain why we face social censure when we violate gender norms and enjoy social sanction when we abide by them (Eareckson and Heilman, 2024), research identifies the strong social pressures we all face to "perform" our gender appropriately.

As we discussed in Chapter Two, the home is a powerful site of socialization and where we learn what is expected of us as men and women. Thus, the consequences of decisions about household division of labor and investment of resources ripple out into the broader community. Consider, for example, UNICEF's (2023) finding that the gap between the time that boys and girls spend on "unpaid care and domestic work" becomes acute in adolescence—just as children start to take on the physical characteristics and social responsibilities of men and women. Thus, as children transition into adulthood, they are quickly saddled with expectations about the type of work they will do as men and women in their communities. These gendered heuristics have life-long effects. Furthermore, these norms shape the size of the labor force and can also shunt men and women into different types of work. Though invisible and difficult to pin down, these expectations play an important role in determining the structure of domestic economies and, ultimately, the global economic system.

Because families want what is best for their children, they often socialize them to adhere to gender norms and associated gendered expectations. Unfortunately, under gender hierarchy, that often means investing in their sons' prospects for a lucrative and stable career, while they may encourage their daughters to "play to the marriage market rather than to acquire market-relevant skills on their own" (Iversen and Rosenbluth, 2010, p. 18). Expectations to "play to the marriage market" persist even in industrialized and advanced economies. As a young woman growing up in Georgia, I was shocked by the widespread expectation that female college students would have a "ring by spring"—meaning that they would be engaged before graduation. It was a regional variation on the idea that women only go to college to get their "Mrs." degree (to find a husband, rather than to further their education or career prospects) (Urban Dictionary, 2007a; Urban Dictionary, 2007b).

Box 4.3: Sticky Norms in Northern Ethiopia amidst Civil War

Norms about who should be responsible for certain kinds of work are hard to change—which can help us understand why women who work for pay are still taking up a disproportionate share of household labor and remain in charge of "feminine" household tasks. The profound stickiness of gender norms was hammered home to me during my dissertation fieldwork. I was conducting research on women's participation in the Tigray People's Liberation Front (TPLF), a rebel group from northern Ethiopia that successfully overthrew the Ethiopian military regime and took power as a political party. The TPLF touted a progressive reform agenda, which included expanding women's legal rights, political participation, and teaching them how to plow the fields so they could contribute to the region's economy. The TPLF overcame mind-boggling odds; their opponent, the Derg, was backed by the Soviet Union and had significant military resources at their disposal. In other words, the TPLF was a capable organization accustomed to facing down daunting odds.

Yet, for all of the TPLF's impressive military successes, it struggled to change gender norms and to shift long-held expectations about what was "men's work" and "women's work." For example, the TPLF quickly abandoned its efforts to teach women how to plow in the face of strong community resistance—norms that governed, for the women of Tigray, just how much progress the TPLF could make. In conversations with veterans of the TPLF, they explained that there were widespread beliefs, "if a woman ploughs, she can't have a baby" or "if a woman ploughs, the rain won't come." Even in the face of a wrenching civil war, these superstitions made it difficult for communities to accept women ploughing the fields to secure a harvest. While norms are rarely written in stone, the process of changing them can be uncomfortable, extended, and deeply difficult (Agarwal, 1997). Even if it no longer makes economic sense to exclude women from some activities, the norms that developed surrounding that initial gendered division of labor can persist to great effect.

Let's think about the gendered expectations parents face and how these expectations shape their behavior. A recent survey by Richard Fry et al. on behalf of Pew Research (2023) revealed that 35% of women surveyed believed that their contributions at home were valued higher by society than their contributions at work. Yet men still get outsized praise for their willingness to engage in any childcare. It is almost a trope in American life at this point about how men doing the bare minimum for their children are lavished with praise, while mothers are rarely acknowledged even when they go the extra mile. As journalist Kristen Bringe (2024) wrote about her own husband: "Everywhere my husband goes with my daughter, he gets applause. *Bravissimo*, young trailblazer, well-meaning women of a certain age cry," as her own care work is taken for granted.

Though American social norms have adjusted to allow men to spend more time with their families, men engaged in feminized roles outside of their immediate families still face social sanction. Men working in care professions like nannies or nurses are often called "mannies" and "murses," nicknames that at best highlight their novelty in such jobs and at worst call their masculinity into question. As Nancy Folbre observes: "In the United States, at least, a liberal and highly individualist form of feminism has prevailed. Everybody has heard of 'Take-Your-Daughter-to-Work Day,'... No one has ever heard of 'Teach-Your-Son-How-to-Babysit Day'" (2002, p. 17).

Around the world, families and communities are grappling with what it means to be involved and caring parents. Globally, we see a diverse mosaic of how families assign these responsibilities, but they almost always stick to the theme of assigning more of this work to women. Consider, for example, a survey that revealed that Indian mothers spent an average of 2.4 hours a day providing emotional support to their children, as compared to just 1.5 hours for men. In Chile, the division was 4.1 hours and 3.6 hours, respectively. In Croatia, there was near parity—2.7 hours for mothers, compared to 2.6 hours for fathers (van der Gaag et al., 2023, p. 29). Gender norms guide these deliberations—creating a feedback loop that shapes intra-household divisions of labor. For example, just 51% of Indian mothers and fathers surveyed disagreed with the statement, "Changing diapers, giving kids a bath, and feeding kids are the mother's responsibility" (van der Gaag et al., 2023, p. 39). This norm is also reflected in and reinforced by India's parental leave policy, which provides no time off for fathers (van der Gaag et al., 2023, p. 68). While the consequences of gendered household dynamics look very different for men and women, patriarchy traps us all, telling us who to be instead of asking us who we are.

Renegotiating the Household Bargain

What I've described thus far paints a pretty bleak picture of home life for women around the world. So why don't women opt out of this crummy bargain by leaving (or threatening to leave) their partners for something (or someone) better? The answer is deceptively simple: in many cases, they lack a credible threat. In general, men have the upper hand because there are desirable and viable alternatives to them outside of the home.

The ability for men and women to credibly threaten to leave the home depends on whether or not they can support themselves independent of the family unit. This is good news for women living in advanced, industrialized economies (at least according to some academics). Iversen and Rosenbluth (2010) observe that as countries have upgraded their economies, men's physical strength has become less and less important, giving women better options in the labor market and making them less dependent on the home (Iversen and Rosenbluth, 2010, p. 22). In such economies, we've seen a shift in the characteristics and durability of marriages, as well as renegotiation within the home regarding roles and responsibilities. Around the world, as countries' economies have moved away from being primarily agricultural and as women have entered the formal workforce, divorce rates have gone up. Iversen and Rosenbluth conclude, "...on average, higher divorce rates and higher levels of female market participation go together" (2010, p. 12). When women are capable of economically supporting themselves (and their children), making bargains at the expense of their well-being becomes less appealing. This is, all things considered, a good thing—women are not trapped in unhappy or abusive marriages simply because they don't have the financial independence to leave.

Of course, not all working women file for divorce when they sign their new hire paperwork. Some renegotiate the expectations placed upon them without exiting their marriage contract. For those that remain in their marriages, we have seen a shuffling of household responsibilities and new expectations about what home life should look like. Beyond—or in conjunction with—changes in women's expectations, men have, on the whole, stepped up and taken on more work at home when their wives enter the workforce. Analysis by Gallup finds that in the United States:

> Since 1996, women have become less likely to be the primary partner handling grocery shopping (down 14 percentage points), laundry (down 12 points), cooking (down 12 points), dishwashing (down 11 points) and cleaning (down nine points). These shifts are accompanied by some combination of increases in the percentage of men primarily performing the tasks or sharing the work equally with their partners (Brenan, 2020).

Beyond secular national-level trends, the data at the household level also suggests couples adjust responsibilities when women go back to work. Gallup noted, "although mothers are more likely than fathers to say they perform most of the housekeeping chores, the division of labor among parents with at least one child under the age of 18 at home varies largely on each parent's employment situation and earnings" (Brenan, 2020, n.p.). When both parents are employed in paid work outside the home, "men shoulder slightly more of the burden of chores than do men in single-income households" and are more likely to share the responsibility of caring for their children (Brenan, 2020, n.p.).

Reshuffling responsibilities, however, does not mean dividing them equally. As we have seen earlier, an unequal gendered division of labor in the home remains even when women go to work. Mothers in dual income households were more likely to do laundry and clean the house than their male counterparts (Brenan, 2020). According to Pew Research, even in households where women and men contribute equally financially, "women pick up a heavier load when it comes to household chores and caregiving responsibilities, while men spend more time on work and leisure" (Fry et al., 2023, n.p.). Even in households where both parents work, but the wife is the breadwinner, women still spend more time on housework and childcare.

There are additional factors shaping women's ability to credibly threaten to leave an inequitable family situation and how they renegotiate their roles in the home, beyond what they expect to encounter in the labor market. Social norms also shape the viability of our exit options, and thus women's ability to renegotiate the household bargain. Indian development economist Bina Agarwal observed, "…women's exit options in marriage would depend not only on their economic prospects outside marriage, but on the social acceptability of divorced women, and their possibilities of remarriage (their worth in the 'marriage market')" (1997, p. 17). She further observes, "divorced and widowed women, older women, women with children, are typically less 'eligible' than men with these characteristics" (1997, p. 17).

Additionally, Nancy Folbre, a feminist political economist, argues that care work is harder to abandon or renegotiate because of the *care* involved. She writes, "People who provide care for pay are also prisoners of love. Nurses are limited in their ability to go on strike, because job actions threaten the welfare of their patients. Teachers are reluctant to impose long absences on their students. Auto workers and airline pilots can make more credible threats to withdraw their services. Not surprisingly, their salaries are a lot higher" (2002, p. 40). The stakes are even higher when we consider care for dependents that cannot provide for themselves—like infant children and elderly parents. Waiting for a father to return from work to change the baby's diaper because it's "his turn" means that your child is sitting in their own waste for hours at a time, risking diaper rash and infections (to say nothing of the smell). When we factor in the care and love that people feel for their families and dependents, it becomes difficult for women to credibly threaten to leave it all behind.

Two relatively recent developments suggest avenues for change to renegotiate how we divide labor in the home, in the hopes of securing more egalitarian communities and countries. First, Icelandic women have demonstrated the possibility and promise of collective action among women. In 1975, women in the country refused to attend work, nor do housework or childcare—all to draw attention to the discrimination they faced on the labor market. Compliance with the strike was remarkable, with an estimated 90% of women participating. The country ground to a halt:

> There was no telephone service. Newspapers were not printed because all the typesetters were women. Theaters shut down because actresses refused to work. Schools closed, or operated at limited capacity, because the majority of teachers were female. Airline flights were cancelled because flight attendants did not work that day. Bank executives had to work as tellers to keep the banks open because the female tellers had taken the day off… Meanwhile the men had to take their kids to work and provide them with food because daycares were

closed and women would not do any of the work they normally did at home (Rennebohm, 2009, n.p.).

The strike reverberated throughout Iceland's political system, long after women returned to work. The next year, the parliament "...passed a law guaranteeing equal rights to women and men" (Rennebohm, 2009, n.p.). Furthermore, the 1975 strike set the stage for another round of collective action in 2023. The Associated Press reported, "Schools, shops, banks and Iceland's famous swimming pools shut on Tuesday as women in the volcanic island nation — including the prime minister — went on strike to push for an end to unequal pay and gender-based violence" (Bjarnason, 2023, n.p.).

Icelandic women's bold actions have inspired women around the world. Polish women "...boycotted jobs and classes in 2016 to protest a proposed abortion ban"; and in 2018, Spanish women held a strike with a theme: "If we stop, the world stops" (Bjarnason, 2023, n.p.). All of these efforts are important—recognizing an injustice is the first step in rectifying it and these demonstrations have demonstrated the radical possibilities of women's collective action.

Secondly, women in South Korea have captured global attention through the "4B movement" in recent years. The name refers to the four things that South Korean women in the movement are refusing to do with men: "bihon (no marriage), bichulsan (no childbirth), biyeonae (no dating), and bisex (no sex)" (Windsor, 2025). The 4B movement is a response, in part, to the country's economic modernization, which has placed a slate of new demands on women but has not offered commensurate support (Windsor, 2025, n.p.). Despite strong economic growth, South Korea still has the ignominious honor of having the highest gender wage gap in the Organization for Economic Co-operation and Development (OECD), with women earning 31% less than their male counterparts. Women in the country also face high rates of intimate partner violence and crushing social pressure to get married and start a family. According to academic Ming Gao (2024), "Against this backdrop, traditional life paths – marriage, childbearing and homemaking – have become less appealing," giving rise to the 4B movement (n.p.).

It's not clear yet whether the 4B movement will have tangible effects on women's economic rights or their ability to renegotiate the household division of labor. According to Jean Nikita Purba (2004), "The movement has sparked discussions on gender inequality, sexuality, and the dynamics of 'power' between women and men in global society. These discussions emphasize agency and self-determination, aligning with many individuals who feel marginalized or oppressed by international gender norms" (n.p.). Following the re-election of Donald Trump, there was a noted uptick in interest in the movement in American culture. Time will tell whether the 4B movement's tactics will become a part of the global feminist playbook.

Conclusion

Sophie's Choice's tragic precipitating event ends in a similarly tragic tone with Sophie dying by suicide. Even though her decision to send her daughter to the gas chamber was a "choiceless choice," she cannot live with herself and the repercussions of that day.

In this chapter, we discuss how examining households like we do factories and firms can help us understand why women have so frequently been saddled with the responsibility for running the home and caring for children, while men have been expected to enter the workforce. Specialization in distinct tasks makes the household more productive overall, yet it is not without consequence. We also consider that choices made in the name of household productivity can come at women's expense. Gender divisions of labor that trap women at home, leave women financially dependent on their partners, and prioritize sons and brothers over daughters and sisters all impact women's well-being.

We have also unpacked how, even when it is no longer economically sound to divide labor in this way, powerful norms and expectations that have emerged around what is "women's work" and what is "men's work" drive many of the choices families make over who does what—and who gets what. In the modern economy, women often bear the dual burdens of working for pay and taking up a larger share of unpaid domestic labor. The decisions that are "rationally" made by each individual household aggregate into a system that devalues women's work while depending on their labor to sustain the global economy.

In this chapter, we have also considered why renegotiating the intra-household division of labor is difficult. There is no global "women's union" that can articulate our demands and organize a strike until they are met and patriarchy is toppled. Without a large-scale movement, we look to changes we can make inside our own homes to improve the status of women. Yet, the cost of shirking our responsibilities in the home—striking from the "second shift"—in the name of an equitable distribution of labor can come at a high cost to those that we love the most. Furthermore, persistent gender discrimination in the labor market undermines women's "exit options."

The most important take-away from this chapter is that the economic decisions we make in our personal lives, our homes, and our relationships have profound political and emotional consequences. How we divide up responsibilities in our home and who we deem responsible for earning income outside of the home sets the terms and conditions for our most intimate and vulnerable relationships —and therefore for the way we interact with the rest of the world. There are good reasons to be cautiously optimistic about the possibility for more egalitarian households in the future. Norms are slow to change—but not entirely frozen in time. While men still do not do their fair share at home, there is evidence that they are doing more than they used to, as women have entered the labor force. Furthermore, same-sex couples offer alternative avenues for families to divide household labor that don't rely on gendered heuristics. The road to gender egalitarianism is long, winding, rocky, and uphill—but it does exist.

Chapter 5
Gender Hierarchy and National Economies

The "green revolution" was hailed as nothing short of a miracle. In the mid-twentieth century, the spread of agricultural technology and new, high-yield strains of certain crops (like wheat and rice) resulted in skyrocketing agricultural productivity. Communities that had previously been stalked by the threat of hunger and even famine found themselves on more secure footing when it came to feeding their families (International Food Policy Research Institute, 2002).

Governments and international organizations patted themselves on the backs for their role in facilitating this transformation. Indeed, their interventions were critical, because the private sector would not have made necessary investments in research, development, and dissemination to propel this innovation. As the Gates' Foundation's Prabhu L. Pingali explains, "Private firms operating through markets have limited interest in public goods, because they do not have the capacity to capture much of the benefit through proprietary claims; also, because of the global, nonrival nature of the research products, no single nation has the incentive to invest public resources in this type of research" (Pingali, 2012, n.p.). Collaborations among governments, farmers, and international actors made technological innovation both possible and more accessible, which produced the Green Revolution.

The rapid growth obscured how those gains were distributed, however. Digging deeper, it becomes clear that large, commercial farms benefitted much more than small farmers (Food and Agriculture Organization of the United Nations, n.d.). Because of this, rural poverty and food insecurity persisted for many farmers.

The gains of the green revolution were also distributed unequally between men and women within farming communities. One study points out that, in Asia, the adoption of high-yield rice "had a major impact on rural women's work and employment, most of it unfavorable" (Harwood, 2013, n.p.). The green revolution required farmers to purchase technology with cash, meaning that they had to find paid employment—a process that often was fraught for women and resulted in more unpaid labor for them (Food and Agriculture Organization of the United Nations, n.d.). Another study, examining the effects of the agricultural revolution in Rwanda, points to the ways in which the "revolution" rewrote social norms, often in ways that disadvantaged women. The Rwandan government had incentivized small farmers to grow cash crops, which were typically associated with men, rather than the subsistence crops that women grew and occasionally sold when they had a surplus. As the researchers explained,

https://doi.org/10.1515/9783111662886-007

the reduction of these crops due to agricultural intensification, coupled with diversion of resources to crops considered by the government to be commercially viable, has impacted women's livelihoods and overall household food security. This was often expressed to us not as a rote matter of preference but as a life or death issue. As one woman put it: 'You can abandon maize and survive but you cannot abandon sweet potatoes and survive' (Clay and Yurco, 2024, p. 7).

The agricultural revolution—spurred by the Rwandan government and international organizations' interventions in these communities—also shifted the dynamics of intra-household economic bargaining in these communities. Some Rwandan women told researchers that the shift towards cash crops made them feel like they were subject to greater oversight by their husbands. According to the study, these women "felt obligated to 'report' their spending, even for relatively inexpensive goods like salt, to their husbands," in ways they did not before (Clay and Yurco, 2024, p. 8).

The effects of the Green Revolution speak to a fundamental truth: there is no such thing as a gender-neutral intervention into the economy. The policies underpinning the Green Revolution were not designed in order to prop up commercial farms, nor were they designed to cement the patriarchal order. But in practice, they did just that. Governments' economic policies—from taxes to industrial policies to the ways they balance their budgets and beyond—are influenced by gender hierarchy and metabolized through that system. In this chapter, we consider how economic decisions made at the national level are intertwined with the gender hierarchy. We first consider how gender hierarchy affects the design and implementation of government economic regulations (including rules around property, labor, and taxation), before then turning our attention to how government spending is intertwined with gender hierarchy. Though this chapter is not a holistic account of the gender dynamics of domestic economic policy, my goal is to provide readers with sufficient examples so that they can identify how gender hierarchy affects domestic economic policy in their own countries and lives.

Gender Hierarchy, Government Regulations, and Taxation

Governments get to make the "rules of the game" for those who live and do business within their borders. These rules determine the who, when, how, and where of economic participation—who can work, when employers are asking too much of you, how economic activity can be taxed to raise money for government spending, and where those tax dollars are spent as social welfare policy. These rules of the game have distinctly gendered dynamics and implications. This creates an interesting "chicken or egg" question—when these rules both reflect gender norms and effect the extent to which women and men can equally participate in economic life, which came first? In reality, we'll never know because the relationship is cyclical and interdependent. Here, we'll consider three kinds of regulation —regarding property, labor conditions, and taxation—that governments undertake to manage their economies and the gendered dynamics of these decisions.

Who Can Have—or be—Property

Governments around the world regulate who or what can be regarded as property, as well as who is capable of owning and transferring property. Let's first consider how governments have regulated who can be property. The most obvious example of this comes from how governments fostered and managed the slave trade.

Let's look at how the English government intervened to regulate, promote, and benefit from the slave trade. The House of Stuart and City of London merchants partnered to found the Royal African Company (RAC) to engage in trade along the West African coast. In the 1660s, the crown granted the RAC a monopoly on English trade in Africa. As a government-founded and -favored company, the RAC played a significant role in the trans-Atlantic slave trade, which became an integral part of the English colonies' economies. Once the crown repealed the RAC's monopoly in the 1690s, however, the company went belly up despite the slave trade continuing apace (Carlos and Krus, 1996). Government regulations allowing Africans to be sold as slaves were accompanied by policies directing who could benefit from that trade.

Regulations surrounding who or what is property and who can hold property have frequently been gendered. In many cases, government regulations have allowed women to be treated as commodities and restricted their ability to legally control property. Indeed, in many cases women were regarded as property, even when slavery as we typically think of it has been abolished.[1] For example, until the early twentieth century, women living in the United States lived under a legal system called "coverture" (Hoff, 2019; Geddes and Lueck, 2022). This meant,

> At birth, a female baby was covered by her father's identity, and then, when she married, by her husband's. The husband and wife became one–and that one was the husband. As a symbol of this subsuming of identity, women took the last names of their husbands. They were 'feme coverts,' covered women. Because they did not legally exist, married women could not make contracts or be sued, so they could not own or work in businesses. Married women owned nothing, not even the clothes on their backs. They had no rights to their children,

---

1 That is not to say that human trafficking is not an issue today.

so that if a wife divorced or left a husband, she would not see her children again (National Women's History Museum, 2012, n.p.).

Coverture was an erasure of women's legal personhood.

The United States did not invent coverture—in fact, its coverture system was an echo of eighteenth century English law (the adoption of coverture in the U.S. reflects its early status as a British colony). Other countries like France and Spain had their own versions of coverture, which robbed women of an independent legal identity and attendant rights (National Women's History Museum, 2012). In Saudi Arabia, the government still operates under a male guardianship system, in which "...every woman has a *wali*, a male guardian who makes decisions on her behalf – typically her father, and then her husband after marriage, although guardians can be brothers, sons, uncles or even male judges" (Carr-Ellis, 2025, n.p.). In this legal system "women are essentially treated as minors, in legal terms, for their entire lives" (Carr-Ellis, 2025, n.p.). Though Saudi Arabia has reformed its guardianship program in recent years, women still remain legally subjugated to men. At the heart of all of these systems is the idea that women are property or that they need male protection.

The roll-back of coverture and similar laws around the world allowed women the opportunity to enter into contracts, earn their own wages, and own their own property. This brings us to the subject of how governments regulate who can own property and how they can exercise those property rights.

As we discussed previously, gender norms can be sticky and hard to change. Despite the formal prohibition of many forms of coverture, women's property rights remain imperfect around the world. As of 2019, women living in half of the countries in the world "are unable to assert equal land and property rights despite legal protection" (World Bank, 2019, n.p.). This is both a function of inegalitarian laws and the difficulty enforcing legal regulations that go against customary practices or social norms.

One striking example of the long-term effects of coverture on women's property rights is American women's limited access to things like credit cards. Until 1974, American women could not get a credit card in their own name—they had to have a male co-signer to access credit (Gariepy, 2024). As of 2020, there were at least 72 countries "where at least some women from specific social groups do not have the right to open a bank account or obtain credit" (World Economic Forum, 2019, p. 11). While credit cards might seem frivolous, access to credit is an important way that individuals can invest in themselves. By making women's access to credit contingent on her relationship to a man, this regulation made it harder for women to own property and invest in their financial futures, while also extending patriarchal control.

The legacies of coverture also extend to women's physical security. Under coverture, raping a woman was not a violent crime against her but rather a property crime against her husband (Sack, 2010). Though coverture laws have, by and large, fallen by the wayside, the norms that surrounded this legal status have made it harder for women to exercise their rights. Consider, for example, "it wasn't until the 1990s that all 50 American states had laws on the books giving wives legal recourse if their husbands raped them" (Filipovic, 2013, n.p.).

Box 5.1: Land Rights as a Critical Property Right for Women

Of particular note in any discussion of women's property rights is women's uneven (and often uneasy) access to land ownership. As Renee Giovarelli and Beatrice Wamalwa (2011) report, "Secure land rights confer direct economic benefits because land is a key input into agricultural production and enterprise development; can be used as a source of income from rental or sale; and can provide collateral for credit where strong, well-regulated land markets and credit infrastructure exist" (p. 2). Land can serve as the foundation upon which economic independence is built—yet women have frequently been excluded from owning or accessing land, either by law or by custom.

Even when governments have tried to secure women's equal rights to own land through legal reforms, enforcement of these regulations has proven difficult. For example, though Indian women enjoy the same rights to land as men do, "less than 10 percent of privately held land is in the name of a woman" (Giovarelli and Wamalwa 2011, p. 4). They attribute this to the operation of social norms, which discourage female ownership of land. In many contexts, land is governed not only by formal laws but also through overlapping (and sometimes contradictory) systems of customary or informal governance. These various systems can all conspire to make it difficult for women to enjoy secure land tenure.

This is not only an issue for gender equality—it has implications for the country's overall economic production and, by extension, the global economy. Like we saw in Chapter 4, when women are dealt a bad hand, they do the best they can under suboptimal conditions. When women's access to land is insecure, they may be forced into making rational but ultimately self-defeating decisions about how to use it. For example, a study in Uganda found:

> When women farmers did not have independent and secure rights to the land they were farming, many chose not to let it lie fallow for an optimal period. Since their rights to use the land were insecure and dependent on a relationship with a man, the women feared that not using the land for one season would affect their longer-term access, thus they overworked the land (Giovarelli and Wamalwa 2011, p. 2).

The agricultural output and incomes of the women in this study suffered as a result of this pattern of overuse. The inadequacy of the land tenure program hampered their ability to provide economic and food security to their families. We cannot blame these women for believing that a bird (or harvest) in hand is worth two in the bush—but we can also clearly see how this rational decision-making process undermines their overall well-being.

Reforms to land tenure systems can give women more power within their homes and communities. A study of a land titling program in Peru, for example, sought to improve women's legal title to land by ensuring that both partners in a married couple had their names listed on the property titles. Academic Erica Field investigated the factors driving this decline and found that having their name on the land title increased women's bargaining power in the home (Field, 2003). Access to land was thus revolutionary in terms of empowering women within their own homes.

The laws that governments adopt with respect to property can curtail or catalyze women's participation in the domestic economy. When governments try to course-correct from an inegalitarian set of property laws, however, they must still grapple with the legacies of earlier regulations. Gendered economic regulations can have long half-lives, because of the ways that regulations are path dependent and because of the social norms that emerge around those regulations.

When Labor is Legal and When it is Exploitative

Governments also set the standards about who can work and under what conditions; these regulations affect not only our experiences in the workplace but also the costs of the goods and services that we consume every day. Let's consider one of the clearest ways that governments intervene into the labor market: by regulating wages, or how much money you earn for the work you do. While individual firms determine what they will pay their employees, many workers are protected by a minimum wage (also known as a "price floor") that prevents employers from paying them too little. As of 2021, Pew Research reported, "In at least 115 countries, the central government (or an official such as a labor minister) sets minimum wages by regulation, order or decree, typically pursuant to some authorizing law" (Desilver, 2021, n.p.). Indeed, Pew Research (2021) could not find information on some form of a minimum wage regulation in only 29 countries around the world. Minimum wages help prevent employers from taking advantage of their workers. Furthermore these regulations can help dampen the gender wage gap (International Labour Organisation, 2020).

Minimum wages, however, are an imperfect protection against exploitation at work. In the United States, for example, the federal minimum wage has been frozen at $7.25 an hour since 2009. Adjusted for inflation, that would be closer to $11 today. But because the federal government has made a political decision not to adjust for inflation, in 2021 a single American would have to work more than 60 hours a week to live above the federal poverty line (Ross, 2024). Given that more than two-thirds of minimum wage workers in the United States are women, the failure of the U.S. government to make the minimum wage a living wage means that too many women are struggling to make ends meet (Byrnes, 2023).

Some governments have passed further protections, aimed at ensuring that workers do not face discrimination on the basis of things like race, religion, or gender. Yet, these important and well-intentioned policies have not prevented discrimination. The gender pay gap is real, and has real implications for women's lives and the domestic economy.

Gender discrimination in pay further compounds women's economic precarity. A government's willingness (or unwillingness) to legally require equal pay for equal work is an economic intervention with clear implications for women's well-being. In Chile, the 2009 Equal Pay for Equal Work Law (which, as the name suggests, prevents gender discrimination in pay) helped shrink the gender wage gap (Cruz and Rau, 2022). There is even evidence that when governments make non-binding commitments to gender equality in the work force, women benefit and wage discrimination becomes less common. For example, one study found that when a country ratifies Convention on the Elimination of Discrimination against Women (CEDAW) and International Labor Organization (ILO) conventions on equality, the gender wage gap falls (Weichselbaumer and Winter-Ebmer, 2007).

While some governments have sought to protect women's rights to equitable compensation and to promote their participation in the workforce, others have adopted restrictions on the types of jobs women can do and, in some contexts, have made it difficult for women to participate in economic life at all. Let's consider workplace regulations in Russia. Despite rolling back Soviet-era restrictions preventing women from working in 350 occupations in 2021, the government maintained restrictions preventing women from working 100 jobs, many in the mining and construction industries (Maynes, 2021). These restrictions were initially passed because of the concerns about how working in these sectors would affect women's reproductive health. The government's paternalistic approach to women's employment overlooks how workplace safety regulations to reduce exposure to harmful chemicals and unsafe working conditions would benefit men and women. Instead, the state has cast itself as a protector of women, preventing them from getting hurt by playing with the boys.

The system of "gender apartheid" established by the Taliban in Afghanistan is a more extreme example of how governments can prevent women from participating in the economy. Activists define gender apartheid as "...the institutionalized pattern of systemic domination and oppression on the basis of gender" (Amnesty International, 2024, n.p.). In Afghanistan it has meant a near-total ban on women's participation in public life—including their ability to work outside of the home. One report asserted, "the loss of employment and restrictions on physical mobility have caused many working women to return to traditional home-based businesses, significantly reducing their incomes. According to the UN, this will cost Afghanistan up to $1 billion, a burden the country can hardly bear during the current economic crisis" (Remedios, 2024, n.p.). The logic is simple: a country's economic growth is hamstrung when half of the population is unable to contribute to the economy. Yet, the logic underlying the Taliban' restrictions is also clear: men benefit from sharply delineating women's roles in the home and maintaining their dominance of the public sphere.

Tax Policies

Taxes accomplish something truly remarkable. Not only do they give us something universal to gripe about, they also allow the government to redistribute wealth by collecting revenues from its citizens in order to finance the programs it runs for the country at large. That includes funding things like public schools, catalyzing research into finding new vaccines to keep us healthy, paying members of the military, and providing care for the elderly. Taxes allow us to accomplish, collectively, what we could not do individually.

While much of the literature focuses on the class dynamics of taxation, tax structures are also thoroughly gendered. Taxes can be designed with both explicit and implicit gender bias. Explicit bias comes when the tax code is explicitly written so that men and women are taxed differently than one another. Until 1995 in South Africa, for example, married women's earnings were taxed at a higher rate than married men's earnings (Barnett and Grown, 2004). The end of the apartheid government came with sweeping changes to the country's economic, political, and social systems.

Though these changes were aimed at putting all of its citizens on equal footing, the tax code continues to place a disproportionate burden on working women —in large part because of the implicit gender bias of the new tax system. In 2022, academic Lee-Ann Steenkamp (2022) explained, "By disadvantaging single-earner households, the revised tax system with its unisex tax tables has in fact deepened inequality in taxation between men and women" (Stellenbosch Business School, 2002, n.p.). More than 4 in 10 households in South Africa are headed by a solo woman, meaning that the tax system's preference for two-earner households comes at the expense of those households' well-being.

Implicit bias in tax codes also emerges as a result of how gender hierarchy conditions men and women's economic positions in society. Not only can tax codes disadvantage single-headed households (which are disproportionately female), when they aggregate married men and women's earnings to tax them at the "household" level they can come at a steep cost to women. Barnett and Grown (2004) observe,

> ...systems of joint filing with a progressive marginal rate schedule often discourage secondary earners because the tax on the secondary income starts at the highest marginal rate of the 'primary' earner. This is known as the marriage penalty... wives generally receive less after-tax income on each dollar they earn than their husbands, which is a significant disincentive to married women to enter the paid labour force. The disincentive effects of high marginal tax rates on married women's labour supply are further exacerbated by their responsibilities in the unpaid care economy during their reproductive years (p. 33).

Such a tax code assumes that assets are shared jointly—even though the couple might not have fully integrated their finances or the husband might be in control of the household's money entirely. By taking the "household" as an undifferentiated unit, such a tax code puts women at a disadvantage.

Without careful attention to the gendered implications of their tax structure, governments may unwittingly pick women's pockets. When women's wages and expenditures are taxed differently than men's, their incentives to participate in the workforce and engage in the economy shift. Failing to pay attention to both explicit and implicit gender dynamics within tax codes could mean that a country is not only standing in the way of gender equality but also hamstringing its own economic productivity.

Box 5.2 Balanced Budgets and Sacrificed Women

Sometimes governments are accused of "overspending" (with critics frequently pointing at domestic assistance programs as the culprit). The budget cuts that the government makes in the name of a "balanced budget" also have gendered implications. In the face of an economic downturn, many governments adopt "austerity programs" that require chipping away at government spending in order to get their economies "back on track." The programs that find themselves on the chopping block are often those that women depend upon. For example, an Oxfam International report notes, "In the wake of austerity policies from 2010 following the economic crisis of 2008, the UK saw the closure of rape crisis centres and domestic violence organizations, which were already underfunded and under-resourced, with demand for such services exceeding supply by an estimated 300 %" (Abed and Kelleher, 2022, n.p.). Or consider the austerity policies adopted after Javier Milei, a right-wing populist and libertarian, became Argentina's president. As a part of getting the country "on the right track," the government shuttered the Ministry of Women, Gender and Diversity and ended a program that gave "...victims of gender violence a monthly subsidy worth about €180 – equivalent to the minimum monthly wage – for a period of six months" (Moloney and Iricibar, 2024, n.p.). Women's rights advocates lamented the loss of the program, which they said had given women the necessary boost to start small businesses or achieve financial independence from their abusers—breaking cycles of violence and dependence.

Furthermore, cutting government budgets can threaten women's employment. According to the World Bank, "The public sector remains a larger employer of women than the private sector. Globally, women represent 46 percent of the public sector workforce compared with 33 percent in the private sector" (Mukhtarova et al., 2021, n.p.). Women and other minorities have often benefited from stable public sector employment, which comes with predictable wage increases and can be subject to more stringent anti-discrimination regulations than the private sector (Cooper et al., 2012). These fiscal policies often mean sacrificing women on the altar of "responsible" spending; this raises the important question of who governments are ultimately accountable to.

Gender Hierarchy and Government Spending

Having created the conditions for economic production and taxed a portion of that productivity, governments then have a choice about how to spend the funds they have raised. Here again, we see that gender hierarchy influences what governments prioritize and how government spending is metabolized through the domestic economy. The economic decisions that governments make at the domestic level have implications for women's well-being in their homes and communities; they also condition women's standing in international economics well beyond their borders (which we will consider in greater detail in the following chapter).

Welfare Programs

Since most of the people classified as living "in poverty" around the world are women and children, government programs to support the poor are inherently gendered. These programs have also been influenced by the gender hierarchy's erasure of feminized, unpaid labor in the home. The invisibility of women's labor in the home and as caregivers (which is, of course, work, even if it is not compensated as such) has led to misconceptions among communities, policymakers, and even women themselves that the work they do is "unskilled" or unimportant (Agarwal, 1997).

Let's consider the United States, which has a particularly caustic relationship with recipients of its (scanty) welfare program. Recipients of such assistance are alternatively vilified, patronized, and written off. Raced and classed assumptions are layered on top of this suspicion of the recipients of welfare. The racist trope of the "welfare queen" is still a mainstay of American politics, nearly 50 years after Ronald Reagan introduced her into the American imagination. Rather than considering the ways in which our economic and social systems are stacked against certain segments of society, we are conditioned to understand welfare recipients as people that made a series of bad decisions or who are too "lazy" to support themselves.

The belief that poverty is a personal failing means that many of the U.S.'s welfare programs are designed to encourage people to "get to work," rather than recognizing the broader social importance of the uncompensated work that they are doing. These program requirements can make program recipients vulnerable to exploitative working conditions—to say nothing of the burnout that they risk while navigating paid work, care work, and the labyrinth of government bureaucracy in order to get meager support (Calaraco, 2024). Joy K. Rice (2002), for example, noted that women on welfare are often employed "in low-paying service industries such as restaurants, bars, nursing homes, home child care, and temporary help service firms," where they are unlikely to receive employer-sponsored health care or have unions to press for better working conditions (p. 360). The precarity and low wages associated with these jobs mean that it is hard for these families to make their way out of poverty.

But it doesn't have to be this way. The United States is unique among industrialized countries for the paucity of its welfare regime. Other countries have provided a more robust social safety net for the poor, with particular implications for the well-being of women and children.[2] Let's consider Norway, which not only provides fairly robust support to those that have been fired or laid off from their jobs but also provides additional funds for each child under the care of an unemployed person (Norwegian Labour and Welfare Administration, n.d.).

Or take into account that the U.K., Australia, and the Netherlands all have "policies have provided a social wage or a mother's wage that acknowledges the worth of caring;" as a result, "social benefits were the key component of the income package of solo mothers," rather than the income they earned through work outside of the home (Sainsbury, 2025, p. 249). These governments recognized that work in the home is still work, and work that contributes to the country's overall welfare. Running these programs is not a matter of financing, it's a matter of political will and whether our representatives see working families as worthy of government support.

---

2 The variation in how countries approach support for women and children does not fall into the clear categories described in the academic literature on "welfare regimes." See Sainsbury, ed. (1999).

Childcare Programs

The remarkable variation among countries' childcare policies and spending on childcare programs has clear implications for women's participation in the economy, both as mothers and as grandmothers. Let's first consider which family members can take leave—and how much—once they become parents. In Egypt, for example, only the mother can take paid time off work—and she gets just 90 days (Herre and Arriagada, 2024). In Russia, mothers get 140 paid days and both parents get an additional 475 paid days to divide between them (Herre and Arriagada, 2024). That two years of leave can give families breathing room during a difficult time—and giving the father time off allows him to form important bonds with his child. In the United States, the Family and Medical Leave Act (FMLA) empowers employees to take 12 weeks of unpaid leave after having a child. Furthermore, only employees that have "... worked for their employer at least 12 months, at least 1,250 hours over the past 12 months, and work at a location where the company employs 50 or more employees within 75 miles" qualify to take FMLA (United States Department of Labor, n.d., n.p.). While employers and states have supplemented this allowance in many cases, American women like myself have to get lucky to get pregnant[3] and get lucky again to get paid leave.

There is also tremendous variation in what degree of childcare governments provide or subsidize once the bundle of joy is out in the world. In recent years, the astronomical cost of childcare has become an increasingly pressing political issue for working families around the globe. In 2023, for example, a World Economic Forum report asserted, "no one ever said having children was cheap, but when childcare costs start to exceed monthly mortgage or rental payments for large parts of the population, it looks like there might be a problem" (Shine, 2023, n.p.). They cited a survey of UK mothers in which 43% of them reported considering leaving their job because of the prohibitive cost of childcare (Shine, 2023).

Governments have, in some cases, intervened to prevent families from being crushed under the weight of childcare costs. Norway, for example, has capped the amount that families pay in nursery fees to NOK 3050 a month—or roughly $269 (TEKNA, 2022). The extent to which governments are willing to intervene into the economy to ensure that quality child care is affordable and accessible has a tremendous influence on women's ability to participate in the workforce. Because of gendered norms linking women to care and the persistence of wage discrimination against women, they are often the ones that give up their career in the face of untenable childcare costs.

---

3 Pun very much intended.

In many places grandmothers have become the unsung heroes of modern childcare. Studies from places like Mexico, China, Spain, the United States, and the Gambia all point to the critical roles that grandmothers play in providing an extra set of (generally unpaid) hands to manage the care and feeding of the next generation (The Economist, 2023; Mansilla-Domínguez et al., 2024; Marcos, 2023). Though there is not a tremendous amount of research on the effects of grandparents serving as caretakers, the studies we do have suggest that grand-mothers stepping in improves children's health, their school attendance, and their mother's ability to go to work (The Economist, 2023). One survey in the U.S. found that two-thirds of those families that rely on grandmothers for child-care reported that they would have lost their job if not for the flexible and free care they receive (The Harris Poll, 2023).

Studies from around the globe suggest that grandfathers (and other male rel-atives) are much less likely than grandmothers (and other female relatives) to pro-vide childcare, reflecting the widespread norms linking women and care. A study of Spanish grandmothers that provide childcare for grandchildren revealed that gendered expectations weighed heavily on their decision to lend a hand. One grandmother reported that she was driven by familial duty: "My daughter works and, in addition, she is studying. Dedication to her work and her child is impossible for her. If I can help my family in any way, I must do it and I feel sat-isfied" (Mansilla-Domínguez, 2024, p. 6). Another suggested that grandmothers are trapped in cycles of gendered reciprocity, telling researchers: "I was working when I had my daughter, so my mother took care of her. My mother put her to bed, fed her, dressed her, how can I not do it now for my daughter?" (Mansilla-Domínguez, 2024, p. 7).

The benefits that families derive from having grandparents lend a hand come at a cost—particularly to grandmothers. In China, women often retire in their fif-ties in order to be available for childcare; this means they leave paid work in order to take up unpaid care work in support of their family (The Economist, 2023). In other places, women may not retire, but instead take on more flexible —but less well compensated—jobs in order to help raise their grandchildren (The Economist, 2023). Furthermore, taking care of young children is physically intensive labor that can be difficult on aging bodies. The extent to which the un-compensated care work that grandmothers do props up the modern economy should make us rethink whether they can truly be considered "retired."

Grandmothers have had to step up because governments around the world have so frequently opted out of providing support to working families (and par-ticularly to working mothers). In Sweden, where the government provides robust parental leave and childcare resources, families are much less likely to rely on grandparents to provide childcare. *The Economist* (2023) notes that, in Sweden,

"Rather than allow a daughter to go back to work, grandparents might enable her to go out to dinner with her husband" (n.p.). Robust welfare states allow grandparents to provide support on their own terms, rather than as an economic necessity for their families.

Box 5.3: Childcare in the United States

The United States, again, stands out among industrialized economies for its paltry support to working families. The absence of government-subsidized childcare acts as a shackle, constraining women's ability to participate freely and comfortably in the economy. Like all shackles though, there is a key to unlock it and shake ourselves free of the weight—it's just one that the United States has decided would be too expensive.

While the United States' government support for childcare today is laughably scant, during World War II the country ran a childcare program that provided care for more than half a million children (Little, 2021). The program was a result of the government needing women to step into the workforce to maintain the war effort. Yet, when the war drew down and men returned, the government withdrew its support, shooing women back into the home.[4] The United States thus stands in stark contrast to other Western, developed economies "…that developed a poignant appreciation of the effort necessary to produce citizens and soldiers," and adopted family allowances and pro-family policies after World War II. A "return to normal" in the United States meant sending women back home and the evaporation of government support to working families (Pettman, 1996).

Development and Industrial Policies

Finally, even state efforts to grow the economy have very different effects for men and women living within their borders. Take, for example, Singapore's "growth miracle." The country grew at an average of 7% per year after independence (The World Bank, n.d.). As academics Brenda S.A. Yeoh, Shirlena Huang, and Katie Willis (2000) observe, the country's "vision charted for the twenty-first cen-

---

4 The jaw-dropping expense of childcare in the United States can force American women to take up jobs in the pockets of time where they can find free or cheap care for their kids. This work is generally poorly paid and ill-protected. Once, as a teenager, I made the mistake of disparaging strippers (and sex workers, generally) in front of my dad about the choices "those" women made. He asked me to consider what I would do right then if I got pregnant and couldn't afford an abortion. Both of my parents were working full-time during the day, so I would only be able to take a job that allowed me to work nights and weekends. In the absence of reliable childcare, I would have to drop out of high school. As a teenager without work experience and a stunted education, I was unlikely to find a job that paid well and provided that sort of flexibility. It became clear to me quickly that it wasn't that "those" women made bad choices: it was that we had a bad system.

tury... [is] driven primarily by the state agenda and programmes, [and] is resolutely couched in global terms" (p. 150). Yet that development agenda has relied heavily on women's un- or under-paid labor in the home. The Singaporean government has adopted a wide range of family policies, aimed at shoring up a "traditional" division of labor between husband and wife. Academic Teo You Yenn (2007) observes that

> In tandem with its aggressive economic agenda, the state has focused sustained attention on the family since the 1960s. The state's contemporary position signals an ever-increasing anxiety over trends toward late marriage and low fertility rates, which have come about with rapid industrialization... the state greatly desires to "protect" the "traditional family" in the face of these changes. To this end, the state has set up national matchmaking agencies, a ministry devoted to promoting marriage and childbearing, and a mandatory savings plan that secures housing ownership for married couples, among other institutional mechanisms (p. 427).

The government has also reified national and racial divisions between women in order to fuel its economic growth. In order to facilitate Singaporean women's participation in formal wage labor, the country expanded the number of work permits granted to (often female) "domestic servants from Thailand, Sri Lanka and the Philippines" (Yeoh et al., 2000, p. 154).

Lee Kwan Yu, the engineer of the country's economic strategy and a Prime Minister, was explicit in his nationalist, eugenicist, and classist approach to his country's population. In a public speech in 1983 he crudely explained to the audience the importance of educated Singaporean women having children: "If you don't include your women graduates in your breeding pool and leave them on the shelf, you would end up a more stupid society ... So what happens? There will be less bright people to support dumb people in the next generation. That's a problem" (The Guardian, 2015, n.p.).

Academic Kamalini Ramdas (2015) concludes, "the legacy of Lee's biopolitical vision for Singapore is, therefore, one that is rooted in heteronormativity and gendered roles within the family to promote a type of familyhood that is a key economic survival and nation-building" (p. 109). The full scope of the Singaporean growth project, then, depended on the right women going to work and having children in service of the state.

Similarly, governments' "industrial policy," or "the strategic effort by the state to encourage economic transformation, i.e. the shift from lower to higher productivity activities, between or within sectors," can inadvertently reinforce gender hierarchy (The Donor Committee for Enterprise Development, n.d., n.p.). Stephanie Seguino (2020) observes, "... industrial policies that promote structural change and the shift to higher valued-added production using more sophisticated technologies can contribute to and exacerbate already existing gender inequality" (p. 437). Consider, for example, the effects of government policies promoting investment in heavy construction. One study of the Canadian economy estimated, "...women account for a mere 2–7 percent of construction, trade, and transportation workers; 12 percent of engineers; 22 percent of primary industry workers; and 31 percent of manufacturing workers," meaning that women were not likely to be the primary beneficiaries of government incentives in that sector (Lahey and de Villota, 2013, p. 90). Without governments intervening to provide strong legal protections ensuring equal pay for equal work and to minimize gender discrimination in hiring decisions, women may be locked out of some of the most dynamic sectors of the economy. That study further noted that the projects themselves would also disproportionately benefit men when they were completed, as they focused on highways (used more frequently by Canadian men than women).

Government efforts to increase women's participation in traditionally male occupations could have unintended consequences for the sector in general. The solution to this problem is not just to "add women and stir." There is compelling evidence that work that's considered a "women's job" is regarded as less prestigious; some have referred to these jobs (or feminized specializations within broader fields) as "pink ghettos." As women become more common in "masculine" work, the prestige of that work is undermined. One study found, "when male managers are told that a high-status occupation is hiring more women, these men tend to evaluate women as less competent, leading them to offer women lower salaries" (The Clayman Institute for Gender Research, 2014, n.p.). Furthermore, a study of the healthcare sector found troubling patterns: in many contexts, as more women joined, the wage gap between men and women increased and compensation suffered in general (Shannon et al., 2019).

Optimism and Caveats about Economic Policies and Gender Hierarchy

Though this chapter has highlighted the gender dynamics of governments' economic policies and has railed against the discrimination women face in the modern economy, it is not all bad news. Governments have also found ways to effectively promote women's economic participation through targeted interventions and regulations. Seguino (2020) observes that

> Public policy can influence the distribution of care work between women and men, and can also reduce the amount of necessary care work through public investment in physical infrastructure (roads, sanitation, and electricity that reduce the time necessary for care activities

such as fetching water and fuel), as well as social infrastructure (spending on publicly fund-
ed care services). These expenditures, which can reduce women's unpaid care burden and
redistribute social reproduction to the state and to men, also support the goals of industrial
policy (p. 439).

In other words: investing in women and taking their gender-specific priorities (as
discussed in Chapter 2) into account is good for the economy.

Similarly, recent decades have seen an explosion of "gender-sensitive budgeting," also called "gender-responsive budgeting" or just "gender budgeting." The
Council of Europe (2005) defines it as "a gender-based assessment of budgets, in-
corporating a gender perspective at all levels of the budgetary process and re-
structuring revenues and expenditures in order to promote gender equality"
(p. 10). According to the International Monetary Fund (IMF), as of 2022, "More
than half of G20 countries," or those countries that belong to the "group of 20" international forum, "have a legal framework in place requiring that gender goals
and activities be incorporated in the budget, and almost all collect gender-disaggregated statistics to some degree" (Curristine et al., 2022, n.p.). These legal and at-
titudinal reforms speak to a growing recognition that the economy is not a gender-
neutral arena. Collecting gender-disaggregated statistics and designing budgets
with gender in mind are important first steps to securing more gender egalitarian
economic development. Gender-responsive budgeting might be the law of the land
in some places, but law cannot compel political will (Alonso-Albarran et al., 2021).
Ultimately, gender budgeting is an imperfect tool but still one that can be useful
for some jobs.

Though it is certainly difficult for governments to manage the economy to promote gender equality, there are both normative and economic reasons that they
should continue to do so. Rather than throwing our hands up in despair about
how gender hierarchy can produce unintended consequences for well-meaning
policies, we must be vigilant in our gendered analysis and flexible in our approach.

Conclusion

It was mostly Rwandan women hard at work swinging hoes to prepare the land
for planting, rather than men, when a group of academic researchers traveled
to the country's southwest to understand the effects of the green revolution.
When the researchers asked why so few men were among them, the Rwandan
women replied with "Ha! Men used to do agriculture here. Now they see no
money in it. They send female servants to work in the fields for them" (Clay

and Yurco, 2024, p. 6). Though agricultural productivity may have increased in the aftermath of the green revolution, this chapter shows us the inaccuracy of the assertion that economic growth is good for everyone. Economic development is designed under and metabolized through a system of gender hierarchy.

The biggest takeaway from this chapter is that states' economic policies are affected by, and contribute to, gender hierarchy. In this chapter, we dug into how the regulations that governments adopt related to property, compensation, and labor all are influenced by gender hierarchy and affect men and women differently. Having discussed the gender dynamics of the economic environment, we then turn our attention to the gender dynamics of government spending. Together, we unpack how welfare regimes, legal restrictions on discriminatory policies, and investment in certain sectors are all influenced by the economic logic of gender hierarchy. Furthermore, this chapter considers how, in the absence of nuanced gendered analysis, well-intentioned government policies can further entrench the discriminatory tendencies of gender hierarchy.

Weaving together Chapters 4 and 5, we can see an interactive relationship between the economic decisions made within households and those made by governments. This chapter highlights that there is no gender-neutral intervention into the economy, because of the ways that gender hierarchy conditions our upbringing and responsibility in the home and undergirds the structure of the domestic economy. In tandem by decisions made in the home, governments can enter into destructive, patriarchal, and mutually-reinforcing cycles—or they can adopt policies that facilitate a more egalitarian economy in the country at large and in the families that make up the nation.

Chapter 6
Gender Hierarchy and International Economics

Before she took a position in her local Empowerment, Knowledge and Transformative Action (EKATA) group in Bangladesh, Mushoumi had not envisioned herself as a strident labor leader. Like so many women that take on leadership roles, she had to be convinced by others that she could make a real difference if she stepped up.

Mushoumi proved them right. As an EKATA leader, she's worked hard to ensure that women aren't exploited in garment factories in her community. When she and nine other workers were fired without cause, she steeled herself and confronted the factory's management. She explained that the conversation went something like this:

> 'Did we do anything wrong?' I asked. 'Is there a complaint about our work?' He said no. 'So why are you trying to dismiss us?' I asked. I asked for four months' salary and notice. And he replies that that's not their procedure. I said that I won't leave. Why would I leave? I have worked here productively for so long (CARE, 2022, n.p.).

With the backing of the EKATA group, Mushoumi threatened to bring the managers to court unless they let her keep her job and paid her what she was owed. She also stood up for the other nine workers that were facing similar circumstances in the factory. Because Mushoumi knew her rights as a factory worker and felt confident in her ability to challenge her managers' decisions, she and nine others were able to keep working to support their families.

Not every factory has a Mushoumi and not every community has an EKATA group. Other garment workers around the world have struggled to obtain fair working conditions and decent pay. This fight has been especially hard for women working in garment factories, who rarely have a strong bargaining position vis-à-vis their employers.

Women hold an estimated 80 % of jobs in the global garment industry—but they are more likely to be found on the line rather than in the C-Suite (Better Work, 2018). In these already generally low-paying positions, some research suggests that women are paid roughly 20 % less than their male counterparts (Better Work, 2018). Women factory workers responsible for making the clothes that you and I are wearing right now have likely faced sexual harassment and discrimination as they sought work or tried to do their jobs.

Despite advocacy by and on behalf of garment workers, meaningful and widespread change has been elusive. The very structure of the international economic

https://doi.org/10.1515/9783111662886-008

system provides incentives for garment factories and similar industries to exploit their workers—many of whom are women. It also provides incentives for countries that import the results of their painstaking labor to look the other way about the conditions that they work under in order to maintain low prices for their citizens.

In this chapter, we consider the relationship between gender hierarchy and international economics. We dive into how women experience international trade agreements, government austerity programs, and economic sanctions differently than men. Together, we also consider how gender hierarchy influences decision-making in all of these domains. As with the previous chapter, this chapter does not purport to be a comprehensive account of how gender hierarchy affects all of the world economy but rather a discussion that spurs critical thinking about how global economic production relates to gender hierarchy and how the functioning of the world economy is linked to decisions made in our homes and communities.

Gender and International Trade

International trade, or "the purchase and sale of goods and services by companies in different countries," is a nearly ubiquitous feature of our modern economy (Heakal, 2025, n.p.). In 2024, economists estimated that international trade was valued at nearly $32 trillion—larger than the U.S.'s entire economy by roughly $5 trillion (United Nations Trade and Development, 2024). I'm typing this now in Colorado on a laptop made with materials from the Democratic Republic of the Congo, assembled in China by a Taiwanese company, and marketed to me by an American company, while I sip a cup of coffee made with beans from El Salvador.[1] Let's unpack how gender hierarchy conditions how individuals navigate economic changes as a result of international trade and how gender hierarchy can influence government decision-making about which industries are considered worth "protecting."

Without subjecting you to a primer on international trade, it is worth reviewing the basics of how trade between nations works. As we briefly discussed in the last two chapters, some of the foundational concepts in international trade are "comparative advantage" and "specialization." Comparative advantage means that a country can "...produce a particular good or service at a lower opportunity cost than its trading partners;" it is the reason that countries benefit from trade

---

1 At Corvus Coffee in Littleton Colorado, which is well worth a visit if you are passing through.

(Hayes, 2024, n.p.). Specialization means that a country focuses primarily on producing a limited set of goods and services—typically in areas where they enjoy a comparative advantage.

Setting aside the unbearably clunky lexicon of economists, this means that trade prompts economies to focus their economic efforts on creating the things that their economies are well-placed to make. Trade shifts the way that economies function, as the sector where they have a comparative advantage becomes more prominent and other sectors take a hit. This means that trade agreements between countries create winners and losers, even while boosting the overall economic productivity of each trading country. As we saw in the last chapter, jobs and industries are characterized by different degrees of male and female participation. This means that international trade does not just create winners and losers at the sectoral level but also among men and women.

Consider, for example, how the North American Free Treaty Agreement (an agreement between the United States, Mexico, and Canada better known by the acronym NAFTA) has meant radically different things to men and women in Mexico. The effect of NAFTA in Mexico, put very simply, was to increase manufacturing and decrease agricultural production.

Given how factory work is often male-coded, one might assume that Mexican men benefited from NAFTA more than Mexican women. However, the reality is more complicated. NAFTA appears to have increased the demand for female labor among factories. One group of economists found that the shift towards higher-tech factory production that accompanied NAFTA decreased the incentives to hire men and resulted in more opportunities for women to enter the workforce as blue-collar workers (Juhn et al., 2014). In other words, as Mexican factory work relied less on physical strength as the result of investments in better technology, these factories became more likely to hire women.

Even though NAFTA opened up opportunities for Mexican women to enter the workforce in manufacturing jobs, this opportunity was a double-edged sword. On the one hand, working outside of the home can mean the sort of financial independence that can improve women's bargaining power in the home (as we discussed in Chapter 5). Further, paid labor can offer a ladder out of poverty for working women and their families. On the other hand, managers at these factors have been eager to hire women because of the belief that they are less likely to form unions and because they can often pay women less than men.

But women's reticence to rock the boat at work reflects their precarity, not particularly humane working conditions. On the contrary, there is evidence these women are exposed to harmful chemicals that affect their health and the health of their children. Additionally, despite Mexican labor laws providing protections for female workers, "Human Rights Watch has documented many cases

of Mexican *maquiladora* plants requiring female job applicants to provide certif-
icates verifying that they are not pregnant, and firing women when they become
pregnant" (Folbre, 2001, p. 190). Discrimination, harassment, and poor working
conditions are rife. NAFTA brought about new opportunities for women—but
also new threats to their well-being.

Furthermore, Mexican women's work outside of the home has not necessarily
been accompanied by less work at home. Marceline White, Carlos Salas and Sarah
Gammage (2003) found that Mexican women face a daunting 'second shift' at
home, writing, "Women work all day in the maquilas and then come home to
care for the house and their children – they work a total of 18 hours a day" (p.
iv). They conclude, "While these jobs may provide increased autonomy for
women, many of these jobs are low-waged, precarious, and exist in difficult working conditions. Simply stated, these types of jobs do not enable women to pull
themselves and their families out of poverty" (p. iv). In the absence of well-en-
forced labor protections, dignified working conditions, and more egalitarian gender norms, the purported "winners" from international trade may find themselves
celebrating pyrrhic victory.

NAFTA is not an anomaly. Around the world, trade has shifted economic production patterns. These changes interact with the pre-existing gender hierarchy
while also providing new sets of incentives to bring women into the paid labor
force or for them to specialize in taking care of the home.

Gender hierarchy also influences what industries are deemed worthy of protection from possible negative impacts of free trade. Because male-coded occupations are more prestigious and there is an expectation that men will work for a
living, they can attract more political protection and consternation. Consider,
for example, the efforts that some politicians have undertaken to protect traditionally masculine industries or those that hold a lot of symbolic or material importance to men. During Donald Trump's first bid for the Presidency, he frequently asserted that free trade had been disastrous for American workers employed in
manufacturing and other heavy industries. According to academic Rachel Brewster "although the argument in favor of more industrial employment could be gender neutral, the Trump campaign sought to frame this issue as one regarding the
loss of traditional forms of male employment" (2020, p. 59). She asserts that
Trump's platform of protectionism "was not only about jobs but the type of
work that would validate a blue-collar male worker" (p. 59).

Box 6.1: A Closer Look at Trump's Gendered Protectionism

After winning the 2016 election, Donald Trump imposed a 25% tariff on steel imports, among a series of other protectionist tariffs. According to economists and workers in these industries alike, the results were devastating for the economy at large—even in industries that the protections were supposed to benefit. One study estimated that 75,000 jobs were lost in "metal-using" jobs as a result of steel and aluminum tariffs, a significant portion of the 175,000 jobs lost overall as a result of the trade war (Reuters, 2020, n.p.). A labor leader within the United Steelworkers Union, Bob Kemper, told journalists in 2020, "I don't see any policy that helped us. We are losing our damn jobs here" (Reuters, 2020, n.p.).

The jobs that were created by the tariff regime came at a hefty cost for American workers. A report from the Brookings Institute noted, "…American consumers paid about $817,000 in higher prices attributable to the tariffs for every job created in the washing machine industry and $900,000 in the steel industry. While policy interventions to support manufacturing jobs may be warranted, there are cheaper ways to do so" (Gertz, 2020, n.p.).

Donald Trump and his allies did not learn their lesson from their expensive dalliance with protectionist policies in his first term. Shortly into his second term, President Trump announced a blanket 10% tariff rate (The White House, 2025). For some countries, notably China, Trump threatened tax rates above 100%. His trade policies were met with frustration from other countries' leaders and panic in the stock market.

Given the credible accounts suggesting that the tariffs produced a net loss for American workers and consumers, we might ask ourselves why the Trump administration still pursued this policy, why the successor Biden administration left some of these tariffs intact, and why Donald Trump adopted similar policies after starting his second term in 2025.

These policies are not purely economic—they are also tied to an often backward-looking vision of what roles men and women should play in society and how they should relate to one another. According to Brewster (2020):

> It is not just that an earlier era had more factory employment, but that society was different as well. There is nostalgia for a time when women were discouraged from entering the work force, and it was socially uncontroversial to discriminate in favor of men both in terms of employment and salary. The political promise to restore the employment status of 'big, strong guys' in industries such as steel rather than electronics manufacturing is, in part, about restoring a previous social order in which these men dominated (p. 64).

Some welcomed the Trump administration's protectionist policies in 2025 as the solution to a "crisis of masculinity" affecting American men. Vish Burra—who previously worked for scandal- tainted, right-wing politicians like Rep. Matt Gaetz and Rep. George Santos—tweeted, "Men in America don't need therapy. Men in America need tariffs and DOGE," a reference to the controversial Department of Government Efficiency (Walsh, 2025). Ariel Messman-Rucker (2025) explains, "The logic goes that with sky-high tariffs, manufacturing will come back to the United States (it won't) and men will start working in physically demanding factory jobs which in turn will make them extra 'manly'" (n.p.).

Put that way, we can see the connections between some protectionist trade policies and the sort of backlash politics we will discuss in Chapter 10. We can see how gender hierarchy influences both how trade policy is brokered and the effects of these deliberations. Americans are clearly willing to pay dearly to protect quintessentially "masculine" jobs—but are reluctant to invest in things like the "feminine" care economy.

Governments are increasingly willing to take the gender dynamics of trade seriously. This has inspired a raft of reforms in trade agreements and a broader shift in how policymakers think about trade. Take, for example, efforts underway in Canada. In line with its "feminist foreign policy," the country has also adopted a "feminist" international trade policy (Government of Canada, 2019, n.p.). This program "...seeks to ensure that benefits and opportunities resulting from free trade agreements (FTAs) and foreign investment promotion and protection agreements (FIPAs) are widely shared, including among women workers, entrepreneurs and business owners" (Government of Canada, 2019, n.p.). A key part of this is integrating "gender-based analysis plus" (GBA+), "an analytical tool used to support the development of responsive and inclusive policies, programs, and other initiatives" (Government of Canada, 2024, n.p.) into Canadian trade agreements (Government of Canada, 2019, n.p.). As a part of this feminist trade policy, Canada has been at the forefront of the effort to include independent gender chapters in free trade agreements, providing important visibility and attention to the fact that men and women are impacted by trade agreements differently (Hannah et al., 2022).

Other countries contributing to this trend of gender-sensitive trade policies include Japan, Argentina, Brazil, the United Kingdom, and Uruguay (Fröhlich, 2023). These efforts have notched some modest gains. A study of gender provisions in trade agreements found that these gender provisions are associated with more female owners and managers of firms (Karam and Zaki, 2024).

These programs have also faced backlash from a range of interest groups. For example, Canada's feminist international trade policy has also come under fire— both from conservatives who "claim that Canada's efforts to place gender equality and environmental sustainability at the centre of its trade policy are nothing more than virtue-signalling" as well as from more progressive circles who take issue with the policy's focus on elites, rather than structural gender inequalities and the experiences of working women (Hannah et al., 2022, pp. 72–73). Feminist academic Jacqui True (2009) asserts that gender mainstreaming within the European Union "... is associated with the transformation of gender equality from a normative goal demanded by women's movements into a technical, bureaucratic (and measurable) repertoire of powerful state and supra-state actors involving indicators, checklists, benchmarks, and other tools" (p. 739). This is meaningful not only because of the shift in discursive power it signals but also because "...gender mainstreaming becomes a form of rationalization in disguise, an argument for getting rid of budget lines devoted to gender expertise and budgets for women's projects" (True, 2009, p. 739). The tangible implications of this is that gender has been "mainstreamed" into oblivion.

Furthermore, there is reason to interrogate the international distribution of power at play in efforts to make trade more gender egalitarian. One study found, "...only 16 % between developing countries (South-South FTAs) and 14 % between developed countries (North-North-FTAs) include gender provisions" (Fröhlich, 2023, pp. 183 – 184). Another study found that gender-provisions in trade agreements can produce positive effects on women's management and ownership also found, "...the positive effect of gender-related provisions in trade agreements on women empowerment holds only for developed countries" (Karam and Zaki, 2024, p. 875). Women in developing countries did not benefit from the inclusion of gender provisions in trade agreements—though these women are more economically vulnerable than their counterparts in developed countries. Who wins and loses from trade depends not only on the country they live in but also the jobs they do and their gender.

Gender and International Austerity Programs and Liberalization

The previous chapter explored some of the connections between gender hierarchy and the dynamics of governments' domestic economic policies. Yet, many government officials ultimately have limited control over decisions about their economy because they are dependent on economic support from more developed countries or international financial institutions. International financial institutions (IFIs) have imposed conditionalities on borrowing countries, called Structural Adjustment Programs (SAPs) (Halton, 2024, n.p.). These recommendations reflect economic orthodoxy, and often include requirements like slashing government spending, opening their domestic markets to international trade and investment, and privatizing government-owned companies. Though these reforms may make sense on paper, they often come at a high human cost. Under the guise of fiscal responsibility, IFIs like the World Bank and the International Monetary Fund (IMF) have demanded that borrowing countries balance their budget even when it comes at the expense of citizen well-being or future economic growth.

SAPs and other economic reforms endorsed by international financial institutions are often felt acutely by women and girls. The compound effect of each of the reforms undertaken in conjunction with a structural adjustment program can significantly reduce women and girls' opportunities, rights, and economic well-being.

Let's first consider the effects of cuts to government programs. While IFIs do not typically have final say on what programs should be cut or reduced, countries undergoing structural adjustment often put social services on the chopping block first. Cutting social spending can be a matter of life and death for women. According to academic Hillary Campbell (2010), "in Tanzania, for example, seventy-one mothers died in the first thirteen weeks of 1988, when economic reforms were in force," which was "four times the maternal death rate of previous years" (p. 9). She concludes, "mothers died because of inadequate health care, which stemmed from a lack of sufficient funding," itself a function of IFI demands for government reform (p. 9).

Tanzanian women's experiences are far from isolated: austerity programs and government cuts have caused women and girls pain worldwide. A recent Oxfam International report (Abed and Kelleher, 2022) goes so far as to describe austerity programs as a form of "gender-based violence" because of the profound negative impacts they have on women's well-being. These programs have curtailed women's ability to support themselves, cut off access to important government programs, subjected them to new expenses, and undermined their rights.

Or we can examine SAP's implications for women's ability to support themselves and their families by farming or getting a job. Though intended to balance countries' budgets, SAPs can be disastrous for women's pocketbooks. The adoption of IMF programs, for example, are associated with significant declines in women's employment (Kern, Reinsberg, and Lee, 2024). One study reported, "When women become unemployed—or leave the labor force altogether—they often take up informal employment, unpaid care work, and absorb the burden of adjustment. Hence, IMF programs unintentionally work as a powerful catalyst to amplify the adverse effects of societal gender norms on women" (Kern, Reinsberg, and Lee, 2024, n.p.). The specific effects of the IMF program also depended on prevailing gender norms in the country adopting the reforms; in countries with higher levels of gender inequality, the effects of IMF programs on women's labor force participation is even greater (Kern, Reinsberg, and Lee, 2024). This means that vulnerable women get an even worse deal. As we discussed in the last chapter, government employment has frequently been a bastion of reliable work for women—meaning that trimming back the government can mean laying off women.

Other studies have examined the broader impacts of these economic reform programs on women's rights, not just how they affect women's experiences as workers and consumers. One study on the effects of IMF reforms found that they were associated with a deterioration in women's economic rights (Detraz and Peksen, 2016). The authors note that even though IMF reforms have, in some instances, increased opportunities for women to enter the workforce, these jobs were often precarious and fraught work environments. They offer Kenyan women working in export processing zones (EPZs) as an example of the double-edged sword that IMF reforms can constitute for women. They write:

> These EPZs were developed as a strategy to address widespread unemployment in the aftermath of IFI interventions. Women's economic rights were routinely violated in the EPZs, with women frequently experiencing sexual harassment and having to work overtime and in unhealthy and unsafe environments. Despite these conditions, they rarely reported the economic rights abuses for fear of losing the jobs on which they relied (p. 87).

The authors conclude, "IMF policies create conditions that shift labor patterns in ways that make it more difficult or less likely for governments to strongly enforce women's economic rights" (p. 87).

Troublingly, many key economic performance indicators used by IFIs and economic policymakers are not designed to disaggregate the impact of these policies on distinct subsets of the population. As Campbell (2010) observes, "initially, it may appear that SAPs are working" because the Gross Domestic Product (GDP, the most common measure of an economy's productivity) "appears to be increasing and debts are being paid off" (p. 6). Campbell further asserts that this rosy macroeconomic picture obscures that this growth is typically concentrated amongst the most well-off in a society. By this point in the book, you should be beginning to appreciate the need for gender-disaggregated data and gender-sensitive analysis.

Supposedly responsible government economic policies—urged by international technocrats in offices in posh international capital cities—often compound women's economic and social vulnerability. These programs have been especially damaging because they were not designed nor implemented with gender hierarchy in mind. These programs reflect both gender hierarchy and international hierarchy, as IFIs provide conditions and suggestions to less powerful governments, who implement them at the expense of women and other marginalized populations.

Gender Hierarchy and International Economic Sanctions

In recent decades, economic sanctions have become a critical part of economic statecraft and a frequently used tool in foreign policy. According to the Council on Foreign Relations, sanctions are levied "to try to alter the strategic decisions of state and nonstate actors that threaten their interests or violate international norms of behavior" (Masters, 2024, n.p.). In other words, economic sanctions are a way by which governments throw around their economic weight to incentivize policy change.

Advocates for sanctions point to a number of different pathways by which they can provoke policy change. Some focus on the effects that sanctions can have on the targeted country's elites. Sanctions can include things like travel bans and locking individuals out of the international banking system (Elliott et al., n.d.). Taken to the extreme, economic sanctions can be a way of expelling actors—individuals and even whole countries—from the benefits of the international economic system.

If the government officials can't be swayed through the sanctions directly, there is some hope for indirect policy change—meaning that sanctions will produce enough domestic frustration that the government officials will be swayed or removed from office. In 2019, then-Secretary of State Mike Pompeo said of sanctions in Iran: "Things are much worse for the Iranian people, and we are convinced that will lead the Iranian people to rise up and change the behavior of the regime" (Rodríguez, 2023, n.p.).

Minimized in Pompeo's model of policy change is the extent of suffering and deprivation necessary to drive people to revolution. The share of the global economy that is subject to sanctions has surged in recent decades. According to a 2023 study from academic Francisco Rodríguez,

> Less than 4 percent of countries were subject to sanctions imposed by the United States, European Union, or United Nations in the early 1960s; today, that share has risen to 27 percent. The magnitudes are similar when we consider their impact on the global economy: the share of world GDP produced in sanctioned countries rose from less than 4 percent to 29 percent in the same period (2023, n.p.).

Like other international economic programs, economic sanctions affect men and women differently, because of the different roles and statuses assigned to them under gender hierarchy. There are multiple avenues by which economic sanctions disproportionately impact women in targeted countries. Among them are the effects that sanctions have on public health, women's employment, social spending, and the overall political zeitgeist.

Firstly, the isolating effects of economic sanctions can be catastrophic for public health. Sanctions are associated with significant declines in life expectancy, especially among marginalized populations like women. One review of nearly 100 sanctioned countries between 1977 and 2012 found that reduced government spending in response to sanctions resulted in a statistically significant reduction in life expectancy, an increase in child mortality, and increased deaths from Cholera (a disease transmitted through fecal matter in food and water) (Gutmann et al., 2021).

Part of the reason for plummeting health in sanctioned countries are drug shortages. In Yugoslavia, economic sanctions resulted in a 50% decline in the availability of essential drugs (Yazdi-Feyzabadi et al., 2024). Economic sanctions in Iran produced shortages in 73 drugs—despite the fact that 32 of these drugs were deemed essential by the World Health Organization and that 70 of them had authorization under Office of Foreign Assets Control (OFAC) to be exported to Iran (Rodríguez, 2023, n.p.). Put simply: economic sanctions dissuaded the sale of permitted medicine to Iran.

Sanctions can even prevent domestic pharmaceutical firms from stepping in to address gaps in drug availability. In Iran and Syria, for example, sanctions affected the availability of raw materials needed to produce drugs or other public health necessities (Yazdi-Feyzabadi et al., 2024). In Cuba, sanctions kneecapped the country's ability to produce chlorine, which resulted in a precipitous decline in the share of Cubans with access to safe drinking water (Yazdi-Feyzabadi et al., 2024).

Unsurprisingly, marginalized communities are often hit hardest by sanction-induced shortages or price hikes—in drugs and other essential goods. Not only can sanctions reduce government spending in critical areas like education and public health—they can also make it harder for families to fill the gaps resulting from those cuts, as everyday necessities are subject to widespread shortages and sky-rocketing prices. Sanctions can be especially onerous burdens for women, who are often responsible for managing their family's health and household budget.

Secondly, when faced with shrinking government revenues as a result of economic sanctions, many targeted states look to trim their government spending. The pattern of these cuts often mirror the cuts made under structural adjustment programs or other austerity programs which we have previously discussed. Just as is the case in countries undergoing structural adjustment, these sanctions-induced cuts hit women the hardest. Indeed, according to academic Kate Perry (2022), government cuts to public education result in sharp declines in women's rights in targeted countries. Thinking back to previous chapters, we can see how these cuts can shift incentives at the household level, making it more economically rational to invest in men and boys, further hamstringing women and girls' opportunities.

Sanctions can also make it hard for women and girls to make up the gap in state funding through international partnerships. Economic sanctions raise the risk of doing business (or providing charity) in a targeted country. This can lock innocent populations out of the international economic system. One report noted the muffling effect of sanctions on civil society in Afghanistan:

> Banks and multinational firms are often hesitant to pay large legal fees to review hundreds of pages of not necessarily binding Treasury Department guidelines to be able to engage in trade with Afghanistan. In the words of a director of the nonprofit organization Women for Afghan Women, 'the moment that the banks see any sanction or any sort of restriction, they

just walk away from doing any transactions ... The banks are not willing to take our business, and no amount of OFAC licenses is going to satisfy their needs' (Rodríguez, 2023, n.p.).

Thirdly, economic sanctions can result in sharp reductions in women's participation in the labor force. One cross-national study, examining the effects of economic sanctions between 1971 and 2005, found that women's economic rights and their participation in the formal workforce in targeted economies were both negatively impacted (Drury and Peksen, 2014). Furthermore, they found that women's participation in the labor force was harder hit than men's (Drury and Peksen, 2014). While everyone's economic opportunities may be curtailed in a sanctioned country, the effects on women's economic fortunes are particularly acute. The decline in women's participation in the economy may also shift household bargaining dynamics, giving women less power in these negotiations and reducing their exit options from abusive situations.

Finally, economic sanctions can produce societal-wide economic insecurity that can cultivate backlash against women, as we will discuss in greater detail Chapter 10. Drury and Peksen (2014) found that women's social rights—which include things like equal educational opportunities, the ability to own property, freedom from female genital cutting, reproductive rights, freedom of movement, and the ability to file for a divorce—are harmed in the aftermath of sanctions, especially in poor countries. Furthermore, they assert, "the economic hardship caused by sanctions will make the violation of women's rights overt" (Drury and Peksen, 2014, p. 466). They offer several examples of how this works, pointing to how women are typically the first demographic laid off during economic contractions and highlighting that economic grievances can percolate into anti-woman sentiment. In times of crisis, a longing for a "return to normal" can take the form of longing for a gendered order in which men could comfortably take care of their families (Pettman, 1996). Challenges to the gender order can become a convenient scapegoat during economic downturns, fueling cycles of backlash politics that we will discuss in Chapter 10.

Box 6.2: The Gendered Effects of Sanctions on Iran

Let's consider the United States' economic sanctions on Iran. Among other policy objectives, these sanctions were intended to dissuade the Iranian government from pursuing nuclear weapons capabilities. While certainly not intended to punish Iranian women—who have functionally no sway over the country's pursuit of nuclear weapons—a number of studies found that the sanctions reduced women's participation in the labor force and decreased girls' education (Moghadam, 2024). A 2022 report from the United Nations Special Rapporteur on the negative impact of unilateral coercive measures on the enjoyment of human rights relayed, in the stale language of multilateral bodies, that

Sanctions and resulting economic pressures undoubtedly have a pronounced gender dimension. Economic sectors traditionally employing women have been particularly affected, including manufacturing, handicrafts and family businesses, and an increasing number of women have had to engage in the informal economy to make a living and to meet the financial needs of their households in the context of rising inflation... The unemployment rate for women is approximately double that of men, with a rate of 36 per cent for young women aged between 15 and 24, compared to 21.2 per cent for young men of the same age. According to an analysis of data from the Iranian Labour Force Survey... 2 of every 3 job losses affected women. Several interlocutors also raised concerns about the precarity of the approximately 3 million female headed households and the vulnerability of the 9 million women in low-income categories who face difficulties in accessing basic services, including health care (Douhan, 2022, p. 13).

Furthermore, Academic Asma Abdi (2025) observes that the Iranian state's response to the crisis has also been "highly gendered" (p. 96). She writes that

This response has entailed, on the one hand, a reinforced emphasis on patriarchal ideologies, increasingly confining women to traditional roles of mothers and wives, and, on the other, a doubling down on neoliberal discourses of women's empowerment to promote home-based informal economic activities for women. These seemingly contradictory policies have been central to the formation of a feminization of survival in the country; they have facilitated the extraction of women's unpaid and underpaid labor, as households and the state have become increasingly reliant on them for their survival (pp. 96–97).

Put another way, the economic sanctions placed on Iran were an intolerable burden on Iranian women. However, there was no meeting in a smoke-filled room where policymakers swirled glasses of expensive scotch and explicitly decided to punish Iranian women. Indeed, many of the sanctions that the United States and other countries levied on Iran in recent years were so-called "smart sanctions," designed to minimize their impact on civilians (Gordon, 2013). Despite these efforts, the gender hierarchy in Iran meant that women were unduly burdened under this sanctions regime.

Conclusion

Mushumi has done her best to advocate for safe and dignified working conditions for herself and her fellow workers through her local labor organization. But Mushumi's and her fellow garment workers' perspectives are not always represented in negotiations surrounding international trade, even though these agreements have massive impacts on their livelihoods and well-being.

In this chapter, we investigated the relationship between gender hierarchy and international economics. Again, we have seen how gender hierarchy both influences economic policies and conditions the effect of these ostensibly "gender neutral" policies. We unpacked these dynamics by examining three components of the international economy: international trade agreements, structural adjustment programs, and economic sanctions. In this chapter, we have considered how the decisions made in technocrats' cushy offices around the world are felt differently by men and women because of gender hierarchy. We have also discussed how gendered political concerns can influence international economic policies.

In conjunction with Chapters 4 and 5, this chapter helps us understand the intertwined relationship between the economy and gender hierarchy. Together, these chapters trace how economic decision-making in the home percolates up to the state and international level. They also help us understand how gender hierarchy is at the heart of economic decision-making, while also conditioning the effect of economic policies on men and women.

This section of the book unpacks the relationship between gender hierarchy and the economy. It illustrates that we cannot detach individual or household economic decision-making from the global economy—and demonstrates the ways that gender hierarchy shapes decision-making at each level. Everything from quotidian decisions about who does the dishes to massive summits on international trade agreements are shaped by gender hierarchy and have implications for women's economic well-being and gender equality globally.

Section III: **Security and Gender Hierarchy**

Chapter 7
Gender Hierarchy and Justifying War

After spending a few hours organizing my notes for this chapter, I took out my phone to reward myself with a few minutes of mindless scrolling. I pulled up X (formally known as Twitter) and was immediately presented with an advertisement for the US Navy that reminded me that there really is no escaping the gendered dynamics of international security. The advertisement was a two-image slideshow, meant to mimic the layout of an Instagram post. The first image is a close-up of a young black woman applying makeup to another young woman's face. The woman applying makeup is in uniform, though the Navy insignia on her shirt is slightly blurred. Stretched out across the bottom of the image is the text: "You can't wear makeup on the ship."

The second image features a smiling young woman of color. Her hair and makeup are immaculate but done in a way that emphasizes effort and skill over ostentatiousness. Her hair is pulled tightly into a low bun and her eye make-up appears to include shadow, liner, and mascara. Her brows are "on fleek" (as cringey millennials like me say) and her lips give off the subtle shine of a tinted lip gloss. She is wearing a pristine white uniform, with her Ensign insignia proudly displayed.

The text at the bottom of this image reads: "If you don't bring it." The tone of the advertisement is very much in line with the #girlboss vibes of the 2010s—the lag between the military's advertisement and the cultural zeitgeist being very much in line with the military's plodding pace. The tweet introducing the ad reads: "Who said serving on a ship or sub means you can't wear a full face of makeup? Not us. Your brows, lashes, eye and lip liner, lipstick and nails are all welcome on board, even if it's permanent" (r/navy, 2024).

I immediately took a screenshot of the advertisement, saving it to introduce the beginning of this chapter and to discuss with both my academic and military friends. The Navy's ad, clearly targeting young women and women of color, speaks to the close connection between warfighting and masculinity—and how armed groups have grappled with the tricky question of how to integrate women into their ranks. It also underscores how ham-fisted and cringe-inducing some of these efforts have been.

In this chapter, we consider how the gender hierarchy and our ideas about what "good" men and women should do can serve as the basis for our decisions to go to war. We discuss how joining the military or a non-state armed group can provide men with the opportunity to prove their masculinity through the conduct of violence. This chapter will help us understand the anxieties and uncertainties

https://doi.org/10.1515/9783111662886-009

surrounding women's participation in warfare, as well as how different armed groups have tried to square the circle of women's participation in the manly art of war. This chapter helps us understand how gender hierarchy—and the expectations of men and women that emerge from it—are at the heart of how and why we mobilize for war.

Why do We Go to War?

Masculinity and Warfighting

In *Captain America: The First Avenger*, a splashy, big-budget comic book movie released in 2011, the protagonist Steve Rogers transforms from a diminutive weakling with a heart of gold into a strapping American soldier and superhero. As a consumer of art and culture, I have unapologetically low-brow taste. I love the whole universe of Marvel movies that *Captain America* takes place in. And I'm not the only one—the movie made more than $370 million dollars, packing theaters around the world.

Part of the reason for Captain America's success as a mainstay of comic book culture is how it renders and recreates masculinity as a function of military service. Neither the original comic book creators, working in the 1940s, nor the writers of the 2011 script were coming up with a novel version of masculinity. The movie played up longstanding links between manhood and fighting. Indeed, around the world and across a variety of time periods, warfighting has been associated with masculinity. This has given rise to the idea of "militarized masculinity" or "militarized masculinities." According to Maya Eichler's study of gender and armed forces, this militarized masculinity means that the "traits stereotypically associated with masculinity can be proven through military service or action" (2014, p. 81).

Militarized masculinities are the result of a variety of different social and political forces. According to Eichler, they "shape, and are shaped by, military practices, but also by state policies, security discourses, education programs, media debates, popular culture, family relations, personal identities, and more" (2014, p. 84). Because of this, militarized masculinities are neither homogenous nor static. They reflect different cultural expectations and adapt in the face of new norms, crises, and opportunities.

While there is wide variation in how militarized masculinities manifest, they all share an important principle: participation in war makes a man, and a man is a good thing to be. Participation in war allows members of armed groups—sol-

diers with shiny dress uniforms and scrappy rebels operating in remote moun-
tains alike—to gain standing in their community.

Another commonality among militarized masculinities is that they are often
predicated on the idea that men are "just warriors" who engage in violence in
order to protect "beautiful souls." According to Jean Bethke Elshtain (1982),
women have been cast as the "beautiful souls" that act "as the collective projection
of a pure, rarified, self-sacrificing, otherworldly and pacific Other" (p. 342). These
narratives help carve up the war into gendered spaces—where women are protected, and men do the protecting. Laura Sjoberg explains that:

> The protagonist in the narrative is the just warrior, who is a hero because he protects (his)
> (innocent) women and children from the evils of the enemy. He sacrifices his time, his body,
> his fear, and even his life for the good of life back home... This story equates women with the
> cause men die for – the life back home. Women are at once the object of the fighting and the
> just purpose of the war. They are 'beautiful souls' who are (incorrectly) pacifists because they
> are naïve about the nature of war. The just warrior fights to protect the 'beautiful soul's in-
> nocence and the quality of her life. War is therefore necessary because the world would be
> unthinkable without innocent women. Women's consent to those wars is not only irrelevant
> but actually undesirable; it would corrupt their innocence (2010, p. 55).

The relationship between just warriors and beautiful souls has been described as
"masculinist protection" because of the way the former is the guardian of the latter (Young, 2003).

Masculinist protection defines the threats that just warriors (in state militaries and rebellions alike) must defend against. The "good" men are those
"who protect their women and children by relation to other 'bad' men liable to
attack" (Young, 2003, p. 228). Without that threat, the promise and purpose of
just warriors and masculine protectors are called into question.

The process of defining these threats matters for how we justify going to war.
Violence against women can become a rallying cry for just warriors; as "a woman
outside the military who has been raped by someone else's soldiers can be remil-
itarized if her ordeal is made visible chiefly for the purpose of mobilizing her
male compatriots to take up arms to avenger her — and their — allegedly lost
honor" (Ray and Enloe, 2002, p. 109). This can mean protecting the wives, daughters, and sisters of a just warrior—but it can also mean deploying far from home
in service of the idea of protecting beautiful souls abroad.

These tropes perpetuate the gender hierarchy, by offering more honor, prestige, and rights to the protector than the protectees. The masculine protector is in a
position of authority over those that they protect; it is not an egalitarian division
of responsibilities. As academic Iris Marion Young (2003) explains, "central to the
logic of masculinist protection is the subordinate relation of those in the protected

position" (2003, 224). She further observes that the inequities of the gender hierarchy are sometimes difficult to identify because it is "masked by virtue and love" (2003, p. 224). But subordination and domination is still oppression, even when it's accompanied by a pat on the head or a kiss on the cheek.

Furthermore, militarized masculinities often rest on the idea that a just warrior will be rewarded with a beautiful soul—who just so happens to also have a beautiful face and body. Armed groups of a variety of backgrounds, objectives, and capabilities have all sought to bring men into their ranks by promising them the opportunity to improve their prospects on the dating and marriage market. These messages can be both explicitly stated and implied.

Box 7.1: The United States' Military, Masculinity, and Access to Women

Let's consider how the United States military (the most well-funded military in the world) has sought to attract young men by connecting military service to successful masculinity and access to women. These messages are repeated during recruitment and throughout military service, to cultivate continued commitment to the organization. Consider the account of one American veteran, who described his recruitment into the armed forces as such:

> Like so many other veterans, I joined the military at least in part to get girls—something my recruiter, drill instructors, and all of 1980s American popular culture assured me was a wise investment of my time and energy. The contract I signed had explicit terms of service, but it also contained an implicit cultural codicil: those who use violence to defend the nation receive something special in return—a manly prestige that brings with it sexual opportunities, if not sexual privileges (O'Connell, 2016, p. 152).

Or consider that during World War II, an American infantry division's circular dedicated to Olivia De Havilland, a pin up girl, included the post script, "We are not only fighting for the Four Freedoms, we are fighting also for the priceless privilege of making love to American women. We assure you we will win that fight" (Martin, 1944, n.p.). While certainly not American soldiers' only motivations, it is important to consider the ways in which the idea of protecting "their women" in the abstract and the prospect of having a woman to call their own prompted men to join and remain in the military.

The American military's services have all cycled through slogans and recruitment campaigns, finding new ways to appeal to young men. Though they have adopted different messages for various audiences and in response to shifting cultural norms, these campaigns have frequently connected manhood to the prospect of professional and romantic success (Brown, 2012a; Brown, 2012b). One study notes that the Navy's recruitment ads:

> hint at the sexual rewards of being a sailor. The traditional pattern of naval life is long stretches of duty at sea, punctuated by liberty in ports of call around the world, where sailors could indulge themselves with women and alcohol. While the ads don't explicitly mention this aspect of Navy life, the references to travel and the images of civilian women subtly evoke it (Brown, 2012a, p. 162).

The Navy's promises have tried to account for changing preferences, addressing head on the most prominent concerns for each generation of recruits. For example, as I was writing this chapter, I was served another advertisement for the Navy that was clearly aimed at young men (though, clearly, the algorithm had missed the mark in showing it to me). This ad was structured similarly to the ad about wearing make-up on a Navy ship that I described in the opening section. The first image shows two young men of color laughing, with the man in the foreground grasping a video game controller. The text at the bottom reads "You can't play video games at sea" in all-caps. The second slide shows a multiracial group of young men laughing and yelling, with the text at the bottom reading: "If you don't play to win." The text in the tweet accompanying the image reads "The only reason you won't be allowed to game aboard one of our vessels is if you're not ready to give it 100. Whether you're gaming on your own console, in a high-stakes group tournament, or as a tabletop player, you better bring your A game."

The ad was striking to me for a number of reasons. The first thing that I noticed was that there were no women visible in either photo, despite featuring a large group photo. The sea is, apparently, no place for a woman. The second thing that jumped out to me was the individualism promised in this recruitment appeal. In the world of this advertisement, you don't need to give up "childish" pastimes in order to become a Navy man—you just need to bring a competitive spirit. This ad reflects the reality of how American teens spend their time; a 2018 Pew Study found, "Substantial majorities of both boys and girls play video games and have access to a video game console, but gaming is nearly ubiquitous among teenage boys," with 92 % of male teenagers having a game console (Perrin, 2018). Taken together, the advertisements about makeup and video games on Navy ships suggest a shift in recruiting that emphasizes the ability to maintain your identity while serving and, perhaps, suggests a reduced emphasis on recruits' romantic prospects.

The association between armed service, masculinity, and access to women is not a modern phenomenon. Writing on the British military in the 1700s, Jennine Hurl-Eamon (2014) observes that soldiers could be enticed both by the military's reputation for swashbuckling womanizing, (consider "the words of an early nineteenth-century ballad refrain: 'storm the trenches court the wenches'" which expressed "key elements of the soldiering life" that appealed to some) (p. 105). She also notes that young men were drawn to the military because marriage may have been easier as a soldier than as an apprentice (Hurl-Eamon, 2014).

Nor is it just a Western phenomenon. Reflecting on the link between military service and masculinity in Bolivia, Lesley Gill (1997) writes that men serve "to earn respect from women (mothers, wives, sisters, and girlfriends) and male peers, both as defenders of the nation and, more broadly, as strong, responsible male citizens who can make decisions and lead" (p. 527). Similarly, Robert E. Upton (2018) argues that India's recruitment drive during the First World War depended heavily on the connection between masculinity and warfighting. As Upton notes, the "conflation of manliness and martiality" in the public discourse in this period "served to valorize martiality in the eyes of these Indians, and accentuate the corresponding and often visible sense of gendered weakness" felt by a largely demilitarized country (p. 1991). That recruitment drive meant navigating ethnic stereotypes that cast certain subsets of the population as inherently more "martial" and thus suited to warfare. Around the world, armed groups have grappled with how to navigate class, race, ethnicity, on top of gender.

Nor is the link between war-fighting and romantic success something that only state-affiliated armed groups have benefited from. Rebels, gangs, and a range of other armed, non-state actors have also tried to attract men to their ranks by promising them the opportunity to become a "just warrior" or another type of "real man." While these organizations may not recruit through glossy magazine ads or expensive, splashy ads during the Super Bowl, they still expend considerable energy trying to bring young men into their ranks. As Maria C. Correia and Ian Bannon (2006) observe, "at the most basic level, boys involved in brutal armed insurgencies become big men by being in control of a setting and being able to exert violence on those around them. In addition to survival, they achieve and wield power" (p. 173). Taking up arms as a part of a non-state armed group can thus be a means by which young men cultivate prestige and gain status as a man.

Box 7.2: Recruiting based on Masculinity in ISIS

The Islamic State provides a helpful case study in understanding how non-state armed groups incorporate masculinity into their recruitment tactics. This Salafi-Jihadist rebel group, which waged a brutal military campaign in Iraq and Syria, sought to establish an Islamic Caliphate, and appealed to both local men and prospective foreign fighters by offering them the opportunity to become "a real man" within the organization. As one academic study notes, "in their slickly edited videos, with fighters in choreographed, slow-motion combat and posing on captured vehicles or over the corpses of defeated enemies... ISIL internet messages compare the dull, isolated and discouraging lives their potential male recruits are supposedly leading to the glories and excitement of being involved in nothing less than apocalyptic battles between good and evil" (Leuven, Mazurana, and Gordon, 2016, p.107). One study of the rebels' recruitment tactics found that the Islamic State designed their messages "to best attract men who feel emasculated or helpless" in their current situation (Speckhard and Ellenburg, 2021, p. 161).

The rebellion has also attracted recruits through "the relative guarantee of marriage and assurance of a home and monthly allowance"—in other words, through a starter pack for a family (Leuven, Mazurana, and Gordon, 2016, p. 108). Consider the account from one 20-year-old Iraqi man, who was drawn to the Islamic State's online recruitment videos: "They affected me because I was poor. I wanted to improve my condition [for] marriage. I wanted us to have a house and for me to get married, and to have money" (Speckhard and Ellenburg, 2021, p. 162). These norms also helped structure internal hierarchy within the group. According to a 2015 CBS report, "the new ISIS ruling class" had taken over the "luxury houses and apartments, which once belonged to officials from the government of Syrian President Bashar Assad" in Raqqa (CBS News, 2015, n.p.). The Islamic State thus links material comfort, providing for one's family, and masculinity with the process of vanquishing the enemy. Living as a "good man," as IS defined it, came with clear benefits (Twaij, 2016). However, it also came with strict enforcement of what IS defined as proper behavior for men, which extended to things ranging from their treatment of sexual slaves to their physical appearance (Roth, 2016).

The Islamic State also plays up the idea that its members are masculine protectors. A 14-year-old Syrian boy recounts that: "We started being taught that Shiites were raping Sunni women, and that Shiites were killing Sunni men" (Leuven, Mazurana, and Gordon, 2016, p. 109). According to the Islamic state, it was their duty as Sunni Muslim men to defend their brothers and sisters. Prestige, material comfort, and a sense of masculine success were all wrapped up with one another in the Islamic State's appeals to young men.

Similar to the appeals made by the military, militarized masculinity in rebel groups can also imply access to women. With Valerie Hudson, I have previously written about how non-state armed groups in Nigeria and South Sudan have offered potential recruits financial support to get married (by covering or reducing the "brideprice" men are expected to pay) (Hudson and Matfess, 2017). These appeals seem especially relevant when social or economic structures have made it difficult for young men to get married and when marriage is considered a rite of passage to adulthood. One South Sudanese government official told researchers, "Some youth are joining the rebels [militias] to loot properties so they can marry" (Sommers and Schwartz, 2011, p. 6). When armed groups help young men get married or facilitate their access to women, they're not just securing companionship for them—they're also offering them the trappings of the good life and a means of leaving behind adolescence.

In summary, militarized masculinities connecting violence, masculinity, and prestige have played an important role in convincing young men to take up arms for a variety of organizations, across different time periods, and in a wide variety of locations. While military masculinities have evolved over time or have been interpreted differently in different contexts, their prominence within armed groups' recruitment tactics has remained constant, helping cement the gender hierarchy by exalting men. Even groups that have met each other on the battlefield—like the U.S. military and the Islamic State—have each relied on their own specific interpretation of masculinity to attract young men to their cause.

Femininity and Recruitment into Armed Groups

Given the well-established link between masculinity and fighting, women joining armed groups can be a thorny prospect. Indeed, armed groups must balance a number of competing dynamics when they open their ranks to women and decide what roles they can play as members. Armed groups have a clear logistical incentive to include as many people as possible. It's hard to win a war if you categorically reject getting help from more than half of the population. Yet including women can rattle the foundation of why (some) men join—how can war be a man's job and a proving ground for masculinity if women are there?

Furthermore, there is some evidence that armed groups can improve their reputations and attract foreign support by showcasing their female combatants—meaning that hanging a "no girls allowed" sign might mean giving up financial support from foreign sponsors (Manekin and Wood, 2020). On the other hand, however, the public's discomfort with women's participation in political violence is evident in the narratives that crop up to explain their presence. Academics Laura Sjoberg and Caron Gentry (2007), for example, outline how violent women are frequently regarded as either "mothers," "monsters," or "whores." If the women in your organization are regarded as "monsters" or "whores," it seems unlikely that they are doing a lot to improve the reputation of your group.

So armed groups work hard to balance women's inclusion with the sense of masculinity that men derive by joining, as well as the desire that some women have to participate in war as a means of protesting—and hopefully unraveling—the oppression they face as women.

In this chapter, we will unpack how state and non-state actors have navigated this fraught relationship while recruiting women. We'll consider how armed groups have alternatively challenged or replicated the gender hierarchy when recruiting women into their organization. We will also then briefly discuss the blowback that women in armed groups can face because of the incongruity of warfighting and traditional constructions of femininity.

Political Violence and the Promise of Equality

A number of armed groups have exploited the sexism and repression that women face as women in order to draw them into their ranks. While women cannot prove themselves as men by going to war, a lot of armed groups have promised them the chance to prove themselves equal to men.

For some groups, gender equality is a part of the organization's broader political objectives; recruiting women and treating them well is a way for the organization to show that they can "walk the walk," not just talk a big game. One of the female veterans of the TPLF in Ethiopia explained to me, "The TPLF came up with the idea that women are also human beings," and deserving of equal rights under the law. That veteran also explained to me that the TPLF had a slogan "no liberation without the participation of women," meaning that the organization was convinced that women were an integral part of their military and political campaign. Many women were drawn to the group because it offered them a vision of a life free from discrimination and oppression—both at the hands of the government and from the patriarchal gender order.

Zerin, a commander in the all-female, Kurdish Women's Defense Units (in Kurdish, Yekîneyên Parastina Jin, or YPJ), a part of the Syrian Democratic Forces, stated, "As revolutionaries, as an army of women, of course our desire is equality, permanent equality. Not only for Kurds and their land, not only for the Middle East, but for the whole world" (Steyerl, 2017, n.p.). Zerin ties her participation in the YPJ as a liberatory process—not just for herself and her comrades-in-arms but also for all those oppressed by systems of hierarchy like gender, racism, and capitalism.

Furthermore, the Revolutionary Armed Forces of Colombia (FARC) has also drawn women into their ranks by portraying life in the rebellion as gender-egalitarian. Joining the FARC, the argument goes, offers women an opportunity to escape the daily discrimination they face as women. In particular, combat was held up as a way by which women could become equal to men and relive themselves of the burdens they faced as civilians. One female fighter recalled:

> I went into (my first combat) with the machine-gun detachment, because there was no discrimination, armed only with a pistol. But if I had to go empty handed, I would have gone. I'm not afraid to fight, because the smell of powder excites me. I've fought in Antioquia, in Choco, Uraba ' [provinces], and never been scared ... for me, it's like going to a fiesta. I sing, skip and jump because it makes me happy, fighting (Herrera and Porch, 2008, p. 618).

The opportunity to be seen as equal to men has also attracted women to armed groups without such high-minded notions of universal equality. Aisha, a Kenyan woman who joined Islamic State, told researchers that she was attracted to the group after scrolling through "pictures of Islamic women, dressed all in black stockings and gloves and niqab and she was holding an AK-47," whom she regarded as "independent," despite the Islamic State's clear gender hierarchy that subordinates women to men (Speckhard and Ellenburg, 2021, p. 163). These individual women's ideals about personal liberty can be distinct from the organization's understanding of gender roles and individual freedoms.

State militaries have also recruited women by appealing to women's yearning for opportunity and gender equality. Consider how the British military has positioned women in its recent advertisements which "do not position women as subordinate," a reflection of its "hopes to recruit beyond its typical pool of white men" (Jester, 2021, pp. 65 – 66). In a 2018 advertisement, for example, the British Army portrays itself as a place where women can escape the quotidian sexism that they face. The ad "...begins by asking 'will I be listened to in the army?' and the answer is swiftly delivered: in contrast with her 'normal job' where 'men talk over me', in the army 'all that matters is that you're good at your job'" (Jester, 2019, pp. 65–66). Whether the British military delivers on this promise of meritocracy in practice is debatable—but it has clearly found utility in using that appeal to bring women into its ranks.

The Swedish military, too, has tried to attract women by offering them a way to avoid the everyday gender discrimination so many women face. One eye-catching advertisement, released in 2018, addresses the common concern "Can I have my period in the field?" An academic study argues that this advertisement offers women the opportunity "to transcend their corporeality," by portraying "military service as a vehicle through which the leaky female body can be freed from its limitations" (Stern and Strand, 2022, p. 4). The Swedish Armed Forces doesn't just turn boys into men but can also turn women into something entirely new. In the military, Swedish women will do exceptional work as exceptional—almost genderless—figures.

In contrast to such messages, the American military has often worked hard to reassure women that they can still be feminine and serve their country. One review of American military recruitment tactics found that the depictions of women in recruitment materials "serve to at once normalize the participation of women in the military and to erase it" (Brown, 2012a, p. 155). Consider an advertisement from the 1970s, which a told prospective female recruits: "We're working on a whole new uniform wardrobe, including some things you can wear right now. A black felt beret, white shirt, gloves and scarf. Smart patent leather, low-heeled shoes, clutch handbag, and a matching umbrella and raincoat" (Brown, 2012a, p. 157). Decades later, the U.S. Navy continued to recruit women by emphasizing that femininity and military life are compatible.

State militaries have grappled visibly with how to attract and include women in their ranks. They often rely on somewhat contradictory messages, promising that service in the military will not compromise women's femininity while also highlighting how the military offers them the opportunity to be equal to men or to transcend gender categories entirely.

Male Pushback and the Limits to Militarism for Gender Equality

As I've alluded to earlier, women's presence in armed groups can challenge the prospects for men in those organizations to prove themselves as men. In particular, women's participation in combat can threaten the basis of militarized masculinity, upending (some) men's motivations for joining in the first place. As such, men have not always welcomed women into armed groups with open arms—even when the groups that they've pledged their loyalty to are enthusiastically recruiting women.

Indeed, when I was talking to female veterans of the Tigray People's Libera-tion Front (TPLF) in Ethiopia, I was frequently struck by how many women ex-pressed frustration that, despite the rebels' gender egalitarian rhetoric and robust efforts to include women in a wide variety of roles, their male counterparts could be stubbornly chauvinistic. One woman told me how the men would needle women by demanding that they do hard physical labor (in addition to their com-bat training) to prove they were as strong as men. She recalled that the women met these challenges with clenched jaws and fierce determination. But equality was still just beyond their grasp.

She also explained to me that—despite women's physical contributions and the TPLF's clear ideological commitment to gender equality—"there was a ceiling for women's advancement" within the TPLF. She claimed that for many years there were no female generals within the TPLF and that there were fewer than 10 at the end of the war—a striking absence, given that roughly 30 % of the people in the organization were women.

Similarly, Natalia Herrera and Douglas Porch (2008) observe that among women in the FARC there was "a feeling that the FARC required them to abandon their femininity and become like men to succeed in the FARC's military system" (p. 627). Some observed that women in the group felt compelled to be even tougher than the men they served alongside. One woman observed that in the FARC "There were many women who were very stud (berracas), really stud when they fight with the army, more than the guys' (Herrera and Porch, 2008, p. 618).

Women in the U.S. military have also faced pushback and sexist discrimina-tion from their brothers in arms. In the Marine Corps, the branch of the US mil-itary that is perhaps best known for its swaggering machismo, a recent report found that more than 13 % of women reported unwanted sexual contact (Mongilio, 2022). The prevalence of sexual harassment and assault degrades intra-organiza-tional trust—and contributes to a culture where women face gender-specific threats, layered on top of the challenges and dangers that all Marines confront. Women Marines have also reported the prevalence of tropes in which they must decide whether they want to be known as a "bitch," a "dyke," or "easy" (Archer, 2013). These stereotypes are all degrading to women and mark women Marines as "the other," presenting a hurdle to gender integration.

It is worth noting here that feminist scholars have often treated the idea that women's participation in the military or in organized violence can be a route to gender equality with profound skepticism. They assert that militarization is anti-thetical to the objectives of a liberatory feminism, which prioritizes equality across race, class, gender, nationality, religion, etc. They argue that the women that thrive in the armed groups do so because they have adopted traditionally male roles, which means that success still requires lauding masculinity over femininity. Given the recruiting difficulties that militaries the world over face, however, it seems unlikely that the appeals to women to take up arms for their country to give themselves a better life and fight for a free-er world will end soon.

Replicating Gender Hierarchy in Armed Groups

In many cases, women's participation in armed groups is an echo of the subordinate roles they play in society in general, rather than an effort to upend the gender hierarchy. Make no mistake, however, these women are also often motivated by the sense that they can build a better life for themselves as rebels than they can as civilians.

As a part of their recruitment efforts, a number of rebel groups offer women the opportunity to live out particular versions of femininity that might not be possible in the civilian world. They can market themselves as a place where women can realize their aspirations to be an "angel of the home," taken care of by a masculine protector and provider. Returning to the example of the Islamic State, a number of reports underscore that women were frequently attracted to the group by the prospect of becoming wives of fighters (Spencer, 2016). It would be dismissive and short-sighted to regard these women lovesick fools; their attraction to marriage is an attraction to a world in which traditional gender norms, in which women were responsible for the home and men were masculine protectors, was exalted. Consider the account of a Belgian woman, Laura, who was recruited to IS by a man who told her "...that women could be nurses and help the orphans. He said women had status there and were precious. We women could go to ISIS to enjoy Paradise there," though she found a very different reality when she arrived in the group's territory (Speckhard and Ellenburg, 2021, p.163).[1] She was drawn in by the prospect of living as a "good woman" in a place where such service would be appreciated.

---

1 Importantly, rebel groups may not offer these opportunities to all women. Their ethnicity, religion, race, and age can all affect the roles that women can play within the organization. For example, the Islamic State's "system of sexual slavery is regulated by rules that define the classes of people who can be enslaved, the conditions under which they can be bought, sold, and released, and limits on sexual access and violence." Only certain categories of women can be held as sexual slaves, including: "Alawites, 'unbelievers who have no allegiance pact [with IS],' Yazidis, Shi'a, and other unbelievers..." (Revkin and Wood, 2021, n.p.). Similarly, there is compelling evidence that young women's tribal affiliations affect how Al Shabaab treats them; women affiliated with more powerful clans are treated better than women from less relevant clans (Speckhard and Ellenburg, 2021). The codes that govern women's behavior and their status within the group reflect the groups' vision for a new, proper society.

I often remind myself that you can't eat gender equality; for women living in situations of severe deprivation, the promise of an easier life may be more appealing than promises of equal rights and responsibilities. I will admit that, as a dyed-in-the-wool Western feminist, I was surprised when women I spoke to in North East Nigeria told me they were attracted to Boko Haram because the group offered near-daily education for women and some material comforts. But through these conversations, I learned that many were drawn to the group because it promised them a better life as the wife of a fighter than what they could hope for as civilians.

In groups that replicate gender hierarchy, women are generally concentrated in non-combat work and feminized tasks. That is not to suggest that the work that these women do is marginal—if an army runs on its stomach, cooks are essential employees. Furthermore, the marginalization of women in society in general can make them especially effective non-combat members of the organization, even when these organizations replicate the gender inequality practiced in their communities. For example, women have been especially effective as clandestine operatives because of gender norms that render them inherently peaceful or apolitical or which make it difficult for male security guards to search them. Consider how the Sandinista National Liberation Front (FSLN), a rebel group in Nicaragua, passed messages during the war; according to one account:

> Realizing that 'maybe the only part of the woman that they [the National Guard] would not search was the vagina ... we made the messages in the form of a tampon. Then the task was to explain to a peasant woman who had never used a sanitary napkin what a tampon was, teach her how it was introduced and how it should be taken out, and how to make this tampon safe so that it would not be destroyed (Luciak 2001, p. 20).

The Women's Activities in Armed Rebellion (WAAR) project estimates that 30% of rebel groups include women in clandestine roles—which could well be an underestimate, given that such activities are by definition secretive and difficult to track (Loken and Matfess, 2023).

Furthermore, armed groups can also benefit from integrating women in their operations when there are strong cultural norms that would make it challenging for men in the security sector to conduct thorough searches of members of the opposite sex. During one of my trips to North East Nigeria, I came face to face with the inadequacies of the male-dominated Nigerian security sector as they sought to protect civilians from Boko Haram attacks—in particular from female suicide bombers. A security guard with a metal detecting wand was posted at the entrance of a large market where I was planning to buy some gifts for friends back home and to kill some time between interviews. I expected some degree of hassle—I had a thick camera hanging around my neck and a bulky iPhone in my pocket, which I felt certain would elicit a string of agitated beeps from the wand. I was shocked when the man languidly waved the wand over me in silence and ushered me forward, the wand remaining silent and (likely) off. His whole job was an exercise in unenthusiastic security theater, fostered in large part by norms that would have made a male security guard patting down a woman unacceptable.

Conclusions

At the same time that the Navy is recruiting women by reassuring them that they can wear makeup on the ship and cajoling men by telling them they can still play video games, there are efforts to rewrite the U.S. military as a "man's place" and to reassert traditional gender roles. Just days into Donald Trump's second term in the office of the President, Admiral Linda Fagan, the first woman to lead the U.S. Coast Guard, was relieved of her command (Rubin, 2025), as was the commander of the Air Force's 613th Air Operations Center, Colonel Julie Sposito-Salceies (Novelly, 2025). Under the leadership of Secretary of Defense Pete Hegseth, the Trump 2.0 Administration has vowed to eradicate "wokeness" in the armed forces. As a part of that effort, the Administration and the Department of Defense leadership seem poised to radically reduce women's roles in America's armed forces—meaning that the ads promising the ability to wear makeup on the ship or play video games may be short-lived recruitment gambits (Walsh, 2025). In this chapter, we considered how gender hierarchy contributes to individuals' decisions to go to war. It introduces us to the concept of masculinist protection, in which masculine authority figures offer women protection in exchange for their willingness to behave in certain ways (Sjoberg and Peet, 2011; Young, 2003).

From this chapter, we have learned how gendered norms and expectations are at the heart of how we mobilize individuals and states into armed conflict. We've dug into how war can be a rite of passage into manhood for men, and we have considered how non-state armed groups and state-affiliated militaries have exploited that association to drive recruitment. We also considered how this association can make it difficult to integrate women into armed groups. In this chapter, we dug into the uneasy rhetorical and political balances that have been struck by state militaries and rebel groups alike as they have drawn women into their ranks. Having unpacked the relationship between masculinity and justifications for war, we can better understand the rhetorical and moral appeals that armed groups make to fill their ranks. In the following chapter, we consider the ways that fighters and civilians alike are socialized in times of war, how that is influenced by the gender hierarchy, and why it matters for the conduct of war and post-war politics.

Chapter 8
Gender Hierarchy and War

My husband and I had very different experiences in college. I attended Johns Hopkins University, an elite university in Baltimore, Maryland; my husband enrolled at West Point, the premier military academy in the United States. Every now and then—more than a decade and a half after we set foot on our respective campuses —my husband and I will say a phrase or a truism we learned at college to the bewilderment of the other.

Most of the time, what we share with each other is goofy. I explained to him that Hopkins had a "shush lady" who used to go around to frat parties to get them to quiet down so that the Baltimore Police would not be called in to deal with rowdy college kids. But other times, some darker parts of time in college are revealed and I am reminded of the ways that our college experiences prepared us for different lives—as a male infantry officer and as a female academic. For example, at a dinner party, a mutual friend brought up a specific fraternity. I recoiled immediately, then explained that they had a reputation for slipping roofies into the "jungle juice" they offered young women at their parties. Even as an adult hundreds of miles away and years removed from college, my knee jerk reaction was still to warn people off lest their drink be spiked. My husband was both shocked by my vitriol and the fact that university administrators took such a laissez-faire approach to the frat's reported behavior (meaning that they depended on whisper networks of young women to get the word out).

Another example came when my husband, our baby, and I caught COVID-19 in the fall of 2024. In classic Lisa Matfess form, my mother sent several pints of Ben & Jerry's ice cream to keep us full and happy as we recuperated. Unpacking them, my husband looked at me conspiratorially. "Do you know what they call these at West Point?" I shook my stuffy head no and he explained that some of the less progressive folks at the academy called them "trou buckets." When I looked at him with evident confusion, he explained that "trou" was a derogatory term for female cadets at the Academy.[1] This was a part of the slang and behaviors adopted in order to make women feel uncomfortable and out of place at West Point after the campus opened to women in 1976. It was, apparently, still in use when my husband attended and was still nestled in the back of his brain more than a decade after he graduated. I wrinkled my nose in distaste.

---

[1] If you don't believe me, see https://www.urbandictionary.com/define.php?term=trou%20bucket.

https://doi.org/10.1515/9783111662886-010

While these may seem like inconsequential vignettes from college life, they reveal the different expectations (both formal and informal) imparted on us as impressionable young adults. "Date rapists" and "Trou buckets" both speak to the threats that young women navigated on our campuses—and the ways that these institutions were still designed for men's comfort and a male default. In very different ways, both of our university experiences reinforced aspects of the gender hierarchy.

In this chapter, we home in on socialization in armed groups and in war zones to consider how gender hierarchy impacts the conduct of war. It builds from the previous chapter to illustrate that gender hierarchy does not merely motivate people to join rebel groups—it also shapes how they learn what it means to be a fighter and how they behave in that role. Through this discussion, we explore how socialization shapes who experiences violence—and in what forms—during war.

This chapter then dives into why it is so hard to unlearn the identities and behaviors we learned during war to return to civilian life. Together, we consider the unique challenges facing demobilizing fighters and the consequences of inadequate programs to reorient them to "normal" life.

Gender Hierarchy and Socialization in Armed Groups

Putting on camouflage is not enough to make you a soldier. Becoming a member of an armed group requires learning a whole new set of behaviors and expectations. Armed groups put their members through a process of socialization, not unlike the socialization that takes place in the home that we discussed in Chapters 2 and 4.

Just as socialization in the home is a multifaceted process, socialization in an armed group can take a wide range of forms. When we think about the process of joining an armed group and becoming a fighter, many people bring to mind the image of a red-faced drill sergeant spraying spit and derision as they shout at recruits struggling to perform perfect push-ups or to haul themselves up and over a wall. This is an example of vertical socialization, where identity formation flows from leaders to subordinates. Another example of vertical socialization comes from political education—in which members of the organization are expected to learn and internalize the organization's political objectives, military doctrine, or history. From places like West Point to remote rebel camps, many armed groups have dedicated significant energy to educating their members what it is they are fighting (and possibly dying) for.

Socialization also emerges between peers. This is called horizontal socialization. When recruits return to the barracks and snicker about the booger hanging from the drill sergeant's nose or his dainty hands, they are also teaching one another what is expected of them as a member of the organization. Other studies have found that rebels' meals, how they relieve themselves, and what clothes they wear all become an important part of armed group culture, maintained primarily through relationships with one another (Gutiérrez, 2023; Parkinson, 2021). In my own work, I've argued that marriage (in rebel groups specifically) is the site of consequential horizontal socialization into group norms and culture (Matfess, 2023).

As Checkel (2017) argues, vertical and horizontal socialization interact with one another. In some instances they are mutually reinforcing; in others they contradict one another. The interaction between these layers can help us understand why socialization can be more or less successful.

In addition to preparing soldiers for the realities of war by exposing them to realistic scenarios as a part of their socialization and training, armed groups also cultivate a culture that reifies those who are competent practitioners of violence. Socialization within armed groups frequently relies on the same connections between prestige, masculinity, and the practice of violence that they used to recruit members into the organization. In a wide variety of armed groups, those that are closest to the practice of violence are regarded as the most masculine and most prestigious. The association between masculinity, violence, and prestige can emerge both through formal and informal socialization processes, organized horizontally and vertically. In the United States military, for example, the term "POG" (an acronym for "Person Other than Grunt") is used to demean those who are not members of the infantry, who are the "ground troops that engage with the enemy in close-range combat" (Today's Military, n.d.). In general, those that are in "combat arms divisions," meaning those that are involved in direct ground combat, are considered more prestigious than those who are assigned to other tasks in the military. These dynamics cement the gender hierarchy by not only elevating masculinity over femininity, but by elevating a certain type of man above all others.

Another factor influencing the success of socialization is how well the group's norms and expectations sit with members' previous experiences of socialization and their pre-existing identities (Checkel, 2017). This includes their previous understandings of gender and their performances of masculinity and femininity, which they've learned at home, in school, from their friends and family, and from their culture at large.

Becoming a soldier or a rebel requires unlearning the prohibitions on the use of physical force that govern civilian life. A landmark—though controversial—study by Lt. Col. Dave Grossman (2014) asserts that the central task of socialization into the military is overcoming the psychological and moral barriers to killing. Indeed, he explores how training in the U.S. military has moved towards ever-more realistic training exercises, to prepare its members for the possibility of taking a life in war. There is compelling evidence that socialization within armed groups can rewrite members' relationships to violence. One study of Burundian ex-combatants, for example, found that, though female civilians had lower levels of "appetitive aggression," which refers to positive feelings towards the perpetration of violence, there was no difference between male and female combatants in appetitive aggression (Meyer-Parlapanis, 2016, p. 6). The study's authors assert that this illustrates "that, in a context in which it is situationally appropriate to directly perpetrate violence against others and when males and females have perpetrated similar types of violent acts, both males and females are capable of experiencing aggression as fascinating or pleasurable" (Meyer-Parlapanis, 2016, p. 6). Other studies find that the more experience people have perpetrating violence, the higher their levels of appetitive aggression (Meyer-Parlapanis, 2016). Being a member of an armed group can literally give you a taste for blood.

Men's Socialization in Armed Groups

Though masculinity and warfighting have historically been connected to one another, men are not "natural fighters." They too must be socialized into the armed group's norms and expectations. Within armed groups, men are encouraged to reach the very top of the gender hierarchy, where they can enjoy status as a big man, a tough guy, or an officer and a gentleman.

Various armed groups have developed different ideas of what it means to be a man in their organization—and the differences in their masculine ideals have implications for how wars are fought, men's identities, and the safety of civilians in those areas.

For example, Henry Myrttinen highlights how several modern rebel groups have developed a culture of "fratriarchy"—a fusing of patriarchy and fraternity —in contention with the "old top-down state patriarchal order" (Myrttinen, 2018, p. 566). These young men see themselves as rebelling against a system dominated by older men, in which they have been forced into a subservient position. He observes that this sense of self shapes the ways that young rebels establish and enforce order within their ranks:

> The armed groups thus give the young men a sense of purpose and identity, fraternal conviviality—but also access to the spoils of war, societal status, and power, at least for the duration of the conflict. In these fratriarchal formations, women remain mostly in subservient or supporting roles, as real or imagined audiences for the men's performances (e. g., as the mothers and sisters addressed in the anasheed) but also as voluntary or involuntary protectees (Myrttinen, 2018, p. 568).

This sense of fratriarchal entitlement is in sharp contrast to the idea of the "new man" that a wide range of leftist groups articulated.[2] A variety of left-wing groups —from Cuba to Ethiopia to El Salvador to Nepal—socialized men into the idea that good men support gender equality. Reflecting on her conversations with veterans of Maoist rebellion in Nepal, academic Heidi Riley (2022) observes that their concept of the "new man" was "built on notions of higher intellectualism and progressive thought, combined with a warrior masculinity that was ready to use violence where required" (p. 111). These men saw themselves as vanguards, leading the less educated rural population toward a more egalitarian future. Riley reflects that the Maoist masculinity balanced commitment to egalitarianism with notions of masculinist protection, which sometimes were in tension with one another.

Peacekeeping forces dispatched by the United Nations to maintain stability in conflict-affected communities offer yet another form of militarized masculinity. Henry Myrtinnen observes, "Unlike other, more conventional military operations, peacekeeping however requires far more 'soft skills,' which in some ways run counter to the performances of military masculinities and femininities that soldiers have conventionally been trained to embody and enact" (2018, p. 568). The mark of a good peacekeeper is not necessarily their marksmanship nor their ability to physically dominate an enemy—rather, a good peacekeeper is one that is restrained in their use of force and capable of gaining the trust of the population they are there to protect.

That's one take. There is some evidence, however, that various peacekeeping operations have been less successful in socializing these expectations. Inadequacies in the socialization of peacekeeping forces can have grave consequences for the civilians living in their areas of operation. One study suggested that mid-level commanders may be unwilling or unable to socialize their members into these norms of militarized masculinity. Stephen Moncrief suggests, "individual units and their commanders develop their own norms and patterns of sexual behavior that deviate from these preferences in missions that are plagued by other types of indiscipline, indicating the inability or unwillingness to constrain the behavior of mission personnel" (2017, p. 725).

In some armed groups, failure to live up to masculine ideals (however the group defines them) renders men suspect and vulnerable to criticism. In the U.S. Navy, for example, those "... who fail to live up to the manly standards ... are reportedly targets of gendered insults," which often demean them as being feminine or homosexual (Kiefer, 2022, p. 49). He asserts that this is only insulting

---

2 See, for example: Guevara and Castro, "Socialism and man in Cuba" (1965).

"...because of an unwritten, shared understanding that women would naturally be more in-clined to complaining as well as physically and mentally not strong enough to endure mili-tary training and combat. It is against the backdrop of this background knowledge which equates women with weakness, that the devaluation of femininity takes place in the mili-tary" (Kiefer, 2022, p. 49).

These dynamics increase pressure to conform and help solidify the gender hierar-chy. Or consider academic and veteran Godfrey Maringira's assertion that the Zimbabwean military rewards the practice of violence and socializes its members to enjoy engaging in violence. He provides the following account from a Zimbab-wean soldier: "forcing civilians brings satisfaction to me; we are trained to make enemies feel the pain, and it is the enemies' pain that makes us feel more than good. Remember we are trained to do violence and that is our mandate" (Maringi-ra, 2021, p. 107). That same soldier told him, "on the first day of training, the mil-itary instructor told us that this place is for real men, and women are those who we have left at home" (Maringira, 2021, p. 105). Similarly, Lesley Gill writes that the Bolivian military's socialization reinforces both raced and gendered hierar-chies. Gill observes that the Bolivian military has engaged in the "symbolic debase-ment of women and homosexuals" by equating soldiers' inadequacies with being "whores," "faggots," or "little ladies" (1997, p. 534). Writing on the Nigerian military God'sgift Ogban Uwen and Anthony Ebebe Eyang (2023) write, "songs in the Army's community of practice, aside from functioning as recreational instruments that boost the morale of soldiers, are also composed with linguistic forms that ac-claim male ruggedness, courage, and resilience." (p. 10). In all of these cases, these insults are a means of upholding the gender hierarchy by connecting failure and femininity.

Box 8.1: Alternative Military Masculinities, Looking at the Farabundo Martí National Liberation Front

Some armed groups have endeavored to construct a military masculinity that is not dependent on the domination of women. One of the most frequently remarked upon examples of this phenomenon is the Farabundo Martí National Liberation Front (FMLN).

The FMLN was a left-wing guerrilla group that fought a civil war in El Salvador from 1979 to 1992 before transitioning to a political party. During the war, the FMLN tried to cultivate a more egalitarian rebel identity. As academic Luisa Maria Dietrich Ortega notes, status and identity within the group were "not based on the devaluation of women in general, but on the temporary construction of par-ticular guerrilla femininities, which allow male-female bonding and comradely complicity, and unveil expressions of guerrilla masculinities beyond the predominant association of men with violence" (2012, p. 491). The FMLN was trying to rewrite the relationship between men and women, with the objective of destabilizing the gender hierarchy.

The FMLN's guerrilla masculinity allowed men to show emotion and care without sacrificing their status as a man. One FMLN commander recalled that men were especially sensitive to the plight of children orphaned as a result of the war and told researchers: "When I realized this tenderness of those otherwise rude men, especially in difficult situations … I was impressed" (Dietrich Ortega, 2012, p. 498). These new masculinities reflect rebel leaders' ideological commitment to radical leftist politics (Kiefer, 2022) and, relatedly, their calculations that they could not win the war without mobilizing women.

Yet even in these supposedly progressive organizations, women have still often struggled to be respected. The term "feminism" was not welcome within the organization and women's issues were not always taken seriously (Kiefer, 2022). Female members of the FMLN, furthermore, reported "widespread sexual violence" that was tacitly accepted (and sometimes perpetrated) by the organization's leadership (Kiefer, 2022). The new process of vertical socialization rebels experienced within the FMLN was challenged by their previous socialization and the horizontal socialization they experienced in the group.

Women's Socialization in Armed Groups

As we previously discussed, the deep connections between masculinity, violence, and prestige can put women who join armed groups in a nearly impossible position. By dint of their biological sex, they are constantly fighting an uphill battle and considered "other" within the organization.

Despite all of the ways that they are marked as "different" within the organization, women are often subject to the same processes of socialization within armed groups—meaning that they have incentives to engage in the same types of behavior that men in the group do. This can have positive and negative effects. For example, Peteet (1991) noted of women in the Palestinian liberation struggle that

> training in guerilla tactics and self-defense and the strenuous routine of daily exercise sessions spawned a self-confidence in their abilities to be equal participants in the national struggle. Women spoke of an 'euphoria,' 'a new sense of who I am and my strengths,' and 'carrying the same load as men.'… Most important, the military experience awakened women to their potential equality to men (p. 150–151).

Socialization within an armed group thus contributed to a feeling of gender egalitarianism and personal accomplishment.

Dara Kay Cohen's study of forced recruitment and gang rape, however, finds that women have been active participants in sexual violence against civilians. For example, within the Revolutionary United Front (RUF), a rebel group that fought in Sierra Leone, female rebels "…not only acted as liaisons to locate potential victims but also restrained victims while they were being raped" (2013, p. 403). She also found, "beyond holding victims down, interviewees witnessed female combatants raping other women with objects" (2013, p. 404). Her interviews with former rebels revealed that these women participated alongside men because they were undergoing the same process of socialization as the men in the organization who participated in these abuses.

While Cohen's work emphasizes the similarity of the socialization of men and women, in other cases, women have been held to different standards than their male counterparts—meaning that their socialization processes are distinct. According to academic Anthony King, women's participation in the US military in the 1970s gave rise to "a new system of cultural classification [which] emerged to define women either as sluts (sexually available) or bitches (sexually unavailable), of which lesbians or 'dykes' (self-evidently unavailable) are a subcategory" (2015, p. 381). It is worth emphasizing that neither sluts nor bitches are labels that women typically aspire to, underscoring the fraught choices women in the military face.[3]

Women face similar pressures in non-state armed groups. As we discussed in the previous chapter, women in armed groups often feel compelled to demonstrate that they are just as physically strong and adept at fighting as men. For example, one woman that rose to a leadership role in the Colombian armed group M-19 recalled that she and other women in the group "had to demonstrate constantly that we could do everything asked of us and more" (Herrera and Porch, 2008, p. 618). Some women fighters in Burundian armed groups reported that they actually took pleasure in extremely brutal acts. One admitted "When I tortured someone, I liked to do it slowly. Using my bare hands, I would scratch

---

3 One female Marine told an academic that she had regrets about how she navigated this tightrope early in her military career. She stated:

There was no 'right' answer. There was no 'right' behavior because if you stayed away from the camaraderie, you were an unapproachable bitch who was never considered part of the team. However, if you were a young woman your male peers found attractive, if you ever acted upon that male–female dynamic, you were automatically labeled a slut or a whore or just, generally, a woman who couldn't be trusted because you were 'fucking' somebody in the unit. Honestly, I can't imagine another environment in the entire world that has these kinds of relationship issues as a day-to-day concern. It's really crazy, but in the Marine Corps, you can't escape it ... It would have been better to be labeled a bitch or a lesbian than to be a slut because 'slut' bleeds into every other aspect of your personal and professional reputation, which then bleeds over into the training and leadership, and once it's there, there's no way to make it go away' (Brownson, 2014, p. 780).

She emphasizes that this is not a dynamic confined to the U.S. military and cites the experience of a woman in the British military who stated, "Men soldiers don't respect WRACs [Women's Royal Auxiliary Corps] at all. If you're in it, you're a lesbian or a slut. And there's real pressure to sleep with men" (King, 2015, p. 381).

and pull off the penis. Sometimes it would take more than an hour" (Meyer-Parlapanis et al., 2016, p. 6). In some cases, female fighters get the reputation of being especially bloodthirsty. In one study of Burundian combatants, many reported that they would rather be taken prisoner by a man than a woman, because women were "more dangerous and cruel" (Meyer-Parlapanis et al., 2016, p. 6). These women are not just behaving like men, their behavior exaggerates traditional masculine traits. They are performing a militarized hyper-masculinity—because they are women.

Box 8.2: Regendering or Over-burdening: Expectations of Women in the South African National Defense Forces

Looking at the experiences of women in the South African National Defense Forces (SANDF) can help us understand the catch-22s and impossible situations that women in militaries around the world face. Women in SANDF navigate contradictory expectations about what their very presence means for the military. Their very integration began as a part of the broader political changes ushered in by the end of Apartheid. South Africa's 1996 constitution expressly forbid discrimination on the basis of gender, race, or sexual orientation; this provision paved the way for women's integration into combat positions in the South African military (Wilen and Heinecken, 2018).

Research from academics Nina Wilén and Lindy Heinecken reveals that women in the SANDF are both expected to perform their jobs "like men," and bring a woman's touch to the military. Their conversations with members of SANDF reveal the tension between the idea that soldiers are interchangeable parts, socialized into the military culture, and the idea that the inclusion of women will fundamentally change the character of the military (Wilen and Heineken, 2018).

Furthermore, their research underscores the three tropes that have emerged around female SANDF members: civilianizing, sexualizing, and victimizing narratives. The "civilianizing" narrative attaches civilian identities to active duty women. Those accounts, for example, may emphasize women's roles as mothers and wives, while active duty men are rarely considered as fathers and husbands. Civilianizing narratives can also place a burden of "normalcy" on the shoulders of women. Wilén and Heinecken relay the account of a male soldier, who opined: "When you have females around you, you are not just a soldier, you are human and they are always trying to uplift you when things are not good" (2018, p. 678). Though appreciative of women, this soldier is saddling his female counterparts with additional emotional labor, beyond what he expects of his male colleagues.

Sexualizing narratives are a way of undermining women's competence. For example, aggrieved soldiers may attribute a woman's advancement to them using their sexuality in order to get "special treatment." These narratives can sow discord among women in the military. Wilén and Heinecken quote a white female soldier who complained that women "… have sexual relationships with higher officers so they don't feel the need to listen to other officers … They also use their gender to get what they want from men, and I don't respect that. So I don't have a lot of respect for women in uniform. Although I am one" (2018, p. 679). Her experiences speak to the extent to which misogyny can be internalized by women active in male-dominated spaces.

Finally, victimizing narratives often emphasize the threats to women in the military and suggest that their male counterparts need to protect them. A male officer recounted to Wilén and Heinecken (2018) that while deployed in Sudan, he and his team were taken hostage by an armed group. He told them "The female emotions came out, they cried and we had to calm them down and tell them keep calm and do what we are trained for" (p. 680). When pressed, he admitted that men cried too. It turns out that it wasn't a female reaction, it was just a human one.

These narratives—which civilianize, sexualize, or victimize women in the SANDF—have significant implications for women's well-being within the military. They speak to the ongoing tensions between military culture, masculinity, and the integration of women.

Anthony King suggests that, with the passage of time, a new option may be emerging for women in the military: the "honorary man" (2015, p. 385). He suggests, "the concept of the honorary man represents a significant development in gender relations in the armed forces; it is a material advance on the slut–bitch categories that have predominated to date and endows them with equal status to their male comrades" (2015, p. 385). However, this new category maintains the status quo in which "Male soldiers remain the primary definers of women and military culture, to which women have to accommodate themselves" (2015, p. 385). Some women within the armed forces have internalized this objective of becoming an "honorary man." A female member of the U.S. Army stated: "Definitely professionalism was critical but there were other factors. I'm physically fit. I could beat most of the guys in running and running is a huge thing in this division. Once you showed you could do PT [physical training] and keep up, you were accepted," tying the respect she enjoyed to her ability to "keep up" with or even beat the guys in a foot race (King, 2016, p. 135). In such a system, status comes not from competence but to the extent to which women in the military can emulate their male counterparts. Honorary manhood is not the same thing as gender equality, even if it is an improvement over the "slut-bitch" binary.

Gender Hierarchy and Patterns of Violence in War

The socialization that members of armed groups undergo matters for how wars are fought. Some socialization processes produce restrained, professional militaries that engage in a narrow "repertoire of violence," whereas other groups adopt and cement norms of unbridled violence or encourage certain forms of civilian targeting (Gutiérrez-Sanín and Wood, 2017; Revkin and Wood, 2021).

These norms and expectations have profound implications for civilians' safety. For example, Cohen's study of rebels in a range of conflicts found that forced conscription of members produced socialization patterns that were linked to higher levels of rape, and particularly of gang-rape, of civilians. For example, she notes that:

...ex-combatants reported admiration, not disgust, for those who had perpetrated many rapes...Ex-combatants reported that those who participated in rape in Sierra Leone were seen to be more courageous, valiant, and brave than their peers. Those who committed rape were respected by their peers as "big men"—strong and virile warriors (2013, p. 405).

Cohen also posits that participation in sexual violence was a means by which abducted rebels cultivated camaraderie and cohesion, marking a transition away from their life as a civilian and their new identity as a fighter (2016).

Socialization within armed groups does not only determine what types of violence will be used and under what circumstances. It also shapes how different populations are targeted during war (Revkin and Wood, 2021). Gender hierarchy subjects men and women to different kinds of violence during war. While there are well-noted difficulties tracking non-lethal violence in conflict zones and gender-disaggregated fatality counts are rare, there are some clear trends in the available data. One of these trends is that men are more likely to die as a result of direct violence during war. For example, the Iraq Body Count, a project dedicated to tallying the human cost of the war in Iraq, reported in 2005 that of the 13,000 civilian casualties where they were able to determine the gender, more than 80 % were adult men (Ormhaug, Meier, and Hernes, 2009, p. 11). This count does not include the number of members of armed groups that were killed in battle, which would likely inflate the proportion of men killed even higher, given the male dominance of both state-affiliated militaries and non-state armed groups in that conflict.

Box 8.3: Why "Civilians" Aren't Just Women and Children

Masculine protection norms also shape who is considered a civilian and who is considered a combatant once military activity has kicked off. Consider, for example, the extraordinarily clumsy system by which many state-affiliated militaries distinguish civilians from combatants in war zones, thereby differentiating "legitimate targets" from "collateral damage." As the United States began to rely more and more on "drone strikes" as a part of its arsenal in the Global War on Terror, guilt was not determined by association with an armed group — it was presumed on the basis of their gender, age, and location (Action on Armed Violence, 2019). Under President Obama, the U.S. government adopted a definition: "in effect counts all military-age males in a strike zone as combatants... unless there is explicit intelligence posthumously proving them innocent" (Becker and Shane, 2012, n.p.). As Action on Armed Violence (AOAV) explains:

Gender is one of several characteristics and behaviours which are used to assess the legitimacy of drone targets. Others include travel, phone calls, and location, but gender remains one of the most important... while proximity to a target is important in determining guilt in the collateral damage count, it is only relevant if you are a man or a boy. This means that military-age males geographically close to suspects when the drone strikes are not even included in civilian casualties. Their gender forces them, in death, into the role of the accused combatant (2019, n.p.).

The assumption that any man of a certain age is a combatant is just one of the ways that the patriarchy hurts men.

This system of classification is almost farcical in its simplicity. The United States has some of the most sophisticated intelligence collection and analysis capabilities in the world—in 2023 the government budgeted nearly $100 million for intelligence programs (Ferran, 2023) — and we are still relying on these crude metrics. This system of accounting for the dead and legitimizing that violence relies on the gender hierarchy associates men with latent or explicit threats of violence. The only world in which considering any 16-year-old boy in a war zone as a combatant makes sense is a world predicated on the logic of masculinist protection against masculine threats.

The other side of this coin is the assumption that all women are civilians—a depiction that is often paired with depictions that rob them of their agency. Cynthia Enloe, the pioneering and unfailingly curious feminist scholar, coined the term *womenandchildren* to describe this dynamic. This term helps us draw attention to how the presumed innocence of women is also a means by which masculine protection is justified. Think of how frequently the harm done to "women and children" is used to cultivate disdain for abusive governments or to justify military action against that government—a subject we will consider in greater detail in Chapter 10 (Eisenstein, 2013). Presuming the innocence and lack of involvement of women in war does not shield them from experiencing violence during war. But these narratives do open up opportunities for masculine protection by emphasizing the particular vulnerability of women and children.

While men are more likely to be killed, women are more likely to be the victims of sexual violence during war.[4] Though some commentators suggest that raping and pillaging is an inherent outgrowth of conflict, this is simply not true. This misconception is dangerous. As Cynthia Enloe notes, the conventional wisdom that "Men caught up in the fury of battle cannot be expected to be subject to the rules of conduct, much less the fine print of memos. Grabbing a stray chicken or a stray woman — it is simply what male soldiers do as they sweep across the landscape," is a "... portrait of battle [that] breeds complacency. It blots out all intentionality" (2000, p. 135). It also obscures the ways that armed groups successfully transform and control the behavior of their members in a variety of ways by socializing them into their identities as a member of the group (Wood and Toppelberg, 2017).

---

4 Furthermore, when men and boys are subjected to sexual violence in wartime, it is often qualitatively different than the sexual violence against women and girls. The rapidly-growing literature on this subject finds that sexual violence against men and boys is often intended to demean them by feminizing them. The harms of sexual violence against men and boys are compounded by the ways that they are made to feel "like women," because of the gender hierarchy that privileges men.

Even in circumstances where sexual violence is a characteristic of war, there is wide variation in the prevalence of this violence and the forms it takes (Cohen, Hoover-Green, and Wood, 2013). Compelling work from academics and conflict analysts also suggests that pre-war gender hierarchy and norms affect the characteristics and frequency of wartime sexual violence (Synenko, 2024). Some argue that sexual violence during war is, in many cases, an extension of the violence that women experience during times of "peace" (Meger, 2016). The socialization that militants undergo within the group is layered on top of their pre-war socialization into what behavior is appropriate, to include attitudes towards sexual violence. That means that the outbreak of war may not fundamentally change the threats of sexual violence that women face—it can intensify their vulnerability to existing threats.

Some feminist academics argue that gender hierarchy and the masculinist protection narratives that emerge from it place a target on women's backs during war. Women's subordination and symbolic importance as symbols of innocence and the recipients of protection makes them a juicy target for enemies looking to break their opponents' will. Women's bodies become mediums through which armed groups seek to undermine one another, because they are taught to view themselves as the defenders of good women against bad men. As Laura Sjoberg and Jessica Peet argue,

> If protecting the feminine is a crucial cause of war, it is also a crucial strategic consideration for belligerents' calculations of their own or their opponents' strengths or weaknesses... Destroying 'beautiful souls' could play a role in destroying both the opponent's will to fight and (symbolically and sometimes physically) the nation itself (2011, p. 171).

Box 8.4: The Chibok Girls and Female Suicide Bombers

With collaborates at West Point's Combating Terrorism Center, I contributed to a report detailing Boko Haram's use of female suicide bombers. By tracking Boko Haram's use of suicide bombers, we found that the group was an anomaly both in terms of the raw number of female suicide bombers (244) and the proportion of suicide bombers (56%) that were female. These are higher numbers than any other rebel group using suicide bombers. Reports surrounding the suicide bombings suggest that some of the women and girls had been coerced into committing the acts (Searcey and Boushnak, 2020).

As we started to analyze the numbers and dig into why Boko Haram was so reliant on female suicide bombers, we realized that all of the female suicide bombings that we could find reports of followed Boko Haram's abduction of 276 schoolgirls in Chibok and the global #BringBackOurGirls campaign that followed. Then-leader of Boko Haram, Abubakar Shekau, referenced the campaign in a propaganda video, saying "You've been going around saying, 'Bring back our girls,'" (Smith, 2014) released shortly after the school girls were taken (Smith, 2014).

We concluded that the campaign to draw attention to the plight of the "Chibok girls" and the threats that women and girls faced in North East Nigeria may have inadvertently made women more vulnerable to violence by demonstrating that such violence drew media attention and helped the organization cultivate a fearsome reputation. As I told reporters after the report's release, "Through the global response to the Chibok abductions, the insurgency learned the potent symbolic value of young female bodies ... that using them as bombers would attract attention and spread pervasive insecurity" (Akwei, 2017, n.p.). The connection between the Chibok abductions, the #BringBackOurGirls campaign, and Boko Haram's female suicide bombers illuminates how norms of masculinist protection put targets on the backs of women and girls.

The Legacies of Wartime Socialization under Gender Hierarchy

The socialization that members of armed groups undergo have profound post-conflict legacies, both for themselves as individuals and for the communities they return to. The end of the war does not flip a switch, turning off all of the behaviors that were learned during war—neither among fighters nor civilians.

Efforts to demobilize and reintegrate former fighters are common features of post-war politics, particularly following civil wars. Many of these initiatives are focused on getting the guns out of former fighters' hands and finding them viable jobs as civilians. In the rush to keep ex-combatants busy, however, these programs often overlook the depths of their wartime socialization.

Furthermore, when these programs fail to offer former fighters the degree of prestige and respect that they garnered (or believed that they could garner) as a member of the armed group, they are on shaky ground. As Correia and Bannon note,

> Ex-combatants face many challenges in returning to civilian life, but for most young men the most troubling concerns are a return to second-class status and of again being powerless and marginalized due to prevailing intergenerational power differentials. Having wielded power, some young men are reluctant to return to settings in which they are subordinate to older adults (2006, p. 176).

Having been socialized into being a fighter who can gain respect through violence, demobilized combatants sometimes struggle to figure out what is expected of them and how they can construct a good life for themselves as a civilian. Riley's (2022) study of Maoist veterans revealed that the models of masculinity practiced during wartime were eroded during the demobilization process; as "a more visibly defined hierarchy" among veterans emerged, so too do "masculine practices more aligned with masculine entitlement and gender divisions" (p. 121). Unsurprisingly, Maoist women were frustrated that the gender egalitarian values their male comrades espoused during the war faded in the aftermath of the conflict.

The failure of these programs can be devastating, both for former fighters and for the communities that they return to. One study noted, "young men interviewed in northern Uganda camps reported a sense of idleness, little hope for the future, and that they may turn to alcohol and other substances" (Barker and Ricardo, 2006, p. 176). And young Somali men living in displacement camps in Kenya told researchers, "...because they could not get married, they would use sexual violence against women" (Barker and Ricardo, 2006, p. 177).

The transition from rebel to civilian can be especially dislocating for women affiliated with armed groups, who may lose some of the liberties that they gained through their participation in armed violence. Compounding these difficulties is the tendency of reintegration programs to overlook or minimize women's contributions. After Mozambique's civil war ended, "no special measures were taken to ensure women's security in the camps and economic assistance such as lump sums were mainly reserved for men, leaving female ex-combatants, especially those with children, in a situation of precariousness and dependence" (Gade, 2019, n.p.). Researcher Seema Shekhawat (2015) observes that: "The euphoria of a violent movement – and, at times, the accompanying glorification of women as the backbone of the movement and their accidental empowerment – are replaced by neglect, apathy and stigmatisation. In the post-conflict situation, female ex-combatants are triply alienated – by 'their' group, by the state and by the community" (p. 8). Similarly, the DDR program that followed the civil war in Liberia included a "fundamental assumption.... that unemployed and 'idle' male ex-combatants were equated with instability. The flip side of the coin was that women were not viewed as constituting any security threat," which one observer tied to the unrelenting demands placed on them as caregivers (Hauge, 2019, p. 210). In many cases, female ex-combatants are expected to slip seamlessly back into their pre-war gendered roles and norms.

In recent years, DDR programs have tried to become more sensitive to women's needs. Yet even when programs incorporate gender-specific components into the disarmament and demobilization process by recognizing that not all rebels are armed and by making special accommodations for women in cantonment programs, reintegration into their communities can still be a fraught process.

It is not just former rebels that struggle to return to civilian life. Veterans of state militaries also frequently struggle when they return home from war or when they leave the military service. Governments have sought to ease the transition from military to civilian life for veterans through a wide variety of programs.

Consider the significant resources the U.S. military spends—an estimated $13 billion dollars each year—trying to help veterans transition to civilian life successfully (Kleykamp et al., 2024). The U.S. Department of Veterans Affairs has engaged in outreach to the civilian world to help them understand what veterans might be going through. In a handout for potential employers, for example, the VA explains that veterans may be disoriented by the demands of civilian life and employment. It writes: "The military provides structure and has a clear chain of command. This does not naturally exist outside the military. A Veteran will have to create his or her own structure or adjust to living in an environment with more ambiguity" (U.S. Department of Veteran Affairs, 2021, n.p.). The handout continues, "providing basic necessities" like "food, clothing, housing" can be a struggle, as "in the military, these things are not only provided, but there is often little choice" (U.S. Department of Veteran Affairs, 2021, n.p.). This handout also noted that veterans may be frustrated that their "Families may have created new routines during absences," which can be disrupted with their return to home life (U.S. Department of Veteran Affairs, 2021).

In 2018, China established its Ministry of Veterans Affairs. Its creation was precipitated by the announcement that 300,000 members of the People's Liberation Army would be discharged by the end of 2017 (Yang, 2025). This Ministry was dedicated to address the grievances of veterans as they returned to civilian lives. Though Kai Yang's (2025) research draws attention to the meaningful shortcomings of the Ministry's efforts to address veterans' grievances, the very dedication of state resources and political capital to veterans' reintegration speaks to the weight of the issue.

Just as inadequate DDR for rebel groups programs pose a threat to post-war stability, there are profound consequences when veterans feel unmoored or if they are not well-supported in their transition to civilian life. The strain is felt both by the veterans themselves and by their families. Consider, for example, rates of suicide among American servicemembers and veterans. A 2020 report found that, "adjusting for population age and sex differences, the suicide rate for Veterans was 57.3% greater than for non-Veteran U.S. adults" (National Veteran Suicide Prevention Annual Report, 2022, p. 7). Another study found that female veterans' suicide rates were 2.1 times higher than the general populations' (Ruiz et al., 2022).

Veterans struggling to adjust to civilian life may also become perpetrators of intimate partner violence (IPV) or domestic violence. One study suggests that a

> possible explanation is that Veterans have returned to civilian life and are home with their families and may have more opportunity to perpetrate IPV compared to AD [active duty] personnel who are potentially not home or with their spouses as regularly. It is also possible that stressors associated with transition from military to civilian life may increase the risk for IPV perpetration (Kwan et al., 2020, p. 13).

Programs designed to smooth veterans' reintegration into civilian life don't just benefit those individual veterans—they can also support the families and communities that surround these veterans.

Gender Hierarchy and the Socialization of Civilians in War Zones

Wars are not fought in a vacuum. The communities whose homes are destroyed and lives are upended by the outbreak of political violence also learn new ways of being. Let's first consider the communities where wars are fought. The gendered pattern of violence previously discussed—in which men are more likely to be killed, whereas women are more likely to experience non-lethal violence —means that women often take up new roles in their homes and communities, where they are socialized into new identities and new ways of being. Indeed, a number of academic studies find that, following the cataclysmic upheaval of war, women and girls experience paradoxical improvements in their rights and representation (Webster, Chen, and Beardsley, 2019). Many point to the new skills and networks that women develop during war as the source of these gains. Though such findings are often greeted with enthusiasm by policymakers and academics, these "gains" come with profound costs.

Furthermore, the women and girls that step up and take on new roles do not always consider this a positive change. While talking with women and girls displaced by Boko Haram, it became clear to me that interpreting metrics like women's employment in formal jobs outside of their home as a sign of empowerment often ignored that women were taking up these positions out of necessity. Their entry into the labor force was not necessarily a triumphant march but a dutiful trudge to ensure their families' survival. Furthermore, men can sometimes resent them because of the feeling of having their masculinity thwarted by women taking up "male" roles. This frustration and resentment can result in the types of backlash we will discuss in Chapter 10.

At the same time that women take up new roles out of necessity, they often face old forms of discrimination. Cross-national evidence has found that displaced women have a harder time getting jobs and going to school in the communities where they settle than their male counterparts do (Klugman, 2024). The obstacles that displaced women face are linked to the gender hierarchies in the communities they leave and in the places that they seek refuge. Even when communities have uprooted their lives in pursuit of security, women may still be hemmed in by gendered expectations. Just as the socialization of fighters is a process layered on top of their pre-war socialization, so too is the socialization of civilians in war zones.

In many situations, there is not just a demand for women to take up *new* tasks but also a heightened demand for the types of work that women already provide. Armed groups also depend on women to provide non-sexual, feminized labor— such as cooking, cleaning, emotional support—though they often denigrate the women that provide these services as "mere" prostitutes. As Cynthia Enloe notes: "When they weren't being reduced verbally or physically to the status of prostitutes, camp followers were performing tasks that any large military force needs but wants to keep ideologically peripheral to its combat function and often tries to avoid paying for directly" (Enloe, 1983, p. 40). Armed groups need women's work but do not want to publicly depend on them, nor compensate them for their contributions nor lend them any of the respect that might come from membership in the organization.

One of the most prominent examples of this is the proliferation of brothels and prostitution rings near army bases (Enloe, 1983). The so-called "world's oldest profession" is deeply interwoven into the political economy of war. A variety of militaries have adopted formal policies regulating sex work, while some non-state armed groups have adopted strictly regulated systems of sexual slavery. These systems often intersect with other hierarchies—including racial, ethnic, and religious categories. Consider, for example, the similarities between the Japanese military's violent subordination of Korean "comfort women" during World War II and the Islamic State's enslavement of Yazidi women. In each, control over members of the armed group was maintained through regulations permitting the sexual domination and abuse of minority women.

Armed groups, state and non-state alike, have worked to convince women that their interests are bound up with the organization's in order to continue benefiting from women's labor. For those who live in communities affected by war, the threat of imminent violence and the promise of security can be compelling arguments. Women in war zones make "patriarchal bargains" with armed groups that can be life or death (Kandiyoti, 1988).

Conclusion

One night at dinner with another "improbable" couple (a male military veteran and a female policy-wonk), my husband described someone as "getting canoe'd." The other man chuckled, while both women cocked our heads in confusion. They explained that it was a military term used to refer to someone being shot in the head. The air went out of the room as we processed the description. The men looked sheepish, realizing how they had developed calluses in the course of their work.

My husband and I discussed later how slang, dark humor, and other ways of distancing ourselves from violence are a means of protecting our mental health. Calluses develop for a reason—to protect the body from a source of repeated friction. When we consider how people are socialized, we should bear in mind how some of their behaviors are a means of protecting themselves.

In this chapter, we have explored how gender hierarchy affects wartime socialization and the conduct of war. By this point, you should not be surprised to learn that there are deep connections between gender norms, socialization, and behavior. We have discussed the complex and multi-faceted dynamics of socialization within both state-affiliated militaries and non-state armed groups. Though these groups are different in many ways, in this chapter we've seen the common trend of socializing members into the close connection between masculinity, violence, and prestige. We discussed how the operationalization of masculinist protection and the protection racket produce distinct patterns of violence for men and women living in war zones. We then discussed the long-term implications of socialization into the norms and behavior of an armed group, as well as the post-war implications of the socialization of civilians living in war zones and those far afield from the fighting.

Throughout, this chapter underscores the close connection between gender hierarchy that privileges men and masculinity and the socialization that emerges during war. Weaving together Chapter 7 and Chapter 8, we can trace individuals' decisions to go to war, their behavior during war, and how civilians living in war zones are shaped by norms about masculinity and femininity. In the following chapter, we consider how gender hierarchy influences states' decisions to go to war and their behavior during conflict.

Chapter 9
Gender Hierarchy and International Security

On November 17, 2001, then-First Lady Laura Bush gave the weekly Presidential radio address. Mrs. Bush took to the airwaves at a uniquely difficult time in American history. The United States was still reeling from the devastating September 11 attacks on the Twin Towers by members of the international terrorist outfit al Qaeda.

But Mrs. Bush was not there to talk about the resilience of the American people. She was not there to commend the remarkable bravery of the first responders who rushed towards the smoldering rubble to save their fellow citizens. She was not there to talk about how Americans could find joy and community during the holiday season in the shadow of this national tragedy.

She was there to talk about the Taliban's oppression of Afghan women.

In a somewhat wooden speech, Mrs. Bush drew a clear contrast between the liberty the American government provides women and the Taliban's oppression of them. She characterized the Taliban as brutes who "threaten to pull out women's fingernails for wearing nail polish." She said, "civilized people throughout the world are speaking out in horror, not only because our hearts break for the women and children in Afghanistan but also because, in Afghanistan, we see the world the terrorists would like to impose on the rest of us." The message was clear: it was America's duty to get the Taliban's boot off Afghan women's necks—for the well-being of those women and for American's own security.

Using women to help justify America's invasion and occupation of Afghanistan was not confined to Mrs. Bush's guest speech. In order to help drum up support for the war, the Bush Administration portrayed themselves as liberators of Afghan women. Furthermore, the US tried to distinguish itself from the Taliban through its treatment of women. In particular, the US military offered women in its ranks the opportunity to act as protectors of women "over there." This was particularly evident in its publicity of Female Engagement Teams (FET) after their establishment in 2009 (Kareko, 2019). American women in uniform were presented as the "secret weapon" in the counter-insurgency campaign. Their very presence in the military was a way for the US to prove its commitment to liberal, democratic, and egalitarian values.

The United States' display of military force in Afghanistan can also be read as a means of proving that America was still the toughest guy on the block, even after 9/11 had revealed weaknesses in the country's defenses. The wars therefore became a vehicle for the US to reclaim its own wounded masculinity by displaying its military might. At home, bumper stickers with phrases like "these colors don't

https://doi.org/10.1515/9783111662886-011

run" became popular, hammering home that the United States would not cower in response to a threat—it would come out swinging.

Often lost in the nationalist fervor and the day-to-day reporting on the war were the perspectives of Afghan women themselves. One report exploring the perspective of a women's group in Kandahar included this statement from one woman: "It is like the Taliban times for women now. We are in the same situation as then. We cannot come out of the house to earn extra money or get an education. The only difference is that our honor was safe then but it is not now" (Ladbury, 2009). The US-led invasion of Afghanistan had not produced a gender-equal utopia for women but instead made them vulnerable in new and devastating ways.[1]

The motivations and justifications for the war in Afghanistan—and the effects of these military operations—underscore that women's subordination is one of the most powerful forces in international security. Afghanistan, as a war characterized by gendered performances of protection that marginalized the perspectives of those that were supposedly being protected, is not a one-off event. As this chapter will show, these dynamics have been at play around the world and throughout history.

In this chapter, we'll take a deeper dive into this relationship between gender hierarchy and international security. We'll consider how women's subordination is linked to global instability and war. We will also discuss how governments around the world have responded to this connection through the development of the Women, Peace, and Security (WPS) agenda and "feminist foreign policy". This chapter will also consider how the rise of this agenda has inadvertently fueled the "logic of masculinist protection" at the state level, and how masculinist protection from states creates further insecurity (Young 2003). We will unpack how masculinist protection influences the policies that states adopt to "protect" their own citizens and even those beyond their borders.

---

1 The willingness of Afghan women to publicly challenge the U.S.'s narrative about the war in Afghanistan catalyzed hard conversations—at least in some circles—about the effects of the military's activities. Iris Marion Young (2003) reflected, "I fear that some feminists adopted the stance of the protector in relation to the women of Afghanistan. What is wrong with this stance, if it has existed, is that it fails to consider these women as equals, and it does not have principled ways of distancing itself from paternalist militarism" (p. 230). The presumptuousness of Western men and women purporting to know what is best for women "over there" became clear as the perspectives of Afghan women hit the global mainstream.

Gender Hierarchy and Likelihood of War

Throughout the course of this book, we have seen how the norms developed within our homes ripple out, affecting the characteristics of our communities, countries, and the world at large. This same ripple effect is at play when it comes to international security.

Valerie Hudson, Donna Lee Bowen, and Perpetua Lynne Nielsen—pioneering scholars in this field—argue that the relationship between men and women is the "first political order" and that the characteristics of the state emerge from that relationship (Hudson, Bowen, and Nielsen, 2020). A range of studies have since noted that women's well-being and security in their personal lives affects the character of the state. Countries with higher levels of gender inequality are more likely to go to war with their neighbors and likelier to experience civil war within their own borders (Caprioli, 2003; Hudson et al., 2020). Furthermore, the disempowerment of women in their homes is also correlated with state use of political terror (Hudson and Hodgson, 2022).

A 2022 study noted, "nearly a hundred studies indicate some type of link between sex and gender inequality and violent outcomes" (Cohen and Karim, 2022, p. 415). That so many studies, which measure women's subordination and state instability in so many different ways, have come to the same conclusions suggest that they are picking up on a meaningful dynamic. This degree of consensus is rare in social science.

This research has helped bolster the rise of the "Women, Peace and Security agenda" (WPS). Though a pioneering agenda that helped get the link between women's welfare and international security on the global agenda, it has faced criticism for instrumentalizing and tokenizing women. The following sections unpack the rise—and potential roll-back—of the WPS agenda. They also consider the unintended consequences of the WPS agenda and the way it has inadvertently (and counter-productively) fueled "masculinist protection" from states.

The Women, Peace, and Security Agenda, Feminist Foreign Policy, and State Security

On an unseasonably warm October 31, 2000, civil society advocates and members of the international community came together to do something about the marginalization of women from deliberations around security concerns and peacebuilding. That day, the United Nations Security Council passed Resolution 1325. The passage of this landmark resolution was the result of decades of feminist advocacy and mobilization by civil society groups, who drew attention to the harm done to women by sidelining them and their experiences (Pratt and Richter-Devroe, 2011). This resolution (known as UNSCR 1325) urges all of the members of the United Nations to integrate women and gendered analysis into peace and security matters. It lays out four areas (also called "pillars") in which member states can advance women's participation and gendered perspectives: participation, protection, prevention, relief and recovery. UNSCR 1325 became a cornerstone of the new Women, Peace and Security Agenda.

Box 9.1: The Four Pillars of the WPS Agenda

The Women, Peace and Security Agenda rests on four pillars: participation, protection, prevention, relief and recovery (United Nations and She Stands for Peace, n.d.)

- **Participation** refers to the inclusion of women in decision-making and planning surrounding matters of peace and security. This pillar emphasizes that women must be included in all-levels of decision-making—from the UN Security Council to community-level deliberations.
- **Protection** refers to the need to pay particular attention to the vulnerability of women and girls to sexual and gender-based violence, particularly in conflict-affected contexts.
- **Prevention** refers to efforts to reduce the vulnerability of women and girls through improved legal status and accountability for violence against women.
- **Relief and Recovery** refers to the need for gendered analysis and planning in humanitarian responses.

Since 2000, there have been nine additional UNSCRs passed on matters related to Women, Peace and Security. These UNSCRs have focused on things like recognizing the threat of sexual violence during war and advising members to train their troops on how to prevent and respond to such violence (UNSCR 1820, passed in 2008; UNSCR 1888, passed in 2009; UNSCR 1960, passed in 2010; UNSCR 2467, assed in 2019), improving women's ability to participate in peacebuilding processes (UNSCR 1889, passed in 2009), providing more support and services to women affected by war (UNSCR 2122, passed in 2013), and engaging more with civil society (UNSCR 2242, passed in 2015) (PeaceWomen, n.d.a.).

To help mainstream the agenda, the United Nations has urged member states to develop their own "National Action Plans" (NAPs), describing how they will pursue the objectives of the WPS agenda. NAPs "outline objectives and activities that countries take, both on a domestic and international level, to secure the human rights of women and girls in conflict settings; prevent armed conflict and violence, including against women and girls; and ensure the meaningful participation of women in peace and security" (PeaceWomen, n.d.b.). As of this writing, more than 100 countries have adopted an NAP; some countries have adopted multiple NAPs.

Alongside the spread of the WPS agenda, some countries have also adopted a "feminist foreign policy." This movement was spearheaded by Sweden, which first introduced the concept in 2014. Since then, Canada, France, Germany, the Netherlands, Spain, Slovenia, Luxembourg, Argentina, Chile, Colombia, Mexico, and Libya have also committed themselves to some degree to a feminist foreign policy (Sikkink and Clapp, 2024). One report further observed, "In the UK, three different political parties have pledged that they will pursue this if in power" and "in the United States, a resolution expressing support for this idea has been brought to the House of Representatives" (UN Women, 2022). Though a number of countries have committed themselves to a feminist foreign policy, it's unclear what such a policy looks like in practice and what its objectives are.

The changes brought about by the WPS agenda and feminist foreign policies are not just rhetorical. In recent decades, we have seen a surge in the number of women peacekeepers, women's inclusion in peace negotiations, and women's involvement in politics. Furthermore, these policies provided activists with a set of commitments that they can hold their governments responsible for making good on.

Box 9.2: The Rise and Fall of Sweden's Feminist Foreign Policy

Though hailed as groundbreaking, Sweden's adoption of a feminist foreign policy in 2014 under Minister of Foreign Affairs Margot Wallström was not necessarily a sharp break from the norm in Swedish politics. As early as 1996, the Swedish government was explicitly concerned with gender equality in its foreign policy (Moss, 2020). Wallström's articulation of feminist foreign policy helped formalize what had long been a focus and characteristic of the Swedish government. This new initiative centered on the "three Rs," which included "rights, representation, and resources" (Moss, 2020, n.p.).

Though the Swedish government prided itself on being a pioneer in feminist foreign policy, the agenda quickly ran into obstacles. One of the most notable challenges to Sweden's feminist foreign policy came in 2015, when Ms. Wallström criticized Saudi Arabia's treatment of women. In response, Saudi Arabia blocked Wallström from giving a speech to the Arab League (BBC, 2015; Crouch, 2015). This ignited a tit-for-tat political row that involved Saudi Arabia recalling its ambassador and Sweden cutting off a weapons sales deal (BBC, 2015).

Though this high-profile showdown between the Saudi and Swedish government hinted at the radical potential of feminist foreign policy, a number of critics have pointed out that Sweden continued to export weapons to a wide variety of states with sub-par human rights records. Some argue feminist foreign policy "did not constitute a radical transformative agenda leading to a real shift in Swedish foreign policy" (Wright and Rosamond, 2024, p. 600).

The country's decision to back down from its feminist foreign policy in 2022 reflects both domestic and international political dynamics. Firstly, the new coalition government was further to the right than its predecessor. Their platform included things like reducing immigration and getting tough on crime. Though the new Prime Minister Ulf Kristersson asserted that he believes in the importance of gender equality, he made it clear in the early days of his administration that a feminist foreign policy was not a priority. Additionally, some believe that the Russian invasion of Ukraine in 2022 has drained away support for Sweden's feminist foreign policy among its citizens. Katharine A.M. Wright and Annika Bergman Rosamond observe that the country is undergoing a "rewriting of Sweden's identity narrative, which centres on its capability to be a 'serious military actor', dedicated to the upgrading of its armed forces and, ultimately, militarism and masculinist leadership. From this perspective FFP is a threat to its quest for NATO membership" (2024, p. 602). At the very moment in which Sweden—and the international community—is in dire need of a gender-egalitarian and sensible foreign policy, we are witnessing a backlash to it.

Yet the WPS Agenda and feminist foreign policy endeavors have come under fire. Criticisms have been levied both by conservatives skeptical of making security "woke" and by feminist activists who think they don't go far enough. As detailed in Box 9.2, Sweden abandoned its feminist foreign policy in 2022. When announcing the decision, Swedish foreign minister Tobias Billström stated that the "feminist" "label has not fulfilled a good purpose and has hidden the fact that Swedish foreign policy needs to be based on Swedish values and interests" (Wright and Rosamond, 2024, p. 601). Billström's comments raise the troubling possibility that the new government doesn't consider gender equality to be a Swedish "value" (Human Rights Watch, 2022).

We've seen similar pushback in Germany, where a leader of the Christian Democratic Union stated: "You can do a feminist foreign policy, a feminist development policy—you can do all that. But not with the budget for the Bundeswehr [the country's armed forces]" (Latella, 2023, n.p.). Even a Liberal German politician criticized the country's feminist foreign policy, stating "I don't think much of the concept of feminist foreign policy because it is less aimed at achieving diplomatic improvements than at the emotional satisfaction of domestic political actors" (Latella, 2023, n.p.). These comments reflect a general skepticism of Feminist Foreign Policy among German citizens. One survey found, "compared to the reference category of the Social Democratic Party (SPD), supporters of the right-wing populist Alternative for Germany (AFD) and the liberal Free Democratic Party (FDP), as well as supporters of the conservative CDU/CSU, display considerably lower support for feminist development policy" (Schneider et al., 2024, p. 292). This means that both the left- and right-wings of the German political system are unsupportive of the endeavor. In an era of political polarization, this portends a rough road ahead for advocates of feminist foreign policy.

The second Trump Administration has also pushed back against the WPS agenda. Secretary of Defense Pete Hegseth announced in April 2025 that he was cancelling the WPS program for the US military. He posted to X, "WPS is yet another woke divisive/social justice/Biden initiative that overburdens our commanders and troops—distracting from our core task: WAR-FIGHTING. WPS is a UNITED NATIONS program pushed by feminists and left-wing activists. Politicians fawn over it; troops HATE it. DoD will hereby executive the minimum of WPS required by statute, and fight to end the program for our next budget" (emphasis in original) (Hegseth, 2025, n.p.). Hegseth's characterization of the WPS agenda conveniently overlooks that President Trump signed the WPS directive into law in 2017 and that the program previously enjoyed support from both Republicans and Democrats.

Criticisms have also emerged from folks that originally championed the agenda. Feminist activists and scholars point to the recipe that WPS implementation follows—"add women and stir"—and argue that it leads to underwhelming results. Merely slotting women into existing patriarchal institutions, they argue, is unlikely to change how they do business. Furthermore, some feminists have pointed to the ways in which the WPS agenda has tried to "make war safe for women" (by focusing on things like reducing sexual violence and the targeting of women in war), rather than bring about an end to war and militarization (Shepherd, 2016). As some friends and I darkly joke: "more female drone pilots" is a far cry from feminist liberation and a world at peace.

Feminist critics also point to the ways that NAPs have been used to further neo-colonial understandings of world politics. The women that are given a platform to "participate" in security matters through the WPS agenda are generally privileged women who often live in the Global North and who attend elite colleges and work prestigious jobs. Left out of this process are women of color, women living outside of the Global North, and women who might not have the academic or professional qualifications to be taken "seriously" by the security establishment (Henry, 2021). NAPs have often redirected attention away from the shortcomings of states' policies towards women in the Global North.

Related to the exclusive and elite process by which NAPs are developed, these documents often replicate colonial models of politics in which the "problems" are understood as being confined to the Global South, and in which the Global North is tasked with helping women "over there" (Henry, 2021, p. 23; Shepherd, 2016; Basu, 2016). This can help cement the sort of masculine protection narratives that we have seen end up making women less secure and which present formidable obstacles to gender equality. Though the architects and advocates of WPS and feminist foreign policy did not intend for these policies to prod states into acting as "masculine protectors," this perverse interpretation of such agendas has cropped up frequently in recent decades.

The effects of this misunderstanding (or purposeful misinterpretation) of the WPS agenda and feminist foreign policy has implications for global stability, civil liberties, and women's well-being the world over. As the following sections unpack, when states cast them as masculine protectors, they frequently replicate the predatory and controlling relationships seen between individual masculine protectors and "their women" discussed in previous chapters. When states are masculine protectors, they frequently adopt bellicose and regressive policies at home and abroad. These sections will discuss how the masculine protector narrative has motivated and been used to justify a range of expansionist foreign policies and repressive domestic policies.

The State as a Masculine Protector

In previous chapters, we discussed how fighters have been drawn into armed groups by the opportunity to prove themselves as masculine protectors. But the idea of being a masculine protector is appealing not just to individuals but also to whole governments and state bureaucracies. To that end, states have also cast themselves as masculine protectors of both its citizens and of feminized populations the world over. At times, states have used WPS and feminist foreign policy to justify such behavior, even though this is a far cry from the objectives of such initiatives. Sjoberg observes that the idea of the state as a masculine protector is one that reproduces patriarchal relations, by suggesting that male states are the protectors of feminized civilian populations. She writes, "These accounts of gender tropes as key to the identity of state and/or nation create a narrative of *that which states defend* — femininity, purity, their capacities as masculine protectors; and *that which states must be to defend* — masculine, tough, protecting, militaristic, and nationalistic" (2013, p. 145).[2] States have cast themselves as masculine protectors of both of their own citizens as well as those far beyond their borders.

Masculine Protectors Abroad

Let's consider, for example, the justifications offered by colonial governments about how their "civilizing missions" (also known as the violent colonization of land and people) were for women's benefits—not to bolster their own power and prosperity. Colonized people and places were often rendered

> ...as feminine: weak, passive, irrational, disorderly, unpredictable, lacking self-control, and economically and politically incompetent. European power wielders (not only men or all men) could then justify military interventions by casting themselves in favorable masculinist

---

2 While masculine protection narratives are an undercurrent running through international security, they become especially prominent during times of crisis when the high cost of masculine protection may seem preferable to uncertainty.

terms: as uniquely rational, sexually and morally respectable, and more advanced economically and politically... Through this lens, military interventions were perhaps a regrettable but nonetheless a necessary component of 'enlightening' and 'civilizing' primitive, unruly (feminized) 'others' (Sjoberg, Via, and Enloe, 2010, p. 21).

Masculine protection helps reinforce social boundaries, recreating and reinforcing raced and gendered hierarchies.

As colonization and imperial expansion have fallen out of fashion, masculinist protection norms have been refashioned to justify other military adventures abroad. As the introduction to this chapter discusses, ideas about masculine protection (layered on top of racist tropes about Arab men and women) were an important component of how the United States justified the War in Afghanistan. Or consider Zillah Eisenstein's characterization of America's condemnations of Syrian President Assad's use of chemical weapons in the country's civil war:

Why invoke 'womenandchildren' when condemning the use of chemical weapons by Assad? Chemical weapons cross a line of human decency – although one might argue that all weapons do so. Calling for the protection of 'womenandchildren' allows leaders to frame wars as matters of national security, under the assumption that women and children must be protected for nations to be secure (Eisenstein, 2013, n.p.).

In recent years, we have seen the development of alternative forms of masculinist protection states. Sweden, for example, has cast itself as a "humanitarian superpower" that uses its military might toward compassionate ends, rather than a means of conquest (Agius, 2018). Furthermore, the country's leaders described its military forays in Afghanistan and Libya as a way of demonstrating its commitment to the NATO alliance and protecting vulnerable women. As Christine Agius (2018) argues,

Debates about intervention and NATO membership are constructed along binaries of being *engaged, proactive,* and *protectionist* rather than *isolationist, reactive,* and facilitating human rights abuses through *inaction* or *passivity.* Within these discourses is a particularly gendered idea of revising state sovereignty and identity, which plays to gender binaries of weak/strong, public/private, moral/immoral, even in areas of 'soft security' such as peacekeeping (p. 75).

Even the Swedish reconceptualization of the masculinist protector state is in contradiction to the government's feminist reputation because it finds itself trying to be a "good man" rather than resisting the urge to perform gender at all.

Similar critiques have been levied at anti-violence and pro-gender equality campaigns run at the multilateral and state-level. David Duriesmith (2018) draws connections between the United Nations' HeForShe campaign, the "American campaign My Strength Is Not for Hurting, the 2013 Australian campaign reminding us that 'Real Men Don't Abuse Women,' and the international 'Man Up' campaign" (60). He argues that these initiatives rely on male spokesmen, in the hopes "that their social cachet will make them effective agents of profeminist change... However, this tactic has also caused considerable disquiet over the ways in which masculine actors engage with feminist politics" and he observes, "This approach does not leave space to substantially question masculinity itself; instead it remains focused on 'deviant' men, at whose feet blame for violence is placed" (Duriesmith, 2018, p. 60). These campaigns also rely on the idea that we need "good" men to protect women from "bad" men—perpetuating the sort of masculinist protection that we've seen connected to so many negative outcomes (Duriesmith, 2018).

We have also seen efforts from "proto-states" to portray themselves as masculine protectors. Examining the Islamic State, Katherine E. Brown (2018) notes that the group has promoted a narrative in which its

> history is one of perpetual conflict, in which the forces of evil have continuously sought to undermine and destroy the world of Islam. It anticipates violence on a global, transhistorical, and cosmic scale, which leads it to justify retaliation against perceived humiliations, injustices, and aggressions through highly organized and spectacular violence filled with symbolic messages. According to its key treatise, The Management of Savagery, the violence of civil war is to be coaxed or disciplined into a future legal order by Daesh. It argues such savagery is natural after centuries of humiliation and is innate to the warrior-monk (p. 184).

The Islamic State and its adherents are thus (in their eyes) locked in an epic battle against the contaminating forces of the West, in which violence by (largely male) warrior-monks to protect female adherents to the Islamic State's ideology is justified.

States and non-state actors that justify their military endeavors on the basis of masculinist protection may also infantilize or feminize their enemies. Consider, for example, one American official's description of North Korean dictator Kim Jong-il as a "spoiled child at dinner time" (Sjoberg, 2013, p. 240). This comment rendered the United States a paternalistic figure, imparting lessons on proper behavior—or, in this case, withholding a nuclear "toy" from an irresponsible kid who couldn't be trusted. Neither finger wagging nor economic sanctions were sufficient to prevent North Korea from developing a nuclear weapons program, however. Despite the demonstrated failure of this approach, such rhetoric remains a mainstay in the relationship between North Korea and the United States. Consider President Donald Trump's response to Kim Jung-un's threat of pressing the "nuclear button" in 2018 which he sent via tweet: "Will someone from his depleted and food starved regime please inform him that I too have a Nuclear Button, but it is a much bigger & more powerful one than his, and my Button works!" (Gambino, 2018, n.p.). The prospect of a world-ending nuclear war became a dick measuring contest on social media.

Those who have been subject to masculinist protection from an invading army have frequently spoken out against it. Consider the Iraqi women who condemned the U.S.'s war and occupation as a neocolonial endeavor. In 2003, Iraqi activists Amal Al-Khedairy and Nermin Al-Mufti came to the United States and spoke with "gender officers of the UN agencies, NGOs and several representatives from Member States" at the United Nations (Gibbings, 2011). These women "... spoke in nationalist terms, condemned the invasion by the USA and UK as imperialist and critiqued the UN for its lack of support" (Gibbings, 2011, p. 524).

Yet these narratives are not necessarily welcome in international policy circles. Indeed "...many of the participants were disappointed and embarrassed by Al-Khedairy and Al-Mufti's performance and labelled their comments as 'angry'" (Gibbings, 2011, pp. 530–531). Those who arranged the activists' talk "...were concerned about the impact on their own credibility within the UN, since the Iraqi women they had invited to speak had presented themselves in a way that did not meet the expectations of attendees" and had been surprised that they had not outlined a positive role for the US in promoting women's rights in Iraq (Gibbings, 2011, pp. 524–525). Their embarrassment reflected a widespread assumption that the United States was looked upon with appreciation as a masculine protector, rather than resented for making decisions on women's behalf without their input.

Masculine Protectors at Home

Masculine protectors have often tried to emphasize the threat to the "natural order" their enemies present. They fear-monger to justify expansions in their authority over civilians. Iris Marion Young (2003) observes that protection comes at the expense of our personal liberties:

> To the extent that citizens of a democratic state allow their leaders to adopt a stance of protectors toward them, these citizens come to occupy a subordinate status like that of women in the patriarchal household. We are to accept a more authoritarian and paternalistic state power, which gets its support partly from the unity a threat produces and our gratitude for protection (p. 2).

Take, for example, modern Türkiye. Academic Elif M. Babül (2015) observes, "designated as the quintessential victims in need of protection, guidance, and care, women and children, as domesticated rights bearers, also help consolidate an image of the Turkish state as the locus of 'masculinist protection.' The hierarchical relationship that underpins this form of protection... demands the grateful obedience of the protected" (p. 118). This form of masculinist protection silences those it purports to care for; she observes, "As victims in need of protection and care, women and children are not expected to speak for themselves in the trainings. They are, rather, spoken about, or on behalf of, which disables them from making claims and demands for themselves" (Babül, 2015, p. 125).

Or let's consider Russia, where academic Cai Wilkinson (2018) describes a narrative of masculine protection in which:

> The basic plot of this deeply gendered tale is that Mother Russia, a long-standing national personification of Russia, has been rescued from a decade of post-Soviet neglect and ignominious destitution, and is now once more being supported by the manly Russian state and his aides to fulfill her natural womanly destiny of (re)producing and caring for the nation (her children). However, a pernicious 'Unholy Queer Peril' is stalking Mother Russia, aggressively trying to tempt her with feminism, unnatural gender roles, and secular Western decadence in order to distract her from her maternal and wifely duties and break up the traditional Russian family (pp. 107–108).

In the name of protecting "Mother Russia," the Russian government under Vladimir Putin has cracked down on the independent media, human rights groups, the political opposition, religious minorities, feminists, and the queer community. In recent years, "dozens of rights groups, charities and other nongovernmental organizations have been labeled 'foreign agents' and outlawed as 'undesirable,'" helping justify the sweeping repression (Litvinova 2024, n.p.). As recently as 2024, the *Associated Press* reported, "the Supreme Court banned what the government called the LGBTQ+ 'movement' in Russia, labeling it as an extremist organization. That effectively outlawed any LGBTQ+ activism. Shortly afterward, authorities started imposing fines for displaying rainbow-colored items" (Litvinova, 2024, n.p.). Father Putin is protecting Mother Russia, defending traditional values from an "assault" from Western decadence—by ruling over Russians with an iron fist (Kratochívl and O'Sullivan, 2023).

Or let's consider the xenophobic narratives of purity and protection that have frequently accompanied tighter immigration controls. Operation Sovereign Borders (OSB) in Australia, for example, was "a military-led border security operation established by the Australian Liberal government in 2013 to deter asylum seekers and refugees from arriving by boat in mainland Australia and its territories" (The Bridge, 2019, n.p.).

The implementation of OSB involved serious human rights violations. The government intercepted and turned back boats of would-be asylum seekers as a part of the operation. The UN High Council on Refugees criticized the Australian government and accused them of breaking international law by forcibly returning asylum seekers to the countries they are fleeing. Those who reached Australian territory have been held in detention camps in deplorable conditions (Taub, 2014).

The politicians responsible for the design and implementation of Australia's immigration policy cast themselves as defenders of "real" Australians from the "threat" of asylum seekers. According to Agius (2018), OSB "entails a masculinist discourse and practice that seeks to reclaim a traditional bounded concept of the state. Militarized border security ostensibly claims to 'protect' vulnerable others but is geared toward protecting the territorial state" (p. 70). Indeed, in a speech honoring Margaret Thatcher in 2015 Former Australian Prime Minister Tony Abbott criticized European countries' immigration policies as being too soft and nurturing, stating, "Implicitly or explicitly, the imperative to love your neighbour as you love yourself is at the heart of every Western polity … but right now this wholesome instinct is leading much of Europe into catastrophic error" (Chan, 2015, n.p.) In this telling, other states are too soft-hearted and womanly to make the "tough choices" that Australia has to protect its citizens.

Masculinist protection narratives are often leveraged by abusive governments to distract from their own shortcomings. As David Duriesmith (2018) notes, countries in the global North have frequently supported multilateral measures to improve women's rights and well-being—but have generally done so in ways that "focused on other states from the global South, which are singled out as particularly problematic" (61). In these deliberations, "little attention is paid to harmful cultural practices from the global North, and those states that advocate for change in the practices of states in the global South rarely demonstrate reflectivity in their involvement.. Instead, the problem of harmful practices is always some *other* state's problem" (Duriesmith, 2018, p. 61). So rather than consider the harmful impact of the roll-back of American women's reproductive rights following the overturning of Roe v. Wade in 2022, American leaders have focused on the harms inflicted on women by "bad" governments "over there." Audre Lorde, the American author, once wrote: "I am not free while any woman is unfree, even when her shackles are very different from my own." An addendum worth considering is: "Freedom will not come by using the oppression of others to distract from repression at home."

Box 9.3 Daddy Duterte and Masculine Protection in the Philippines

During his time in office, former President of the Philippines Rodrigo Duterte put himself forward as a masculine protector. Some of his supporters "view him as a father figure" and some go so far as to refer to him as "Tatay Digong" (Daddy Digong) (Santos, 2018, n.p.). In his public statements, Duterte cultivated an image as a womanizing, swaggering tough guy. For example, Duterte once ignored the questions posed by a female reporter regarding his cabinet secretaries' performances, and instead chose to wolf-whistle at her and serenade her with a love song. Sharmila Parmanand (2020) details how

> Duterte's jokes about how he cannot resist women or his encouragement of adultery just for men position him as a traditional macho male who is unapologetic and proud of his sexual entitlement and desire for women in an era where establishment-endorsed norms of decency disallow it. However, because they are 'just jokes' they disarm his audience and reposition his critics as prudish disciplinarians, but still portray him as a transgressive hero who restores respect for the desires of ordinary men (p. 14).

But Duterte's machismo is more than a performance. It is also a part of his governing philosophy. It influences how he justifies his government's actions. Consider, for example, "His regular use of rape imagery—of the need to protect women and children from crazed drug users—in justifying his violent war on drugs" (Parmanand, 2020, p. 9) She observes, "Duterte's portrayal of women and children victims brutally raped and murdered by drug users produces a context that legitimises the killings in his drug war, often by representing the population as helpless and vulnerable, the drug users as violent criminals, and himself as a tough and benevolent protector" (Parmanand, 2020, p. 17). Or consider that "he has spoken about female victims of domestic violence and rape who came to see him when he was the mayor of Davao City and how he threatened their abusers" (Parmanand, 2020, p. 9). In those stories, Duterte casts himself as a "good man," protecting vulnerable women from "bad men." Duterte's public image relies heavily on the idea that he is a masculine protector—one that uses both his power as a man and the power of the state to "protect" vulnerable Philippinos.

Furthermore, Duterte's masculine protection relies on a clear contrast between men and women's inherent characteristics and ties those differences to the roles that they should play in the Philippines. In one statement he argued, "We [men] grew up with a mindset that is sometimes prone to violence. Women are prim and proper. With just one look of their mothers, they will melt. And you will make them cops? It's not that I don't trust them. I believe in the woman, their competence and capability, but not in all aspects of life" (Alqaseer and Pile, 2020, p. 39). This statement underscores how the masculine protection that Duterte offers relies on the submission and subordination of women.

Of course, that protection only applies to the women that Duterte deems worthy. Against his political opponents, Duterte has released a stream of sexist criticisms. For example, he threatened Senator Leila De Lima, with the possibility "that he would make Pope Francis watch a supposed sex video of Senator Leila de Lima to make him regret giving her a rosary" (Go, 2019, p. 34). He's gone so far as to encourage violence against certain women. When speaking with members of the military, he told them "If you rape three women, I'll say I did it" (Alqaseer and Pile, 2020, p. 45). Duterte also stated that the Philippine military would not "kill" female communist rebels, but would instead "just shoot your vagina" (Tanyag, 2018, n.p.). As Maria Tanyag observes, "this military command is supposedly more effective than others because without a vagina women are deemed useless" (Tanyag, 2018, n.p.). As is the case with all masculine protectors, the security they provide some women comes at a high cost.

Conclusions

The United States' military withdrawal from Afghanistan marked a low point for America's reputation in the world; after more than 20 years, more than 2 trillion dollars, and thousands American lives lost, the invasion and occupation had accomplished functionally none of its objectives (Watson Institute, 2001). It was a humiliating moment for the world's only superpower.

American embarrassment pales in comparison to the situation Afghan women found themselves in, however (Akbari and True, 2024). Both the presence of the American military and the resurgence of the Taliban once they left created new threats to Afghan women's well-being. In the rush to protect Afghan women, the United States failed to consider the ways that a full-scale counter-insurgency campaign would make their lives harder.

The War in Afghanistan is a glaring—but not unique—example of how the logic of masculinist protection drives state behavior. In this chapter, we've considered how gender hierarchy predisposes some states to go to war. We have also discussed the rise (and fall) of the Women, Peace and Security agenda and Feminist Foreign Policy, which came about in recognition of the pernicious effects of the exclusion of women from security deliberations.

Furthermore, we have also investigated how some states have taken up the mantle of masculine protectors, both at home and abroad. We considered how the rise of the WPS agenda and Feminist Foreign Policy have perversely facilitated masculinist protection. This chapter also briefly considers the devastating effects of masculinist protection on civil liberties and women's well-being the world over.

Section IV: **The Fight Ahead**

Chapter 10
Gender Hierarchy and Backlash

My social media algorithms quickly picked up that I was pregnant. And as my stomach expanded, so too did the share of my social media diet that was dedicated to well-lit, idyllic depictions of motherhood. And, as embarrassing as it is to admit: they got me. Accompanying each of "share" and "save" of parenting-related content was an unspoken, gnawing anxiety that if I didn't do all that stuff I would be failing my daughter. Even while I shared these videos, part of me understood that I would never be like those women. Domesticity has never been a strength of mine and these women looked more polished at the start of their "get ready with me!" videos than I did on my wedding day. But I wanted to be a "good mom," and I wasn't quite sure how to do that while maintaining my own identity.

Then the algorithm started serving me more extreme versions of this aspirational motherhood content. That's when I was introduced to the TradWife phenomenon—a portmanteau of "traditional" and "wife." Now it was not enough to make sure my child had healthy snacks and aesthetically pleasing lunch boxes—I was also being served content about the importance of homeschooling, the perils of hormonal birth control, the dangers of vaccines, and thinly veiled references to white nationalism.

That's where they lost me. My aspirational scrolling turned into rubbernecking and incredulity. Any content I shared with friends and family was accompanied by commentary like "you've got to be fucking kidding me." But others have been drawn to the deceptively simple message that TradWife influences peddle: that the road to happiness is a time machine back to a time when women kept the house and men made the money.

The TradWife movement is one of the newest manifestations of backlash against gender equality, compelling us to "go back" to find our way forward. Some of the more explicitly political TradWife influences and acolytes point to feminism as the reason that women have been "trapped" into the modern rat race, rather than "free" to play their "natural" role of wife and mother. Indeed, many TradWives see themselves as battling a culture that disparages pregnancy and motherhood; their weapon of choice is not screeds in the *New York Times* but rather performative displays of feminine, maternal serenity on various social media platforms. As academic Megan L. Zahay (2022) notes:

> Trad wives offer an idealized image of pregnancy that is easy because it is the ultimate expression of their natural role. Even more pointedly, it is presented as a desirable alternative to the grind and hustle culture of contemporary 'boss babe' feminism that the trad wives

https://doi.org/10.1515/9783111662886-012

reject. By presenting their experience through a pastoral aesthetic that calls up images of an idyllic and peaceful life, motherhood is forwarded as a blissful, natural alternative to the drudgery pushed on them by elite feminists (p. 176).

TradeWife influencers wax poetic about an imagined past. Many of these influences aspire to return to the 1950s, either explicitly or implicitly through their visual strategies. The past that they are referencing is a work of fiction. It conveniently overlooks that marital rape was legal, racial discrimination was commonplace and institutionalized, and women could not have credit cards in this "golden era." Their nostalgia is selective and ahistorical. As journalist Carter Sherman (2024) observes: "Tradwives portray a fundamentally conservative and individual solution to that societal failure: retreat not only into the home, but also into history. Using the iconography of an idealized past, they evoke the economic and emotional fantasy that families, and especially women, can opt out of the complexity of modern society" (n.p.).

Furthermore, these videos about homemaking and family rearing often include subtle nods to White nationalist ideology. As academic Catherine Tebaldi (2023) notes, "in conspiratorial discourses on gender and sexuality, tradwives defend the national family from gay globalists and trans tyrants through a form of subversive submission to male authority" (p. 15). The solution to our modern ills, TradWifism suggests, is a return to the past and to conservative values.

One of the most striking aspects of TradWife-ism as a political movement is that it is dominated by women and bolstered through the invisible operations of social media algorithms. That is part of what makes it so insidious and so effective. Even as I was "hate-scrolling" through this content (a term my husband and I use for deliberately looking at content that we know will only make us mad), I could understand how so many women were sucked in.

I had a relatively easy pregnancy and yet I still spent most of my time uncomfortable, covered in crumbs, and steeling myself for the next hot flash and attendant waves of sweat. It would have been nice to feel sun-kissed and blissed out; it would have been a relief to feel like I would naturally step into my role as a mother; it would have been a gift to not have to struggle through the brain fog to get my work done before my maternity leave started. TradWives offer up the promise of an easier, better life if we are just brave enough to set aside our feminism and submit to the gender hierarchy. The promise is false but can be appealing to those who find themselves struggling to get by in an economic and political system that is stacked against them, or to those who are desperately seeking direction and fulfillment.

The prominence of women within TradWife messaging makes it a particularly potent form of backlash against women's rights and gender equality. A common misconception about backlash is that it only comes from men in response to a perceived threat to their status. And while that is certainly one way in which backlash manifests, women have also championed backlash campaigns in a wide variety of contexts.

To unpack the nebulous and wide-reaching phenomenon of backlash against women's rights, this chapter is broken into two main sections. First, we consider the definition of backlash and the sources of backlash against gender equality (or even a slight lessening of the gender hierarchy). Then we consider the myriad manifestations of backlash against women's rights and inclusion, exploring rhetorical, legal, and violent responses. This section considers how backlash manifests, as well as where (meaning internationally, domestically, or inter-personally) it operates. This section also considers intersectionality and backlash politics, by examining how certain categories of people are more likely to be targeted by backlash.

Probing the dynamics of backlash is not an exercise in academic navel-gazing. It is critically important to the fight for gender equality. By considering the sources, forms, and targets of backlash, this chapter provides a broad overview of how backlash functions in modern politics.

Backlash: What is it and Where Does it Come From?

In previous chapters, we discussed how gender hierarchy—the privileging of masculinity over femininity—is a system of power that shapes how people engage with politics and influences how political power is wielded. Yet we have not yet broached the subject of what happens when that distribution of power is threatened.

Backlash is defined by academics Karen J Alter and Michael Zürn (2020) as a movement characterized by "retrograde objectives, extraordinary goals and tactics, and the threshold of entering mainstream public discourse" (p. 564). With such a broad definition, backlash can emerge in response to a range of developments. In this chapter, we are concerned with one of the most common forms of backlash—which comes in response to improvements in women's rights, representation, or status.

American journalist Susan Faludi provided the landmark study of how backlash against gender equality (referred to as just "backlash" throughout the remainder of this chapter for stylistic reasons) manifests in her 1991 book, *Backlash: the Undeclared War against American Women*. Writing with more flare and emotion than most academics who work on this subject, Faludi (1991) observed, "...the antifeminist backlash has been set off not by women's achievement of full equality but by the increased possibility that they might win it. It is a preemptive strike that stops women long before they reach the finish line" (p. 11). Backlash is not the defeated wails of the vanquished, it's the rallying cry for an army on its back foot.

Importantly, in her account of it, backlash is not the result of nefarious secret societies meeting in smoke-filled rooms and pulling the strings behind the scenes. One of Faludi's most significant contributions in *Backlash* was to show the ways that backlash sprung organically from American society in response to the modest gains women made in the 1980s (Faludi, 1991).

If only Faludi's work could be read as a time capsule of a time long-since past! Unfortunately, public opinion polling suggests that I am writing this book during an acute period of backlash. A 2022 survey reported, "62 percent of young Republican men say feminism is a net negative for society, and 46 percent of young Democratic men agree" (Grady, 2023, n.p.). Feminism is once again serving as a whipping boy for broader anxieties and frustrations with American life in pop culture and politics.

It is not just the United States, however. As we will discuss later in this chapter, around the world, conservative political movements are mobilizing around "family matters"—such as reproductive rights, women's economic freedom, and gender identity—in ways that ultimately limit women's autonomy.

Backlash is fundamentally about maintaining an unequal status quo (Skewes, Fine, and Haslam, 2018); this resistance to gender equality comes from both men and women who think they are better served by gender hierarchy than by the uncertainty of a progressive future. I assert that we can tie backlash to both men and women's fear of losing their status in the current system. To understand why men engage in backlash, we have to unpack the precarity of masculinity and consider how men shore up their masculine identity in the face of that frailty. To understand why women participate in backlash politics, we have to consider how women "bargain" with patriarchal systems (making compromises and deliberate choices to protect themselves) and why they may fear a renegotiation of these deals (Kandiyoti, 1988). The following two sections will briefly unpack these dynamics.

The Precarity of Masculinity and Backlash Politics

"To be a man is not a one day job" is a common saying among men in southeastern Nigeria (Smith, 2017). This aphorism speaks to the ways that men must repeatedly "prove" their masculinity; defending and demonstrating one's masculinity becomes a part of their daily routine, just like brushing their teeth. In southeastern Nigeria and around the world, threats to one's status as a "real man" lurk constantly in the background.

Psychologists have run a wide variety of studies to try to understand why masculinity is so fragile and to probe how men respond to threats to their masculine status. The results are disheartening. One study found that challenges to one's masculinity elicited different responses than threats to other parts of their identity; a threat to their masculinity produced "more public discomfort, anger, guilt, and shame" than threats to other aspects of their identity (Vescio et al., 2021). Another study used a series of experiments and found that when men were told that they were performing like women or worse than women on a task, they were more likely to act aggressively or try to demonstrate their dominance (Vescio et al., 2021).

Some studies have probed how different categories of men respond to challenges to their masculine status. One study found that younger men were more likely to be triggered by threats to their masculinity. The study author explained that this was not a function of youthful hormones but rather because young men's masculinity is so dependent on how they are perceived by others. The study's lead author explained in an interview, "the more social pressure a man feels to be masculine, the more aggressive he may be" (Jones, 2021, n.p.). Young men's volatility and displays of masculinity reflect that they have something to prove.

Men's individual sense of masculinity thus has implications for how they engage in public life and politics. In some situations, men's frustrations with threats to their masculinity have resulted in men being frustrated with the system in general. One academic study of gender equality in Rwanda suggested that the country's efforts to increase women's representation in office had incentivized men to "give up" on politics because they didn't think it was "worth it to try" (Burnet, 2011, p. 323). It's not an unreasonable leap to tie men's trepidation about their masculinity to the difficulty women face in being elected to office or to the specific threats they face as female candidates—something that we will revisit later in this chapter.

Across the board, these studies find that men frequently respond with aggression and anti-social behavior when they think that their masculinity is at risk. The stability of that finding speaks to a simple fact: life under gender hierarchy provides rewards for being a man. When men feel as if their access to those benefits is threatened, they act out in stereotypically masculine ways to reclaim their position in the hierarchy. If men's reactions can be understood as an attempt to maintain their high-status position under hierarchy, how can we understand women's participation in backlash?

"Good Girls" and Backlash

Women that benefit from the current system in some ways often act to preserve it —which can lead them to participate in or support backlash against gender equality. As previous chapters underscored, gender hierarchy is just one of many systems of ranking that shape our lives. Women's race, class, ethnicity, sexual orientation, and a range of other identity characteristics intersect with the gender hierarchy to determine the opportunities and obstacles they face. Consider, for example, that 53% of White women voted for Donald Trump in the 2024 presidential elections (Sanders, 2024). These women thought that their interests—derived from their many overlapping and intersecting identities—were better served by voting for a man convicted of sexual assault than a woman of color.

Deniz Kandiyoti's notion of "bargaining with the patriarchy" is a helpful framework for understanding both how women navigate life under gender hierarchy and why they may be resistant to egalitarian reforms (Kandiyoti, 1988). "Bargaining with the patriarchy" refers to the compromises that women make in order to improve their status and security under gender hierarchy. Conforming to the expectations of what a "good woman" acts like is a way for women to find a sense of security and even prestige within an oppressive system. The specifics of the bargains that women make depend upon the specific construct of the gender hierarchy in their society, as well as how other aspects of their identity constrain or open up their opportunities to negotiate.

Having made bargains with the patriarchal system, women may resist changes that could threaten the fragile position they have secured for themselves. Kandiyoti observes, "broken bargains seem to instigate a search for culprits, a hankering for the certainties of a more traditional order, or a more diffuse feeling that change might have gone either too far or badly wrong" (Kandiyoti, 1988, p. 284). As such, she notes that conservatism is a logical response to life under a patriarchal system. She notes that women can intensify their commitment to their bargain as a way of resisting change. She asserts that when certain patriarchal orders come under threat, "many women may continue to use all the pressure they can muster to make men live up to their obligations and will not, except under the most extreme pressure, compromise the basis for their claims by stepping out of line and losing their respectability" (Kandiyoti, 1988, pp. 282–283).

A bargain with the patriarchy is also a bet that the system will last. And when it becomes clear that it is a losing gamble, women face a choice: either double down on their strategy in a game that is stacked against them or walk away from the table. Women that participate in backlash politics are all-in on the system, even if they'll never walk away as the night's big winner.

In summary, both men and women have incentives to uphold the gendered status quo. Thus, both men and women can be found in support of backlash politics. The following section considers where backlash manifests and how, paying attention to distinct processes at the international, national, and individual levels.

How and Where Backlash Manifests

The following sections consider backlash internationally, nationally, and interpersonally; they describe how that backlash manifests, including through political movements and through physical violence. This chapter cannot consider all of the forms that backlash takes—rather, this chapter provides you, the reader, with the ability to identify backlash when you see it "in the wild."

The International Community and Backlash

Backlash in international politics can produce strange bedfellows. There are few issues globally that one might expect the Vatican, evangelical Protestant Christians, the Organization of Islamic Cooperation (OIC), and conservative American think tanks like the Heritage Foundation to all find themselves on common ground (UN Women, 2020). Yet it is precisely this sort of alliance that has been at the forefront of backlash against gender egalitarianism in the international arena.

According to a group of academics working on this issue, "anti-gender equality actors have organized around a wider range of sexuality and gender policy issues, and with particular vehemence on abortion and lesbian, gay, bisexual, transgender, intersex, and queer (LGBTIQ) rights, with the aim of questioning the relevance of gender equality as a central public policy objective" (Zaremberg, Tabbush, and Friedman, 2021, p. 528). Indeed, Shruti Rana (2020) argues that despite their rhetorical disdain for "cosmopolitan" international organizations like the United Nations, right-wing populists of a variety of stripes "are intensifying their engagement with the transnational forum focused on gender equality" (p. 160).

This coalition has cooperated to raise concerns about how gender egalitarian trends, policies, and even mere aspirations to those ends constitute a threat to morality and the family. This alliance has thwarted efforts to advance gender equality at the United Nations and through other multilateral forums. Words and terminology have become the locus of much of the international backlash. According to one study, the language used in UN documents is now "a battleground of feminist and conservative concepts, with feminists advancing theirs under the banner of 'gender rights' and conservatives opting for 'the natural family'" (Cupać and Ebetürk, 2021, p. 1183). Another study notes, "a key strategy has been to co-opt and dilute UN and human rights language, in order to derail the collective progress made since the 1990s" (Khan, Tant, and Harper, 2023, p. 5).

The wrangling over words and agendas mean that feminist movements are in a defensive crouch, rather than pushing forward an affirmative agenda. Writing in 2023, a group of academics noted, "Instead of building on their achievements, feminist movements are firefighting to contend with backlash at home and a dismantling of gender justice consensus internationally" (Khan, Tant, and Harper, 2023, p. 4). International backlash means that there is now a roiling debate on the world stage about whether gender equality is a universally desirable goal.

The current international backlash has also manifested through lobbying to reimpose the gender binary and deny the queer community their basic human rights (Edström, Greig, and Skinner, 2024). Connections between powerful evangelical Christian churches in the United States and religious communities in sub-Saharan Africa and Eastern Europe have been linked to a tidal wave of homophobic sentiment and even laws criminalizing homosexuality (Sanderson, 2023; Human Rights Campaign, 2023). As Nigerian journalist Caleb Okereke (2023) asserts:

> Proponents of ex-gay and anti-gay philosophies depend on the permanence of gay people for their message to be relevant. They require an enemy for their fight to be valid, and they go to great lengths to construct this enemy as a well-funded and all-powerful foreign movement while falsely presenting the local anti-gay movement as a grassroots underdog, despite its heavy reliance on U.S. evangelicals for publicity (n.p.).

The trans and non-binary communities have been subject to particularly fervent backlash (Edström, Greig, and Skinner, 2024). Outside of the 2019 Convention on the Status of women, the Vatican and conservative NGOs were responsible for holding events titled "Biology Is Not Bigotry" and "Protecting Femininity and Human Dignity in Women's Empowerment," both of which reflect concern about the growing norm of gender as a spectrum rather than a fixed binary (Goetz, 2020, p. 169). Such backlash reflects resistance to a movement that lays bare the ways in which gender is a performance and the ways in which gendered expectations constrain us all.

Backlash at the National Level

Backlash has also frequently manifested in domestic politics, through both government programs and social movements. In China, for example, the government "has silenced feminists as it tightens social control, imposing strict censorship policies, including by banning feminist terms and content they see as 'harmful speech' or 'inciting conflict between the genders,' according to the advocacy group Human Rights Watch" (Bergsten and Lee, 2023, n.p.). Feminism is a convenient scapegoat for governments seeking to distract from the ways that they are responsible for their citizens' frustrations.

As we previously touched upon in Chapter Two, domestic backlash has recently focused on concerns about women delaying marriage and, relatedly, low or falling birthrates. The President of Tanzania, John Magufuli, told Tanzanian women in 2019 to "set your ovaries free" in order to help the country build a bigger, stronger economy (Al Jazeera, 2019). Just the year before, the government banned the broadcast of family planning advertisements through a US-funded project and characterized those who were in support of managing population growth as "too lazy to take care of their children" (Aljazeera, 2019, n.p.). The government was clearly promoting larger families—but doing so in a way that demeaned those who decided to have a small family (or no family at all), rather than extending support to those who chose to have a large biological family.

Similar rhetoric has emerged in South Korea, which has the lowest fertility rate in the world. In 2024, President Yoon Suk Yeol proposed the creation of a "Ministry of Low Birth Rate Counter-planning." He explained, "We will mobilize all of the nation's capabilities to overcome the low birth rate, which can be considered a national emergency" (Yeung, Stambaugh, and Seo, 2024, n.p.). That same year, "a government think tank recommended that girls start school earlier than boys, so that classmates would be more attracted to each other by the time they were ready to marry" (Mackenzie, 2024, n.p). There is something deeply dystopian about government officials thinking about public education as a matchmaking service.

These policy proposals have been accompanied by finger-pointing and finger-wagging at South Korean women. In 2024, a Seoul City councilor asserted that his country had "begun to change into a female-dominant society" because of women's entrance into the workforce. He blames women working for low marriage rates and even the suicide rate among men (Mackenzie, 2024). The month before, another Seoul city official "published a series of articles on the authority's website encouraging young women to take up gymnastics and practise pelvic floor exercises in order to raise the birth rate" (Mackenzie, 2024, n.p.). Such accusations and deeply misguided suggestions add fuel to the fire of the country's anti-feminist movement, which has surged in recent years. A reporter for the *BBC* notes that this movement is "led by disillusioned young men, who argue they have been disadvantaged by attempts to improve women's lives" (Mackenzie, 2024, n.p.).

Box 10.1: Backlash and fertility in Hungary.

Though the Tanzanian and South Korean governments' approach to family and fertility are shocking, they pale in comparison to the fertility-focused backlash politics in Hungary under Prime Minister Viktor Orbán. As previously discussed, Orbán's justifications for his pro-natal policies include not-so-subtle nods to the "great replacement theory," a racist ideology "that posits white people are being replaced by immigrants, Muslims, and other people of color in their so-called 'home' countries" (Global Project Against Hate and Extremism, 2024, n.p.).

Orbán's Hungary has adopted a range of policies to encourage Hungarian women to have more children. According to Eva Fodor, a Hungarian academic, "Since the mid-2010s, the Hungarian government has introduced a long line of policies offering grants and loans to parents and would-be parents. Those who have, or pledge to have, children, are eligible for a baby grant of 10 million forints (roughly five years' minimum wage). Families who choose to have three or more children can access especially generous tax breaks and highly subsidised mortgages" (Fodor, 2024, n.p). She also observes that there are other government incentives, which range from "discounts on basic administrative services, to entrance fees to entertainment venues, to subsidised loans for buying SUVs and renovating apartments" (Fodor, 2024, n.p.).

Yet the country is hardly a parenting paradise. The eligibility criteria for these benefits leave many parents behind; Fodor notes, "people living in non-traditional families, those raising children alone, those who are older parents or who are simply not in well-paid jobs all find themselves excluded from at least parts of the childcare benefit system" (Fodor, 2024, n.p.). Furthermore, these policies have infringed on women's reproductive rights. Anyone seeking an abortion must listen to the fetal heartbeat before termination (Cursino, 2022). They are also required to participate in counseling sessions with doctors who may try to dissuade them from going through with the procedure (Population Matters, 2024). All the while, these policies have also come alongside a sharp closing of political space in Hungary, where Orbán proudly touts a model of "illiberal democracy" (Suleiman, 2021, n.p.).

Some female politicians have contributed to the moral panic about falling fertility rates. For example Katalin Novák, a Hungarian politician and former president, has been a vocal proponent of pro-natalist policies (Strzyżyńska and Kumar, 2023). She is one of the politicians that has "worked to put Hungary on the map of anti-LGBTQ+ and women's rights efforts, and to establish relations with the global network of anti-sexual and reproductive health and rights (SRHR) actors" (Balint, 2021, n.p.).

Hungary is not an anomaly. According to Population Matters, an NGO looking at population and environmental issues, "almost 30 percent of countries globally now have pronatalist policies—up from 10 percent in the 1970s" (Population Matters, 2021, n.p.). These efforts have largely been ineffective. This raises the scary possibility that states will rely on sticks more than carrots as they try to build their population numbers.

In other contexts, domestic backlash has couched itself in the language of anti-colonialism or anti-Westernism. Political analyst Daniel Volman (2024) notes that:

> African political leaders and religious zealots (both Christian and Muslim) have used homophobia as a tool for political and religious power for many years. They say that same-sex relations and gay rights are imports from the west. They have used homophobia to portray

themselves as nationalists and defenders of African and religious values. They have used homophobia to frighten and divide people to mobilize popular support and votes" (n.p.).

The Kenyan President Ruto, for example, commented, "constitution is very clear, that marriage is between a man and a wife, and that Kenyans should pray for our judges so that they can make decisions not to please the Western world" (Edstrom et al., 2024).

Mona Eltahawy, an Egyptian-American journalist, notes, "In my part of the world, we're often told feminism is a Western import, it's not part of our culture or religion," but that this is a misinterpretation of what women are asking for. She continues

all of these women are saying, we're tired of having to choose between racism and sexism,' and having to fight Islamophobia and xenophobia in parts of the world where Muslims live as minorities, having to fight against that and having to fight against misogyny. More and more women are saying, 'It is our right and it is our role to criticize the misogyny from within and without, and also fight those who are attacking Islam (Eltahawy, 2016, n.p.).

Claiming that those working towards a more egalitarian world are Western plants is a means of making them seem foreign and illegitimate, and positions the practitioners of backlash as the defenders of the "natural order."

Domestic backlash has also often manifested through physical violence, punishing women who challenge the gender hierarchy or who threaten men's masculinity. Both elite women who publicly challenge the gendered status quo and everyday women who quietly engage in non-normative behavior can face violence for their actions. Such violence is startlingly common. The frequency of violence against women involved in politics and government has spawned a new subfield of academic studies and advocacy addressing "violence against women in politics" or VAWIP. The International Parliamentary Union (IPU) found in a cross-national survey of elected officials that nearly every woman had experienced psychological violence as a part of their time in office. One in four were targeted with physical violence and one in five experienced a form of sexual violence (Inter-Parliamentary Union, 2016). Country-level studies confirm that women in politics face profound threats to their safety and well-being. A study done by the National Democratic Institute found that nearly all of the women running for office in Afghanistan in 2010 that they spoke to had received threats via phone (Krook and Restrepo Sanín, 2020). In Malawi, more than half of the women running for office in 2009 quit before votes were cast because of threats they faced as candidates (Semu-Banda, 2008).

Box 10.2: Backlash and female politicians: the case of Marielle Franco.

Marielle Franco was a rising star and formidable force in Brazilian politics. As the Councillor of Rio de Janeiro, Franco was an unflinching advocate for women, *favela* residents, and the queer community. She had also frequently and loudly condemned the Brazilian police's penchant for extrajudicial killings and brutal violence. Her activism grew out of her experiences—she had grown up in a *favela*, given birth at just 19 years of age, had experienced the devastating impacts of police violence, and was engaged to a woman. She was, in so many ways, the type of politician that the international community had pinned its hopes on as it promoted women's inclusion in politics through gender quotas and targeted outreach efforts.

On March 14th, 2018, Franco took part in an event about how young black women were working for political change (Swift, 2018). Just a few hours after that event, a car sidled up to Franco's; two former police officers squeezed off nine shots, four of which hit Franco and cut her life short. She was just 38 years old. Years of investigations would suggest that Franco's assassination was far from a random act of violence. Her death was a targeted hit that was ordered and covered up by some of the city's political elites, who bristled against her demands for better governance (NBC News, 2024).

The nascent research in this field finds that some categories of women in politics are more vulnerable to violent backlash. Again, we cannot understand gender hierarchy without intersectional analysis. Some female politicians, like Marielle Franco (see Box 10.2), are more vulnerable to backlash because they challenge multiple systems of oppression. A study of Swedish politics found some evidence that female politicians "are penalised more than men for substantively representing minorities, suggesting that challenging hegemonic power structures has higher costs for women than men" (Håkansson, 2021, p. 517). Furthermore, an Amnesty International study examining online violence against British parliamentarians found not only that female politicians were subject to more "abusive tweets" than men but also that minority women were especially frequently targeted (Amnesty International, 2018).

As Knock and Sanín (2020) note, there are clear connections between backlash and the violence that so many women face when active in politics, even though they are distinct phenomena. She writes that:

> [v]iolence against women in politics is used to maintain the status quo of politics, while backlash actors are concerned with maintaining a particular social order centered on the heterosexual family as the basis of society. While women's inclusion in politics is an expression of that changing social order, women politicians are attacked regardless of their ideology, policy position, or political party—by members of the opposition but also by members of their own party (p. 303).

Not every instance of violence against a female politician or representative is a function of backlash, though there is evidence that there is a particularly large overlap in that particular Venn diagram.

Backlash at the Individual Level

In some instances, backlash manifests as domestic, interpersonal, or intimate partner violence. There is evidence from a range of countries that women are likelier to experience intimate partner violence (IPV) when they get a job outside of their home. For example, a study done among women living in Indian cities found that married women that worked for pay were statistically significantly likelier to experience intimate partner violence than married women who did not earn a wage (Dhanaraj and Mahambare, 2021). A study from Sweden, a country frequently lauded for its gender egalitarianism, came to similar conclusions: women that worked outside of the home can trigger violent male backlash (Ericsson, 2019). Women's entry into the workforce does not need to be a grand declaration of feminist independence to trigger violent or coercive responses from those they share their homes and lives with.

Women also confront violence directed against them as a result of backlash seeping into the zeitgeist. This chapter opened with a brief discussion of the Trad-Wife phenomenon and the impetus it puts on women to conform to patriarchal ideals. While this is one of the most aesthetically pleasing forms of backlash in popular culture, it is just one of many.

A study I conducted with Marie Berry and Roudabeh Kishi found that as more women joined Kenya's parliament, so too did the number of women subject to political violence. This study suggests that as women become more visibly involved in politics, women in the public sphere in general become more vulnerable to violent backlash—even when they were not candidates for political office or engaged in clearly political behavior. Such a sentiment has been echoed by women living in countries where women have taken on visible political roles. In Uganda, where roughly one third of parliamentary seats are held by women as of the time of writing (Inter-Parliamentary Union, n.d.), one woman told a researcher "to men there will be violence against women by men because men will not allow women to command them as they now do" (Wyrod, 208, p. 812).

Men too, face intense pressure to conform to gender norms and backlash if they fail in that endeavor. The demands for "women to act like women" (interpreted in the most gender-essentialist way) means that men are now under pressure to perform a caricature of masculinity. Just as TradWife content has flooded my algorithms, young men have been barraged with a slew of aggressive and extreme performances of gender.

Consider, for example, the crazed efforts that some pundits and internet personalities have undertaken in an effort to "reclaim" their "masculinity." In 2022, Tucker Carlson, the bow-tie wearing personality on the conservative Fox News, encouraged his viewers to tan their testicles, ostensibly to counter low testosterone levels (Schwartz, 2022). Qualified healthcare professionals rushed to clarify that this practice could actually be harmful for men's ability to have children (Schwartz, 2022). These hare-brained schemes designed to improve men's virility actually threatened the health of their sperm—in short, it was both stupid and counterproductive. Men have also put their health on the line in the pursuit of masculinity through the "carnivore diet." The diet, popularized by Canadian psychologist and manosphere icon Jordan Peterson, advises adherents to eat primarily meat and animal products. By eschewing things like fruits and vegetables, however, dieters miss out on critical vitamins, minerals, and fiber (Baylor Scott and White Health, 2024).

In the social media era, the algorithm feeds young men and young women extreme performances of traditional gender norms. It would be foolhardy to ignore how these messages constitute a profound part of modern backlash politics.

Conclusions

In the years since I gave birth, the onslaught of content and opinions and pressure to be a good mom (whatever that means) has only gotten more intense. I've become more comfortable with the prospect of adding "mother" to the list of hats that I wear but it remains a work in progress. Sometimes the pressure to be a good mom is a good thing—good moms vaccinate their kids, which provides us all with protection against easily preventable diseases. But in other cases, the pressure to be a good mom is a thinly disguised form of backlash, which serves to tie women up in time-consuming and emotionally-draining domestic tasks and care work.

In this chapter, we unpacked what happens when the gender hierarchy is challenged. We have considered the dynamics of "backlash" against gender egalitarian reforms. This chapter dispels some of the misconceptions about who is responsible for backlash by discussing why both women and men might seek to preserve gender hierarchy.

What can we take from this chapter? Firstly, we need to be cognizant of the myriad sources of backlash. It is not as straightforward as "women support gender equality and men oppose it." In many cases, men have been staunch allies in the fight for gender equality, while women have vociferously upheld discriminatory systems.

Secondly, we need to consider the many forms that backlash can take. In this chapter, we have unpacked how backlash has manifested in rhetoric, policies, and physical violence at the interpersonal, national, and international levels. There is no political venue that is somehow inoculated against the possibility of backlash.

Understanding the dynamics of backlash is not to say that we should abandon the fight for gender equality. Operating under the misguided belief that gender equality will be nearly-universally understood as a positive development puts activists at risk and fundamentally misunderstands how gender-egalitarian reforms will be received. Anticipating backlash—from a variety of sources, in a range of forms—is critical for designing more effective and accessible campaigns to challenge gender hierarchy. The next chapter considers how we can push for a more egalitarian world—a fight in which backlash is almost guaranteed.

Chapter 11
Conclusions and the Way Forward

"Don't you ever want to write about something happy?" My dad has been asking me this, mostly as a joke, for roughly a decade. He makes a good point: I do mostly write about stuff that depresses or infuriates me. This book has been no exception.

Academics like myself often try to present ourselves and our work as objective and removed; I find it hard to do so when thinking and writing about patriarchy. It is hard to think through all of the harm that patriarchy has caused; I'm guilt-ridden when I think about the ways I have benefitted from these systems; I'm embarrassed when I think about the ways that I contorted myself to fit into the system's ideals; I'm frustrated when I think about how much work there is to be done to notch even marginal and temporary gains against patriarchy.

It is hard for me to even think about writing about 'the way forward' because I feel guilty that I've not been an active, progressive, or good enough feminist to weigh in on the matter. There is, sometimes, an idea that unless you are a perfect feminist, you need to keep quiet. But none of us will be perfect feminists because that simply doesn't exist. We are all making patriarchal bargains, pushing the system to change in the ways that we can, when we can. That doesn't make us bad feminists, it makes us humans living in a deeply entrenched, unjust system.

Each section of this book has explored how patriarchy manifests in our personal lives, our national governments, and in the international system. It can feel overwhelming to think about all of the places that gender hierarchy reigns. Each chapter in this book explores a facet of how gender hierarchy manifests in politics, economics, and security matters. Not a single one of them is an especially happy story. This book illustrates that gender hierarchy both motivates how people act and conditions the effects of those decisions. It is both the cause and the effect—and wrapping our minds around this can be dizzying, exhausting, infuriating, and depressing.

This book does not purport to provide a holistic account of all of the ways that gender hierarchy operates. Rather, I hope that it provides readers with the tools they need to recognize gender hierarchy at play in the world around them and in their personal lives.

One of these tools is the ability to see how gender hierarchy is a driver of global affairs. Throughout this book, we've unpacked how the prioritization of men and masculinity over women and femininity drives decision-making. We've seen how the different roles ascribed to men and women by patriarchy results in men and women having different political priorities—and different opportunities to express those preferences. We've seen how families respond to the incen-

https://doi.org/10.1515/9783111662886-013

tives created by a patriarchal world by investing more time, energy, and resources in their sons, relative to their daughters. And we've seen how ideas about men as protectors of the vulnerable can drive individuals and whole nations to go to war. Having read this book, you should now feel equipped to interrogate how patriarchal norms condition decision-making in politics, economics, and security matters in settings ranging from the kitchen table to the United Nations Security Council.

The other tool is the ability to see how gender hierarchy conditions the effects of ostensibly gender-neutral political, economic, and security decisions. In this book, we've looked at how things like pandemics, tax structures, international trade agreements, and even the outbreak of war affect men and women differently because of the different positions that they're assigned in society under patriarchy. This book has revealed that there is no such thing as a gender-neutral intervention when patriarchy is woven so deeply into the fabric of our society.

Furthermore, this book has detailed how challenges to the gender order often provoke sharp backlash. This backlash can manifest in response to challenges to men's privileged position in politics, economics, and security-related matters. It shapes dynamics at the international, national, and individual level. Backlash is all around us, working to counter any threat to the prevailing order. Recognizing this means that gendered analysis cannot be regarded as some fringe demand but is fundamental to good governance. So what can we do with this set of tools? What can we do with all of this new insight and motivation?

Way Forward:

Eroding Gender Hierarchy

Frustratingly, there is no straightforward path to ending gender hierarchy. There is no thermal exhaust port in the patriarchy's Death Star—no one fatal design flaw that we can exploit quickly and watch crumble around us. If it were that easy, patriarchy would be a thing of the past. Instead, the fight against the gender hierarchy is going on at all fronts, all the time, which means that there are limitless opportunities to undermine the patriarchal order.

In the face of all of the incentives to keep our heads down and go with the flow, how can we encourage people to challenge gender hierarchy in their everyday lives, demand that governments adopt gender-egalitarian policies, and push the international system towards a more just order? The following sections detail a few things that we can do in our personal lives, in our national politics, and in the international system to press for a more egalitarian future. This is not a holistic list but a starting point for leading an internationally-minded, feminist life.

In Our Personal Lives, We Can:

Adopt a "Feminist Curiosity" in All Aspects of our Lives

A curious feminist (Enloe, 2004) finds all aspects of women's lives worth investigating and valuing; it's a person that turns their attention to things that may be considered unserious in order to better understand how patriarchy manifests and maintains itself. A curious feminist is interested in how gender hierarchy shapes so many different aspects of our lives—and how that hierarchy intersects with so many other forms of power and domination. This book has, hopefully, kickstarted your feminist curiosity and given you the tools to identify patriarchy in practice.

Recognize that the Personal is Political

As a part of cultivating our "feminist curiosity" (Enloe, 2004), we need to take "personal" matters seriously. This means taking a critical (but loving) eye to our home lives. When we acknowledge how the personal is political, we can start making changes in our relationships and homes that can undermine patriarchal order. We can try to take an objective look at how we divide up responsibilities in our home through things like chore audits. We can question whether the men and women in our homes are shouldering an equal burden and if the tasks they are responsible for reflect their interests and capabilities, or if we have defaulted to a patriarchal norm. This can be a difficult process; it requires accepting that the ones that we love—and who love us—might be treating us unfairly because structural conditions have made it so easy to do so.

Furthermore, we can critically interrogate why the personal, private spheres have been depoliticized and who that serves. Suggesting that our home lives are not political ignores how often governments intervene into our homes and families. By recognizing the political aspects of private matters, we can demand more egalitarian government policies. Additionally, we can push back against the denigration of femininity and celebrate healthy, egalitarian expressions of masculinity in our homes and communities.

Celebrate Marginal Gains

It can be daunting to think about all that needs to be done. It can also be appealing to think about "burning the whole system down." Revolutionary rhetoric is mobilizing and inspiring, but we need to be cognizant of how upheaval can leave marginal populations even more vulnerable to exploitation. Recall how in Chapter 4, we explored how patriarchy entrenched itself through marginal economic benefits in the home. We can undermine the system through incremental, marginal change in our homes and communities, then eventually in our countries and around the world.

Develop Diverse, Joyful Communities of Support

Breaking down the patriarchal order cannot be a solitary endeavor. It will rely on diverse communities coming together, recognizing the harms that patriarchy has visited upon us all, and imagining a more egalitarian future where we pursue happiness without gendered or sexed restraints. Within these groups, we must use whatever privilege we have to push where we can and protect who we can. Some research suggests that women's groups can undermine patriarchal norms in the home and spur women's political participation (Prillaman, 2023). Carving out time and space for women to develop relationships outside of their homes and families helps undermine patriarchal order. Friendship and other communities of care can be a radical force for change.

As a part of building these communities, we need to extend one another some grace. Purity tests about practicing "the right feminism" can backfire and make people hesitant to advocate for gender egalitarian changes. Cultivating communities of support means accepting that our communities will be imperfect, people will make mistakes, disagreements will arise, and that sometimes the messaging will be off. In the fight for gender equality, we will all make missteps. We need to be able to welcome each other back with open arms.

Be Ready for Backlash:

As Chapter 10 discussed, gender-egalitarian gains are often met with tremendous pushback. In that chapter, we discussed the various forms and venues in which that backlash manifests. If we can anticipate resistance to gender-egalitarian reforms, we can better prepare our activists and better design our campaigns. Anticipating backlash is not defeatist; it's realistic and it can help us keep each other safe.

In National Politics, We Can:

Rethink "Essential" Functions of the Government

Governments should serve the people. In democratic systems, voters can tell governments what they want them to do. That means that we can tell our representatives that we want economic, political, and social policies that support a more egalitarian future. As former American President Joe Biden once said: "Show me your budget, and I'll tell you what you value." Working towards a more egalitarian future requires adjusting our national budgets to reflect a focus on human security, community well-being, and gender equality.

We can demand gender-sensitive analysis in all areas of government. Gender-sensitive budgeting and gendered analysis do not need to be radical propositions. Rather, we can present them as a means of improving democracy. By showing the relative impact of policies on men and women, we are providing voters with more information about the effects of proposed reforms. Mainstreaming such analysis can also help us move away from the idea of men as the "default" and women as the "other" when it comes to policy analysis.

As a part of this new policy agenda, we must demand policy change to support dignified working conditions for men and women. As Chapter 5 detailed, women's ability to support themselves outside of the home has been an important determinant of women's well-being. Though women's formal labor force participation is an imperfect metric for considering their economic independence, ensuring that women can participate freely in the economy and that all workers enjoy protection from discrimination and a living wage is a critical step towards a more egalitarian future. Furthermore, we must demand that governments provide support to working families that empowers them to make decisions about what is best for them.

Demand Legal Protections for Equal Rights for Men and Women

While laws can only go so far, they can also represent important milestones that activists can use to push for changes in cultural norms and every day practices. Passing laws guaranteeing legal equality between men and women provides activists and advocates with a reference point and legal recourse for addressing harm and discrimination.

Furthermore, we must demand the earnest implementation of these laws. Alongside these gendered protections, we must push for other policies to eradicate discrimination along a range of identity characteristics. Feminist liberation means a more egalitarian future for everyone, not resting on our laurels when we notch gains that benefit some narrow subset of women.

Resist Nostalgic Narratives and Hyper-Gendered Performances

Arguments in favor of the gender hierarchy often rely on false promises that a return to the "natural order" (interpreted to mean men's domination of women) is the key to political stability and prosperity. In our personal lives and in our national politics, we need to resist the false promises of nostalgic political appeals. We need to recognize and call out that these are hollow claims, based on fundamental misunderstandings of the past and the nature of power.

Closely related to nostalgic appeals are hyperbolic performances of gender. As curious feminists, we must be critical consumers of the public images presented by politicians and how they intersect with gendered expectations. We need to recognize how politicians perform gender so that we can resist appeals promising the return of a "masculine protector" by male politicians and be wary of the "tough as nails" performances of female politicians.

Furthermore, we must consider how gendered expectations shape government officials' decision making in office, as discussed in Chapter 3. Taking a critical eye to these processes can help us resist the possibility of being drawn into wars of choice driven by concerns about being sufficiently "tough." It can also help us detangle descriptive representation of women from the substantive representation of women's interests.

Accept that Government Policies will Lag behind Activists' Demands

Changing how a government operates is akin to changing the trajectory of an ocean-liner. Working with government bureaucrats (or working within a government bureaucracy) can be painstakingly slow and frustrating. Bureaucrats are famously stuck in their ways and may not greet gender-egalitarian reforms and new policy initiatives enthusiastically.

That doesn't mean that we should give up on engaging with policymakers or working within government agencies, but it means that we have to be both patient and strategic. Getting "buy-in" from bureaucrats often requires showing them how this new gender egalitarian policy will make them better at their jobs or will make their jobs easier. There are some risks to instrumentalizing gender equality, but it can be a helpful tool for winning over skeptical audiences.

Continued engagement with government bureaucrats and institutions doesn't just benefit the folks on the government side of the equation. Robust relationships and frequent consultations between activists, academics, and bureaucrats can help troubleshoot when policies are going awry or when there are unintended consequences of their implementation.

Furthermore, if we can anticipate that government actors and institutions are going to be slow to change and that they may be more conservative than activists or academics, we can plan accordingly. Those of us working outside of the government also need to recognize that the process of turning political aspirations into actionable government policy is one that often flattens and thins out the original idea. That can happen even when the government officials and agencies have the best intentions at heart.

A friend of mine who worked promoting the Women, Peace and Security agenda within the United States' Department of Defense once told a classroom full of my students that government officials needed activists and academics to push the ball forward, understanding that the government would always be years behind. It's not that gender equality advocates are at loggerheads with government officials, they are simply at different stages.

We Can Also Push for Change in the International System:

Resist Racist and Sexist Narratives Justifying Wars of Choice

Members of the international community have frequently tried to portray militarism as white, Western nations being the saviors of black and brown women globally. These narratives and justifications preserve gendered and raced hierarchies. These narratives of masculine protection come at the expense of civilians' well-being and the prospect of freedom around the world. Related to this, we can press for national security policies and military campaigns that center human security and well-being. This will require troubling definitions of "civilians" that rest on unfounded gendered assumptions. It will require us to consider the possibility of an innocent "military-aged male." It will also require recognizing the ways that women have been complicit or active participants in armed groups' activities.

An important part of resisting these narratives comes from developing robust international connections among like-minded groups of people. Substantive relationships with those that policymakers would purport to "save" are critical for understanding the significance of any potential military operations.

Press for More Accountability in International Systems

Efforts to promote international cooperation to promote global security and prosperity may have altruistic motivations (or at least rhetoric) but in practice, they have frequently served to reify power differentials. A more just international order—in which the autonomy of nations and respect for human rights is promoted—is possible. Key to this is ensuring that bad actors can be held accountable for violations of human rights—regardless of their position in the international system. We can work towards holding elite actors—in politics, economic, and security—accountable for the harms that they have caused.

Cultivate International Networks of Support and Cooperation

Just as it is important to develop networks of support and cooperation locally to us, international solidarity is an important part of undermining patriarchal systems. Previous academic research has shone a light on how cooperation between activists in the Global North and Global South furthered women's rights around the globe (Keck and Sikkink, 2014). Patriarchy is a global system, with different manifestations in different contexts. By developing networks of like-minded feminists from around the world, we can learn what tactics work to resist different manifestations.

Being a Feminist in Public

Of course, all of those demands and reforms are easier said than done. And there are a lot of incentives to shut up and go with the flow. Being a feminist in public (at least in the United States) means dealing with invitations to "lighten up" or "take a joke." The "jokes" that we are supposed to laugh at are often designed to silence women or embarrass them out of taking a stand against their own oppression or the oppression of others. Think about the frequency with which men on the internet reply to women's posts with something along the lines of "make me a sandwich" (Knowyourmeme.com, n.d.). The line is unoriginal (with roots in a skit from the 1995 season of *Saturday Night Live*), sexist, and trite, yet it remains popular because it is a culturally accepted shorthand for "shut up" and because any response to it can be waved away with "take a joke."

The accusation that feminists are joyless and humorless harpies is long-standing; it is up there with the idea that feminists are ugly hags that can't get a man in the hall of fame of anti-feminist tropes. Feminist writers and activists have recently taken on this trope of the "humorless" feminist. Sara Ahmed (2017), for example, writes in defense of the "feminist killjoy" and explains why she is so reviled:

> When you expose a problem you pose a problem. It might then be assumed that the problem would go away if you would just stop talking about it or if you went away. The charge of sensationalism falls rather quickly onto feminist shoulders: when she talks about sexism and racism, her story is heard as sensationalist, as if she is exaggerating for effect. The feminist killjoy begins as a sensationalist figure. It is as if the point of making her point is to cause trouble, to get in the way of the happiness of others, because of her own unhappiness (p. 37).

Similarly, Roxanne Gay (2019) writes: "It's hard not to feel humorless, as a woman and a feminist, to recognize misogyny in so many forms, some great and some small, and know you're not imagining things. It's hard to be told to lighten up because if you lighten up any more, you're going to float the fuck away" (p. 189). Being humorless or a killjoy are not accusations that we can argue our way out of, because there is nothing funny about arguing that you're funny and can take a joke.

What's worked for me to maintain my sanity as a public and imperfect feminist (which is not to say that this will work for everyone) is to recognize the power of laughter. As Margaret Atwood once (supposedly) observed, "Men are afraid that women will laugh at them. Women are afraid that men will kill them."[1] If someone wants to make me feel conscious of my vulnerability or subordination, I will make them acutely aware of their ridiculousness. For me, laughter is both a means of disarming anti-feminist forces and drawing more people to the cause.

This isn't just an act, though sometimes it has been a way for me to mask my rage. It's a reflection of my belief that the best comedy is subversive; political movements that are designed to subvert systems of power are simpatico with comedy. Humor that "punches down" in favor of the system isn't just problematic—it also just isn't funny. Suggesting that sexist men don't understand real comedy and pitying them for not understanding also flips the script on them. It's a sort of feminist judo, using the force of the attacker to land them on their backs.

But working towards a gender egalitarian world will take more than laughing at antiquated ideas and making bullies feel small. It means having hard conversations with people that mean well but may not have a thorough understanding of how gender hierarchy operates. This means that we need to be open-hearted and compassionate educators. We are asking people to leave behind the security of the world that they know and set aside the gendered performances and patriarchal bargains that have kept them safe. That can be scary. The feminism I believe in is one that invites those who have benefitted from the system to feel uncomfortable but not irredeemable by dint of their position in this system. This means a feminism that is inclusive of men and a feminism that recognizes the ways that men are harmed by patriarchal systems. As bell hooks (2004) wrote:

> The first act of violence that patriarchy demands of males is not violence toward women. Instead patriarchy demands of all males that they engage in acts of psychic self-mutilation, that they kill off the emotional parts of themselves. If an individual is not successful in emotionally crippling himself, he can count on patriarchal men to enact rituals of power that will assault his self-esteem (p. 66).

Hurt people hurt people; liberating men from the unreasonable expectations and perverse incentives of patriarchy is an important means by which we can erode gender hierarchy.

---

1 This crops up in a number of places, including in the T.V. adaptation of Atwood's *The Handmaid's Tale.* https://www.imdb.com/title/tt7435252/trivia/

Closing on a Note of Hope

Change is possible and it is worth fighting for. I've seen it in my own family's history. My grandmother and I were born less than 100 years apart—just the blink of an eye in the grand sweep of human history—yet her life is almost unrecognizable to me. Far too often, she was crushed under a gender order that prioritized men's happiness over women's well-being—and which taught women to expect that as a matter of course.

I know that my ability to go to college and graduate school, to pursue a career that I love, to decide when and how I wanted to start a family, and the everyday liberties that I take for granted are all a function of the women who came before me who pushed for me to be able to live a life of their own choosing. I know that too many women—in the United States, and around the world—do not enjoy these luxuries. And I know that the wins that the women that came before me notched are not set in stone; in fact we are living in a time now where they are under acute assault.

So I know that we have to keep fighting, even when it seems like the odds are stacked against us. We are all the scrappy underdog boxer Rocky Balboa, trying to "go the distance" against the polished pro boxer Apollo Creed; the point isn't whether we win, it's that we keep fighting. For ourselves, for our families, for our communities, and so that future generations can grow up in a more egalitarian world.

Works Cited

Abdi, A. (2025) 'A feminist international political economy of sanctions: crises and the shifting gendered regimes of labor and survival in Iran', *International Feminist Journal of Politics*, 27(1), pp. 81–104. https://doi.org/10.1080/14616742.2025.2454462

Abed, D. and Kelleher, F. (2022) 'The Assault of Austerity: How Prevailing Economic Choices are a Form of Gender-Based Violence'. *Oxfam International*, 21 November 2022. Available at: from: https://oxfamilibrary.openrepository.com/bitstream/handle/10546/621448/mn-assault-of-austerity-prevailing-economic-choices-are-gender-based-violence-221122-en.pdf?sequence=2 (Accessed: 7 March 2025).

Action on Armed Violence (2019) '"Military Age Males" in US Drone Strikes', *AOAV*, 28 November. Available at: https://aoav.org.uk/2019/military-age-males-in-us-drone-strikes/ (Accessed: 7 March 2025).

Agarwal, B. (1997) '"Bargaining'" and Gender Relations: Within and Beyond the Household', *Feminist Economics*, 3(1), pp. 1–51. https://doi.org/10.1080/135457097338799

Agius, C. (2018) 'Rescuing the State? Sovereignty, Identity, and the Gendered Re-articulation of the State', in *Revisiting Gendered States: Feminist Imaginings of the State in International Relations*, pp. 69–84. Available at: https://academic.oup.com/book/25553/chapter-abstract/192857563?redirectedFrom=fulltext&login=false (Accessed: 7 March 2025).

Ahmed, S. (2024) 'Living a feminist life', in *Feminist Futures: Theories and Practices.* Cham: Springer, pp. 229–232. Available at: https://link.springer.com/chapter/10.1007/978-3-031-55397-4_18 (Accessed: 7 March 2025).

Ahmed, S. (2017) *Living a Feminist Life.* Durham: Duke University Press.

Akbari, F. and True, J. (2022) 'One year on from the Taliban takeover of Afghanistan: re-instituting gender apartheid', *Australian Journal of International Affairs*, 76(6), pp. 624–633. https://doi.org/10.1080/10357718.2022.2107172.

Akwei, I. (2017) 'Why Boko Haram uses more girls for suicide bombing than any other insurgency', *AfricaNews*, 15 August.

Al Jazeera. (2019) 'Set your ovaries free: Tanzania leader seeks population growth', *Al Jazeera*, 10 July. Available at: https://www.aljazeera.com/news/2019/7/10/set-your-ovaries-free-tanzania-leader-seeks-population-growth (Accessed: 7 March 2025).

Alesina, A., Giuliano, P. and Nunn, N. (2013) 'On the Origins of Gender Roles: Women and the Plough', *The Quarterly Journal of Economics*, 128(2), pp. 469–530. Available at: https://doi.org/10.1093/qje/qjt005.

Alqaseer, S. C. and Pile, J. C. T. (2020) 'The President's Monologues', *Philippine Journal of Social Development*, 13, p. 35–51.

Alonso-Albarran, V., Curristine, T. R., Preston, G., Soler, A. and Tchelishvili, N. (2021) 'Gender Budgeting in G20 Countries', *International Monetary Fund*, 12 November. Available at: https://www.imf.org/en/Publications/WP/Issues/2021/11/12/Gender-Budgeting-in-G20-Countries-506816#:~:text=IMF%20Working%20Papers&text=Gender%20budgeting%20(GB)%20can%20help,gathered%20from%20an%20IMF%20survey.#:~:text=IMF%20Working%20Papers&text=Gender%20budgeting%20(GB)%20can%20help,gathered%20from%20an%20IMF%20survey (Accessed: 7 March 2025).

Alter, K. J. and Zürn, M., 2020. 'Conceptualising Backlash Politics: Introduction to a Special Issue on Backlash Politics in Comparison', *The British Journal of Politics and International Relations*, 22(4), pp. 563–584. https://doi.org/10.1177/1369148120947957.

https://doi.org/10.1515/9783111662886-014

American Association of University Women (n.d.) 'The Motherhood Penalty'. *American Association of University Women*. Available at: https://www.aauw.org/issues/equity/motherhood/ (Accessed: 18 February 2025).

Amnesty International (2024) *Global: Gender apartheid must be recognized as a crime under international law*. Available at: https://www.amnesty.org/en/latest/news/2024/06/gender-apart heid-must-be-recognized-international-law/#:~:text=Amnesty%20International%20advocates% 20the%20legal,Callamard%2C%20Amnesty%20International%27s%20Secretary%20General (Accessed: 7 March 2025).

Amnesty International (2018) 'Online violence against women: Chapter 1 – A toxic place for women', 21 March. Available at: https://www.amnesty.org/en/latest/research/2018/03/online-violence-against-women-chapter-1-1/ (Accessed: 7 March 2025).

Angelou, M. (2008) *Letter to My Daughter.* New York: Random House.

Archer, E. M. (2013) 'The Power of Gendered Stereotypes in the US Marine Corps', *Armed Forces & Society*, 39(2), pp. 359–391. Available at: https://wwwjstororg.du.idm.oclc.org/stable/48609184 (Accessed: 17 February 2025).

Archie, A. (2022) 'Interracial and same-sex marriage: A history of legal challenges and wins', *NPR*, 9 December. Available at: https://www.npr.org/2022/12/09/1141819649/interracial-same-sex-marriage (Accessed: 7 March 2025).

Ashwin, S., and Utrata, J. (2020) 'Masculinity Restored? Putin's Russia and Trump's America', *Contexts*, 19(2), pp. 16–21. doi: https://doi.org/10.1177/1536504220920189. (Accessed: 7 March 2025).

Atwood, M. (2019) 'Margaret Atwood on the real-life events that inspired The Handmaid's Tale and The Testaments', *Penguin Books*, 8 September. Available at: https://www.penguin.co.uk/articles/2019/09/margaret-atwood-handmaids-tale-testaments-real-life-inspiration. (Accessed: 7 March 2025).

Avolio, B., Pardo, E. and O'Brien, J. (2004) 'Gender inequality in time allocation across life stages: a comparative study in a Latin American country', *Community, Work & Family*, pp. 1–24.

Babül, E. M. (2015) 'The paradox of protection: Human rights, the masculinist state, and the moral economy of gratitude in Turkey', *American Ethnologist*, 42(1), pp. 116–130. https://doi.org/10. 1111/amet.12120

Balint, K. (2021) 'Hungary's Pivotal Role in the Global Network against Sexual & Reproductive Rights', *Institute for Strategic Dialogue*, December 17. Available at: https://www.isdglobal.org/digital_dispatches/keeping-it-in-the-family-hungarys-pivotal-role-in-the-global-network-against-sexual-and-reproductive-rights/ (Accessed: 7 March 2025).

Barker, G. and Ricardo, C. (2006) 'Young men and the construction of masculinity in sub-Saharan Africa: Implications for HIV/AIDS, conflict, and violence', in Bannon, I. and Correia, M. (eds.), *The other half of gender: men's issues in development*. Washington, DC: World Bank.

Barnett, K. and Grown, C. (2004) *Gender impacts of government revenue collection: The case of taxation* (Vol. 10). London: Commonwealth Secretariat.

Barrera, J. (2022) *Linea Nigra: An Essay on Pregnancy and Earthquakes*. Two Lines Press.

Basu, S. (2016) 'The global south writes 1325 (too)', *International Political Science Review*, 37(3), pp. 362–374.

Baylor Scott & White Health (2023) 'Meat madness: The risks of the carnivore diet', *Baylor Scott & White Health*, 26 September. Available at: https://www.bswhealth.com/blog/meat-madness-the-risks-of-the-carnivore-diet (Accessed: 7 March 2025).

BBC (2015) 'Saudis recall Sweden ambassador amid diplomatic row'. Available at: https://www.bbc.com/news/world-europe-31831601 (Accessed: 7 March 2025).

BBC (2014) 'Central African Republic MPs elect Catherine Samba-Panza', 20 January. Available at: https://www.bbc.com/news/world-africa-25811250 (Accessed: 7 March 2025).

Beauchamp, Z. (2022) 'Hungary's CPAC 2022 speech: Orbán's embrace of the Great Replacement theory', *Vox*, 19 May. Available at: https://www.vox.com/2022/5/19/23123050/hungary-cpac-2022-replacement-theory (Accessed: 7 March 2025).

Becker, A. (2021) 'Trump wielded toxic masculinity as a weapon. It hurt America', *The 19th*, 19 January. Available at: https://19thnews.org/2021/01/trump-toxic-masculinity-harm/ (Accessed: 7 March 2025).

Becker, R. (1995) 'Review of 'The Social and Political Economy of the Household', Anderson, M., Bechhofer, F. and Burshuny, J.,' *European Sociological Review*, 11(3), pp. 321–324. Available at: https://doi.org/10.1093/oxfordjournals.esr.a036367 (Accessed: 19 February 2025).

Becker, G. S. (1986) *An Economic Analysis of The Family*. Chicago: University of Chicago Press.

Becker, J. and Shane, S. (2012) 'Secret 'Kill List' Tests Obama's Principles', *The New York Times*, 29 May. Available at: https://www.nytimes.com/2012/05/29/world/obamas-leadership-in-war-on-al-qaeda.html (Accessed: 7 March 2025).

Bergsten, S. S. and Lee, S. A. (2023) 'Global backlash against women's rights', *Human Rights Watch*, 7 March. Available at: https://www.hrw.org/news/2023/03/07/global-backlash-against-womens-rights. (Accessed: 7 March 2025).

Bergvall, S. (2024) 'Women's Economic Empowerment and Intimate Partner Violence', *Journal of Public Economics*, 239(105211). https://doi.org/10.1016/j.jpubeco.2024.105211

Bernhard, R., Shames, S. and Teele, D. L. (2020) 'To Emerge? Breadwinning, Motherhood, and Women's Decisions to Run for Office', *American Political Science Review*, 115(2), pp. 379–394. https://doi.org/10.1017/S0003055420000970

Better Work (2018) 'Global Gender Strategy'. Available at: https://betterwork.org/reports-and-publications/global-gender-strategy/ (Accessed: 11 March 2025).

Bianchi, S. M. and Robinson, J. (1997) 'What Did You Do Today? Children's Use of Time, Family Composition, and The Acquisition of Social Capital', *Journal of Marriage and the Family*, 59(2), pp. 332–344. https://doi.org/10.2307/353474

Bjarnason, E. (2022) 'Iceland Women Strike For Equal Pay', *AP News*, 24 October. Available at: https://apnews.com/article/iceland-women-strike-equal-pay-970669466116a2b1a5673a8737089d46 (Accessed: 7 March 2025).

Borresen, K. (2023) 'There's A Key Difference Between The Chores Men And Women Take On', *HuffPost*, 20 March. Available at: https://www.huffpost.com/entry/men-women-chores-difference_l_64022fe9e4b01f84dab715a7 (Accessed: 7 March 2025).

Bos, A. L., Greenlee, J. S., Holman, M. R., Oxley, Z. M. and Lay, J. C. (2022) 'This one's for the boys: How gendered political socialization limits girls' political ambition and interest', *American Political Science Review*, 116(2), pp. 484–501. https://doi.org/10.1017/S0003055421001027 (Accessed: 7 March 2025).

Bose, A., Tanupriya, and Singh, A. (2024) 'Hegemonic Femininity in Popular Culture: Heteronormative Appropriation of Lesbian Sexualities in Contemporary India through Neeraj Ghaywan's 'Geeli Pucchi'', *Monthly Review*. Available at: https://monthlyreview.org/2024/01/01/hegemonic-femininity-in-popular-culture-heteronormative-appropriation-of-lesbian-sexualities-in-contemporary-india-through-neeraj-ghaywans-geeli-pucchi/ (Accessed: 7 March 2025).

Brenan, M. (2020) 'Women Still Handle Main Household Tasks in U.S.', *Gallup*, 29 January. Available at: https://news.gallup.com/poll/283979/women-handle-main-household-tasks.aspx (Accessed: 10 February 2025).

Brewster, R. (2020) 'Gender and international trade policy: Economic nostalgia and the national security steel tariffs', *Duke Journal of Gender Law & Policy*, pp. 59–68. Available at: https://scholarship.law.duke.edu/djglp/vol27/iss1/6 (Accessed: 7 March 2025).

Bringe, K. (2024) 'How Overly Praising 'Good Dads' Stalls Gender Equality', *The Bump*, 18 March. Available at: https://www.thebump.com/a/stop-praising-good-dads (Accessed: 19 February 2025).

Brown, K. E. (2018) 'Violence and Gender Politics in the Proto-State "Islamic State', in Swati Parashar, J. Ann Tickner, and Jacqui True (eds.), *Revisiting Gendered States: Feminist Imaginings of the State in International Relations*, Oxford Studies in Gender and International Relations. New York: Oxford Academic, pp. 174–190.

Brown, M. T. (2012a) '"A Woman in the Army Is Still a Woman": Representations of Women in US Military Recruiting Advertisements for the All-Volunteer Force', *Journal of Women, Politics & Policy*, 33(2), pp. 151–175. https://doi.org/10.1080/1554477X.2012.667737

Brown, M. T. (2012b) *Enlisting Masculinity: The Construction of Gender in US Military Recruiting Advertising during the All-Volunteer Force* [online]. Oxford University Press. https://doi.org/10.1093/acprof:oso/9780199842827.001.0001

Brown, R. (1997) 'Social identity theory: Past achievements, current problems, and future challenges', *Journal of Social Psychology*, 37(6), p. 50. Available at: https://bpspsychub.onlinelibrary.wiley.com/doi/pdf/10.1111/j.2044-8309.1997.tb01118.x (Accessed: 11 March 2025).

Brownson, C. (2014) 'The Battle for Equivalency: Female US Marines Discuss Sexuality, Physical Fitness, and Military Leadership', *Armed Forces & Society*, 40(4), pp. 765–788. https://doi.org/10.1177/0095327X14523957.

Brulé, R. and Gaikwad, N. (2021) 'Culture, capital, and the political economy gender gap: evidence from Meghalaya's matrilineal tribes', *The Journal of Politics*, 83(3), pp. 834–850. https://doi.org/10.1086/711176

Burnet, J. E. (2011) 'Women have found respect: Gender quotas, symbolic representation, and female empowerment in Rwanda', *Politics & Gender*, 7(3), pp. 303–334. https://doi.org/10.1017/S1743923X11000250

Butler, J. (1990) *Gender Trouble: Feminism and the Subversion of Identity*. New York: Routledge.

Byrnes, B. (2023) 'Report Provides Latest Data About Minimum Wage Workers in the US', *Camoin Associates*. Available at: https://camoinassociates.com/resources/current-data-about-minimum-wage-workers-in-the-us/#:~:text=49.9%25%2C%20respectively (Accessed: 11 March 2025).

Calarco, J. (2024) *Holding it together: How women became America's safety net*. Penguin.

Campbell, D. E. and Wolbrecht, C. (2006) 'See Jane run: Women politicians as role models for adolescents', *The Journal of Politics*, 68(2), pp. 233–247. https://doi.org/10.1111/j.1468-2508.2006.00402.x

Campbell, H. (2010) 'Structural adjustment policies: A feminist critique', *Sigma: Journal of Political and International Studies*, 27(1), pp. 2–14. Available at: https://scholarsarchive.byu.edu/sigma/vol27/iss1/2 (Accessed: 11 March 2025).

Caprioli, M. (2003) 'Gender equality and state aggression: The impact of domestic gender equality on state first use of force', *International Interactions* 29(3,) pp. 195–214.

CARE (2022) 'Raising their voices for change: women garment workers speak up', *CARE*, March 8. Available at: https://web.archive.org/web/20241210020539/https://www.care.org/news-and-stories/raising-their-voices-for-change-women-garment-workers-speak-up/ (Accessed: 11 March 2025).

Carlos, A. M. and Kruse, J. B. (1996) 'The Decline of the Royal African Company: Fringe Firms and the Role of the Charter', *The Economic History Review*, 49(2), pp. 291–313. Available at: https://doi.org/10.2307/2597917 (Accessed: 3 March 2025).

Carr-Ellis, E. (2025) 'The laws on what women can – and can't – do in Saudi Arabia', *The Week*, 16 January. Available at: https://theweek.com/60339/things-women-cant-do-in-saudi-arabia (Accessed: 20 February 2025)

Cassese, E. C. and Holman, M. R. (2018) 'Party and gender stereotypes in campaign attacks', *Political Behavior*, 40, pp. 785–807.

CBS News. (2015) 'ISIS fighters get marriage bonuses, including honeymoon', *CBS News*, 26 May. Available at: https://www.cbsnews.com/news/isis-fighters-get-marriage-bonuses-including-honeymoon (Accessed 4 February 2025).

Centers for Disease Control and Prevention (CDC) (2024). 'Milestones for 4-Year-Olds', *CDC*. Available at: https://www.cdc.gov/ncbddd/actearly/milestones/milestones-4yr.html (Accessed: 11 March 2025).

Chan, G. (2015) 'Tony Abbott urges Europe to adopt Australian policies in refugee crisis', *The Guardian*, 27 October. Available at: https://www.theguardian.com/world/2015/oct/28/tony-abbott-urges-europe-to-adopt-australian-border-policies (Accessed: 11 March 2025).

Chandler, D. and Munday, R. (2011) 'Gender Essentialism. In: A Dictionary of Media and Communication' (1 ed.) [online]. Oxford University Press. Available at: https://www.oxfordreference.com/display/10.1093/acref/9780199568758.001.0001/acref-9780199568758-e-1089 (Accessed 31 January 2025).

Chattopadhyay, R. and Duflo, E. (2004) 'Women as policy makers: Evidence from a randomized policy experiment in India', *Econometrica*, 72(5), pp. 1409–1443. https://doi.org/10.1111/j.1468-0262.2004.00539.x

Checkel, J. T. (2017) 'Socialization and violence: Introduction and framework', *Journal of Peace Research*, 54(5), pp. 592–605. https://doi.org/10.1177/0022343317721813.

Cheng, M. (2024) 'Global fertility rates to plunge in decades ahead, new report says', *CNN*, 20 March. Available at: https://www.cnn.com/2024/03/20/health/global-fertility-rates-lancet-study/index.html (Accessed: 11 March 2025).

Childs, S. (2006) 'The complicated relationship between sex, gender and the substantive representation of women', *European Journal of Women's Studies*, 13(1), pp. 7–21. https://doi.org/10.1177/1350506806060003

Childs, S. and Hughes, M. (2018) '"Which men?" How an intersectional perspective on men and masculinities helps explain women's political underrepresentation', *Politics & Gender*, 14(2), pp. 282–287. https://doi.org/10.1017/S1743923X1800017X

Chitando, E. and Mlambo, O. B. (2024) '"I Have Got Stamina!" Yoweri K. Museveni, Masculinity and the Physical Right to Rule in Uganda', in E. Chitando, O. B. Mlambo, S. Mfecane, and K. Ratele (eds.), *The Palgrave Handbook of African Men and Masculinities*. Cham: Springer International Publishing, pp. 297–311. https://doi.org/10.1007/978-3-031-49167-2_15

Clay, N. and Yurco, K. (2024) 'Beyond the 'gender gap' in agriculture: Africa's Green Revolution and gendered rural transformation in Rwanda', *Journal of Rural Studies*, 112, pp. 1–12.

Clements, B. (2012) 'Men and women's support for war: Accounting for the gender gap in public opinion', *E-International Relations*. Available at: https://www.e-ir.info/2012/01/19/men-and-wom

ens-support-for-war-accounting-for-the-gender-gap-in-public-opinion/ (Accessed: 11 March 2025).

Coaston, J. (2019) 'The Intersectionality Wars', *Vox*, 28 May. Available at: https://www.vox.com/the-highlight/2019/5/20/18542843/intersectionality-conservatism-law-race-gender-discrimination (Accessed: 11 March 2025).

Coffe, H. and Bolzendahl, C., (2010) 'Gender gaps in political participation across sub-Saharan African nations', *Social indicators research*, 102(2), pp. 245–264. https://doi.org/10.1007/s11205-010-9676-6

Cohen, D. K. (2016) *Rape during civil war.* Cornell University Press. Available at: https://books.google.com/books?id=p-6vDAAAQBAJ (Accessed: 11 March 2025).

Cohen, D. K. (2013) 'Female Combatants and the Perpetration of Violence: Wartime Rape in the Sierra Leone Civil War', *World Politics*, 65(3), pp. 383–415. https://doi.org/10.1017/S0043887113000105

Cohen, D. K., Green, A. H. and Wood, E. J. (2013) 'Wartime Sexual Violence: Misconceptions, Implications, and Ways Forward', *United States Institute of Peace*. Available at: https://www.usip.org/publications/2013/02/wartime-sexual-violence-misconceptions-implications-and-ways-forward (Accessed 6 February 2025).

Cohen, D. K. and Karim, S. M. (2022) 'Does More Equality for Women Mean Less War? Rethinking Sex and Gender Inequality and Political Violence', *International Organization*, 76(2), pp. 414–444. https://doi.org/10.1017/S0020818321000333.

Conger, C. (2012) 'Do men really have more upper body strength than women?', *HowStuffWorks*, 12 December. Available at: https://health.howstuffworks.com/wellness/diet-fitness/personal-training/men-vs-women-upper-body-strength.htm#:~:text=Secreted%20by%20the%20pituitary%20gland,strength%20for%20the%20long%20haul (Accessed: 11 March 2025).

Congressional Research Service (2024) 'Statistics on Women in National Governments Around the World' CRS Report R45483, *Congressional Research Service*. Available at: https://sgp.fas.org/crs/misc/R45483.pdf (Accessed: 11 March 2025).

Connell, R.W. and Messerschmidt, J.W. (2005) 'Hegemonic masculinity: Rethinking the concept', *Gender & society*, 19(6), pp. 829–859. https://doi.org/10.1177/0891243205278639

Council of Europe (2005) *Gender Budgeting.* Available at: https://rm.coe.int/1680596143 (Accessed: 23 February 2025).

Cooper, C., Gable, M. and Austin, A. (2012) 'The public-sector jobs crisis: Women and African Americans hit hardest by job losses in state and local governments', *Economic Policy Institute*, 2 May. Available at: https://www.epi.org/publication/bp339-public-sector-jobs-crisis/ (Accessed: 11 March 2025).

Correia, M. C and Bannon, I. (2006) *The Other Half of Gender: Men's Issues in Development.* Washington, DC: World Bank.

Crenshaw, K. (2013) 'Demarginalizing the intersection of race and sex: A black feminist critique of antidiscrimination doctrine, feminist theory and antiracist politics', in: *Feminist legal theories*. Routledge, pp. 23–51.

Cronqvist, H. and Yu, F. (2017) 'Shaped by their daughters: Executives, female socialization, and corporate social responsibility', *Journal of Financial Economics*, 126(3), pp. 543–562. https://doi.org/10.1016/j.jfineco.2017.09.003

Crouch, D. (2015) 'Sweden's foreign minister unrepentant over Saudi flogging row', *The Guardian*. Available at: https://www.theguardian.com/world/2015/jun/08/swedens-foreign-minister-unrepentant-over-saudi-flogging-row (Accessed: 11 March 2025).

Cruz, G. and Rau, T. (2022) 'The effects of equal pay laws on firm pay premiums: Evidence from Chile', *Labour Economics*, 75, 102135.

Cupać, J. and Ebetürk, I. (2021) 'Backlash advocacy and NGO polarization over women's rights in the United Nations', *International Affairs*, 97(4), pp. 1183–1201. https://doi.org/10.1093/ia/iiab069

Cupać, J. and Ebetürk, I. (2020) 'The personal is global political: The antifeminist backlash in the United Nations', *The British Journal of Politics and International Relations*, 22(4), pp. 702–714. https://doi.org/10.1177/1369148120948733.

Curristine, T., Tchelishvili, N. and Weerathunga, S. (2022) 'Gender Budgeting Is More Widespread But Implementation Remains a Challenge', *IMF Blog*, 8 March. Available at: https://www.imf.org/en/Blogs/Articles/2022/03/08/gender-budgeting-is-more-widespread-but-implementation-remains-a-challenge (Accessed: 11 March 2025).

Cursino, M. (2022) 'Hungary decrees tighter abortion rules', *BBC News*, 13 September. Available at: https://www.bbc.com/news/world-europe-62892596 (Accessed: 11 March 2025).

David Reynolds, Summits: Six Meetings That Shaped the Twentieth Century (New York: Basic Books, 2007).

Davidson-Schmich, L. K. (2016) *Gender quotas and democratic participation: Recruiting candidates for elective offices in Germany*. University of Michigan Press.

Desilver, D. (2021) 'The U.S. differs from most other countries in how it sets its minimum wage', *Pew Research Center*, 20 May. Available at: https://www.pewresearch.org/short-reads/2021/05/20/the-u-s-differs-from-most-other-countries-in-how-it-sets-its-minimum-wage/ (Accessed: 11 March 2025).

Detraz, N. and Peksen, D. (2016) 'The effect of IMF programs on women's economic and political rights', *International Interactions*, 42(1), pp. 81–105. https://doi.org/10.1080/03050629.2015.1056343

Dhanaraj, S. and Mahambare, V. (2021) 'Male Backlash and Female Guilt: Women's Employment and Intimate Partner Violence in Urban India', *Feminist Economics*, 28(1), pp. 170–198. https://doi.org/10.1080/13545701.2021.1986226

Dietrich Ortega, L. M. (2012) 'Looking Beyond Violent Militarized Masculinities: Guerrilla Gender Regimes in Latin America', *International Feminist Journal of Politics*, 14(4), pp. 489–507. https://doi.org/10.1080/14616742.2012.726094.

DiMuccio, S. H. and Knowles, E. D. (2020) 'The political significance of fragile masculinity', *Current Opinion in Behavioral Sciences*, 34, pp. 25–28. https://doi.org/10.1016/j.cobeha.2019.11.010

DiRita, P. (2014) 'Economic Rationality Assumption', in C. A. Michalos (ed.), *Encyclopedia of Quality of Life and Well-Being Research*. Dordrecht, NL: Springer, pp. 1803–1806.

Ditonto, T. M., Hamilton, A. J. and Redlawsk, D. P. (2014), 'Gender stereotypes, information search, and voting behavior in political campaigns', *Political Behavior*, 36, pp. 335–358. https://doi.org/10.1007/s11109-013-9232-6

Douhan, A. (2022) 'Visit to the Islamic Republic of Iran: report of the Special Rapporteur on the Negative Impact of Unilateral Coercive Measures on the Enjoyment of Human Rights', *United Nations*, 17 August. Available at: https://www.ohchr.org/en/documents/country-reports/ahrc5133add1-visit-islamic-republic-iran-report-special-rapporteur (Accessed: 7 March 2025).

Drury, A. C. and Peksen, D. (2014) 'Women and economic statecraft: The negative impact international economic sanctions visit on women', *European Journal of International Relations*, 20(2), pp. 463–490.

Duriesmith, D. (2018) 'Manly states and feminist foreign policy', in S. Parashar, J. A. Tickner, and J. True (eds.), *Revisiting Gendered States: Feminist Imaginings of the State in International Relations, Oxford Studies in Gender and International Relations.* Oxford Academic, pp. 51–68. https://doi. org/10.1093/oso/9780190644031.003.0004

Eareckson, H. B., and Heilman, M. E. (2024) 'Explaining Penalties and Rewards for Gender Norm Violations: A Unified Theory', *Sex Roles*, 90(12), pp. 1701–1716. https://doi.org/10.1007/s11199-024-01540-8

Edström, J., Edwards, J., Lewin, T., McGee, R., Nazneen, S. and Skinner, C. (2024) *Understanding Gender Backlash: Southern Perspectives.*

Edström, J., Greig, A. and Skinner, C., (2024) 'Patriarchal (Dis) orders: Backlash as crisis management', *Signs: Journal of Women in Culture and Society*, 49(2), pp. 277–309.

Eksi, B. and Wood, E. A. (2019) 'Right-wing populism as gendered performance: Janus-faced masculinity in the leadership of Vladimir Putin and Recep T. Erdogan', *Theory and Society* 48 (5), pp. 733–751.

Eichler, M. (2014) 'Militarized Masculinities in International Relations', *The Brown Journal of World Affairs* [online], 21(1), pp. 81–93. Available at: http://www.jstor.org/stable/24591032 (Accessed 3 February 2025).

Eisenstein, Z. (2013) 'The lie of 'women and children'', *Al Jazeera*, 2 October. Available at: https://www.aljazeera.com/opinions/2013/10/2/the-lie-of-women-and-children. (Accessed: 11 March 2025).

Elliot, K. A., Hufbauer, G. C., and Oegg, B. (n.d.) 'Sanctions', *Econlib.* Available at: https://www. econlib.org/library/Enc/Sanctions.html (Accessed: 11 March 2025).

Elshtain, J. B. (1982) 'On beautiful souls, just warriors and feminist consciousness', *Women's Studies International Forum*, 5(3–4), pp. 341–348. https://doi.org/10.1016/0277-5395(82)90043-7.

Eltahawy, M. (2016) 'How to fight the patriarchy', *Lit Hub.* Available at: https://lithub.com/mona-eltahawy-how-to-fight-the-patriarchy/ (Accessed: 11 March 2025).

Engelbrecht, M. (2020) 'The 'Sickly Boy' and the 'Real Man': Kennedy, Castro, and Competing Masculinities', *The ascendant historian*, 7(1), pp. 57–67. Available at: https://journals.uvic.ca/index.php/corvette/article/view/20012 (Accessed: 11 March 2025).

Enloe, C. (2013) *Seriously!: Investigating Crashes and Crises as If Women Mattered.* Berkeley: University of California Press.

Enloe, C. (2004) *The Curious Feminist: Searching for women in a new age of empire.* Berkeley: University of California Press.

Enloe, C. (2000) *The International Politics of Militarizing Women's Lives.* University of California Press.

Enloe, C. (1991) *Bananas, Beaches and Babes: Making Feminist Sense of International Politics.* Berkeley: University of California Press.

Enloe, C. (1983) *Does Khaki Become You.* Washington: University Of California Press.

Ericsson, S. (2019) 'Backlash: Undesirable effects of female economic empowerment', *Lund University, Department of Economics and Centre of Economic Demography*, Working Paper 12, pp. 1–42.

Everytown (2024) 'Guns and Violence Against Women', *Everytown*, 24 June. Available at: https://everytownresearch.org/report/guns-and-violence-against-women-americas-uniquely-lethal-intimate-partner-violence-problem/. (Accessed: 11 March 2025).

Fallaci, O. (1975) 'Indira's Coup', *The New York Review of Books*, 18 September. Available at: https://www.nybooks.com/articles/1975/09/18/indiras-coup/. (Accessed: 11 March 2025).

Faludi, S. (1991) *Backlash: The undeclared war against American women.* Crown Publishers.

Farris, S. R. (2017) *In the name of women's rights. The rise of femonationalism*. Duke University Press.

Feng, E. (2021) 'The legacy of the lasting effects of China's 1-child policy', *NPR*, 21 June. Available at: https://www.npr.org/2021/06/21/1008656293/the-legacy-of-the-lasting-effects-of-chinas-1-child-policy. (Accessed: 11 March 2025).

Feng, W., Gu, B. and Cai, Y. (2016) 'The end of China's one-child policy', *Brookings Institution*, 30 March. Available at: https://www.brookings.edu/articles/the-end-of-chinas-one-child-policy. (Accessed: 11 March 2025).

Ferran, L. (2024) 'ODNI, Pentagon reveal FY23 intelligence budget at nearly $100 billion', [online] *Breaking Defense*, 30 October. Available at: https://breakingdefense.com/2023/10/odni-pentagon-reveal-fy23-intelligence-budget-at-nearly-100-billion/. (Accessed: 11 March 2025).

Field, E. (2003) *Fertility responses to urban land titling programs: The roles of ownership security and the distribution of household assets*. Mimeo: Harvard University.

Field, B. N. (2021) 'Ministers, gender, and political appointments', *Government and Opposition*, 56(4), pp. 722–743. https://doi.org/10.1017/gov.2020.10

Filipovic, J. (2013) 'Rewriting our rape laws in light of Steubenville', *Aljazeera*, 27 March. Available at: https://www.aljazeera.com/opinions/2013/3/27/rewriting-our-rape-laws-in-light-of-steubenville#:~:text=Traditionally%2C%20rape%20wasn%27t%20a,if%20their%20husbands%20raped%20them (Accessed: 20 February 2025)

Fodor, E. (2024) 'Getting paid to have children? Hungary's carefare regime', *The Loop*. Available at: https://theloop.ecpr.eu/getting-paid-to-have-children-hungarys-carefare-regime/. (Accessed: 11 March 2025).

Folbre, N. (2002) *The Invisible Heart: Economic and Family Values*. New York, NY: The New Press.

Food and Agriculture Organization of the United Nations (n.d.) *Women and the green revolution*. Available at: https://www.fao.org/4/x0171e/x0171e04.htm#:~:text=The%20rapid%20modernization%20of%20agriculture,%C2%B7 (Accessed: 3 March 2025).

Freedom House (2024) 'Rwanda: Freedom in the World', *Freedom House*. Available at: https://freedomhouse.org/country/rwanda/freedom-world/2024 (Accessed: 11 March 2025).

Fridkin, K. L. and Kenney, P. J. (2009) 'The role of gender stereotypes in US Senate campaigns', *Politics & Gender*, 5(3), pp. 301–324. https://doi.org/10.1017/S1743923X09990158

Friedman, R. (2018) 'Female LTTE and Social Reintegration in PostWar Sri Lanka', *International Studies Quarterly*, 62(3), pp. 632–642. Available at: https://www.jstor.org/stable/48619856 (Accessed 4 Feb. 2025).

Fröhlich, M. (2023) 'Promoting Gender Equality in International Trade Agreements: Pioneering or Pipe Dream?', in *Legal Issues of International Law from a Gender Perspective*. Cham: Springer International Publishing, pp. 179–197.

Fry, R., Aragão, C., Hurst, K. and Parker, K. (2023) 'In a Growing Share of U.S. Marriages, Husbands and Wives Earn About the Same', *Pew Research Center*, 13 April. Available at: https://www.pewresearch.org/social-trends/2023/04/13/in-a-growing-share-of-u-s-marriages-husbands-and-wives-earn-about-the-same/ (Accessed: 19 February 2025).

Funk, K. D., Hinojosa, M. and Piscopo, J. M. (2021) 'Women to the rescue: The gendered effects of public discontent on legislative nominations in Latin America', *Party Politics* 27(3), pp. 465–477.

Gade, B. (2019) 'When women take up arms and what that means for DDR processes', *Polis180*, 18 January. Available at: https://polis180.org/polisblog/2019/01/18/when-women-take-up-arms-and-what-that-means-for-ddr-processes/ (Accessed: 12 February 2025).

Gager, C. T. and Sanchez, L. (2004) 'Whose time is it? The effect of gender, employment, and work/family stress on children's housework', in *Annual meeting of the American Sociological Association.* San Francisco.

Gambino, L. (2018) 'Trump boasts nuclear button is 'much bigger' than Kim Jong-un's', *The Guardian*, 3 January. Available at: https://www.theguardian.com/us-news/2018/jan/03/donald-trump-boasts-nuclear-button-bigger-kim-jong-un (Accessed: 11 March 2025).

Gao, M. (2024) '"A woman is not a baby-making machine": a brief history of South Korea's 4B movement – and why it's making waves in America', *The Conversation*, 10 November. Available at: https://theconversation.com/a-woman-is-not-a-baby-making-machine-a-brief-history-of-south-koreas-4b-movement-and-why-its-making-waves-in-america-243355 (Accessed: 19 February 2025).

Gay, R. (2019) *Bad Feminist: Essays.* Translated by A. Spielmann. Munich: btb Verlag.

Gariepy, L. (2024) 'Women and Credit: A Look at the History', *U.S. News and World Report*, 22 March. Available at: https://money.usnews.com/credit-cards/articles/women-and-credit-a-look-at-the-history (Accessed: 20 February 2025).

Geddes, R. and Lueck, D. (2022) 'The Gains from Self-Ownership and the Expansion of Women's Rights', *The American Economic Review*, 92(4), pp. 1079–1092. Available at: https://doi.org/10.1257/00028280260344623 (Accessed: 20 February 2025).

Gertz, G. (2020) 'Did Trump's tariffs benefit American works and national security?' *Brookings Institution*, 10 September. Available: https://www.brookings.edu/articles/did-trumps-tariffs-benefit-american-workers-and-national-security/ (Accessed: 11 March 2025).

Geva, D. (2020) 'A double-headed hydra: Marine Le Pen's charisma, between political masculinity and political femininity', *Norma* 15(1), pp. 26–42.

Ghaffary, S. (2022) 'Sheryl Sandberg's mixed legacy at Meta', *Vox*, 2 June. Available at: https://www.vox.com/recode/23151743/sheryl-sandberg-resigns-meta-facebook-lean-in. (Accessed: 11 March 2025).

Ghose, S. (2017) 'Indira Gandhi: The alpha female who was attracted to alpha males', *Scroll.in*, 25 July. Available at: https://scroll.in/article/844878/indira-gandhi-the-alpha-female-who-was-attracted-to-alpha-males (Accessed: 11 March 2025).

Gibbings, S. L. (2011) 'No Angry Women at the United Nations: Political Dreams and the Cultural Politics of United Nations Security Council Resolution 1325', *International Feminist Journal of Politics*, 13(4), pp. 522–538. https://doi.org/10.1080/14616742.2011.611660.

Gidengil, E., O'Neill, B. and Young, L. (2010) 'Her mother's daughter? The influence of childhood socialization on women's political engagement', *Journal of Women, Politics & Policy*, 31(4), pp. 334–355. https://doi.org/10.1080/1554477X.2010.533590

Gill, L. (1997) 'Creating Citizens, Making Men: The Military and Masculinity in Bolivia', *Cultural Anthropology*, 12(4), pp. 527–550. https://doi.org/10.1525/can.1997.12.4.527

Giovarelli, R. and Wamalwa, B. (2011) 'Land Tenure, Property Rights, and Gender Challenges and Approaches for Strengthening Women's Land Tenure and Property Rights', *USAID*, Property Rights and Resource Governance Briefing Paper #7.

Global Affairs Canada (n.d.) 'Gender equality in trade', *Government of Canada.* Available at: https://www.international.gc.ca/gac-amc/campaign-campagne/inclusive_trade/gender-genre.aspx?lang=eng (Accessed: 11 March 2025).

Global Project Against Hate and Extremism (2024) 'The "Great Replacement" Conspiracy Theory: From The Fringe Of White Supremacist Circles To The Mainstream', *GPAHE*. Available at: https://globalextremism.org/the-great-replacement/ (Accessed: 11 March 2025)

Go, M. G. (2019) 'Sexism is president's power tool: Duterte is using violent language and threats against journalists, Rappler's news editor explains', *Index on censorship*, 48(4), pp. 33–35.

Goetz, A. M. (2020) 'The new competition in multilateral norm-setting: Transnational feminists & the illiberal backlash', *Daedalus*, 149(1), pp. 160–179. Available at: https://www.jstor.org/stable/48563039 (Accessed: 11 March 2025)

Gordon, J. (2013) 'The human costs of the Iran sanctions', *Foreign Policy*, 18 October. Available at: https://foreignpolicy.com/2013/10/18/the-human-costs-of-the-iran-sanctions/ (Accessed: 11 March 2025).

Gothreau, C. (2021) 'How Gender Shapes Public Opinion in American Politics', *Center for American Women and Politics*. Available at: https://cawp.rutgers.edu/blog/how-gender-shapes-public-opinion-american-politics (Accessed: 11 March 2025).

Gottlieb, J., Grossman, G. and Robinson, A. L. (2018) 'Do men and women have different policy preferences in Africa? Determinants and implications of gender gaps in policy prioritization', *British Journal of Political Science*, 48(3), pp. 611–636. https://doi.org/10.1017/S0007123416000053

Government of Canada (2024) 'What is Gender-based Analysis Plus.' Available at: https://www.canada.ca/en/women-gender-equality/gender-based-analysis-plus/what-gender-based-analysis-plus.html (Accessed: 11 March 2025).

Government of Canada (2019) 'Global Affairs Canada's Trade Policy and Negotiations Branch's Gender Pledge.' Available at: https://www.international.gc.ca/gac-amc/campaign-campagne/inclusive_trade/gender-genre.aspx?lang=eng&_ga=2.127726792.45772515.1731508854-346457247.1731508854 (Accessed: 11 March 2025).

Gowrinathan, N. (2022) *Radicalizing Her: Why Women Choose Violence*. Boston, MA: Beacon Press.

Grady, C. (2023) 'Me Too, backlash, and the culture wars', *Vox*, 3 February. Available at: https://www.vox.com/culture/23581859/me-too-backlash-susan-faludi-weinstein-roe-dobbs-depp-heard (Accessed 11 March 2025).

Grant, R. (1992) 'The Quagmire of Gender and International Security', in V. Peterson (ed.), *Gendered States: Feminist (Re)Visions of International Relations Theory*. Boulder, USA: Lynne Rienner Publishers, pp. 83–98. https://doi.org/10.1515/9781685859305-006

Grossman, D. (2014) *On Killing: The Psychological Cost of Learning to Kill in War and Society*. New York: Open Road Media.

Guevara, E. and Castro, F. (1965) *Socialism and man in Cuba*.

Gutiérrez D. J. A. (2023) 'Eating, shitting and shooting: a scatological and culinary approximation to the daily lives of rebels', *Studies in Conflict & Terrorism*, 46(10), pp. 1817–1839.

Gutiérrez-Sanín, F. and Wood, E. J. (2017) 'What Should We Mean by "Pattern of Political Violence"? Repertoire, Targeting, Frequency, and Technique', *Perspectives on Politics*, 15(1), pp. 20–41. https://doi.org/10.1017/S1537592716004114

Gutmann, J., Neuenkirch, M. and Neumeier, F. (2020) 'Sanctioned to Death? The Impact of Economic Sanctions on Life Expectancy and its Gender Gap', *The Journal of Development Studies*, 57(1), pp. 139–162. https://doi.org/10.1080/00220388.2020.1746277

Guttmacher Institute (2024) 'One in four US women expected to have an abortion in their lifetime', *Guttmacher Institute*, 17 April. Available at: https://www.guttmacher.org/news-release/2024/one-four-us-women-expected-have-abortion-their-lifetime (Accessed: 11 March 2025).

Håkansson, S. (2021) 'Do women pay a higher price for power? Gender bias in political violence in Sweden', *The Journal of Politics*, 83(2), pp. 515–531. https://doi.org/10.1086/709838

Halton, C. (2024) 'What Are Structural Adjustment Programs (SAPs)?' *Investopedia*, 16 September. Available at: https://www.investopedia.com/terms/s/structural-adjustment.asp#:~:text=A%20structural%20adjustment%20program%20(SAP)%20is%20a%20set%20of%20economic,competitive%20and%20encourage%20economic%20growth (Accessed 11 March 2025).

Hamilton, L. T., Armstrong, E. A., Seeley, J. L. and Armstrong, E. M. (2019) 'Hegemonic femininities and intersectional domination', *Sociological Theory*, 37, pp. 315–341. https://doi.org/10.1177/0735275119888248

Hannah, E., Roberts, A. and Trommer, S. (2022) 'Canada's "Feminist" Trade Policy?', in *Canada and Great Power Competition: Canada Among Nations 2021*. Cham: Springer International Publishing, pp. 71–96.

Harwood, J. (2013) 'Development policy and history; lessons from the Green Revolution', *History and Policy*, 14.

Hauge, W. I. (2019) 'Gender dimensions of DDR – beyond victimization and dehumanization: tracking the thematic', *International Feminist Journal of Politics*, 22(2), pp. 206–226. https://doi.org/10.1080/14616742.2019.1673669.

Hayes, A. (2024) 'What Is Comparative Advantage?' *Investopedia*, 26 June. Available: https://www.investopedia.com/terms/c/comparativeadvantage.asp (Accessed: 11 March 2025).

Hegseth, P. (2025) 'Post on Social Media.' Available at: https://x.com/PeteHegseth/status/1917203362396639518?ref_src=twsrc%5Etfw%7Ctwcamp%5Etweetembed%7Ctwterm%5E1917203362396639518%7Ctwgr%5E44dce5e07c92891e6a79b3e2d34320228493f9c5%7Ctwcon%5Es1_&ref_url=https%3A%2F%2Fwww.militarytimes.com%2Fnews%2Fpentagon-congress%2F2025%2F04%2F29%2Fhegseth-cancels-womens-leadership-program-despite-past-trump-support%2F (Accessed: 11 March 2025).

Herre, B. and Arriagada, P. (2024) 'The form and extent of government support for early childcare varies a lot between countries', *Our World in Data*, 8 August. Available at: https://ourworldindata.org/data-insights/the-form-and-extent-of-government-support-for-early-childcare-varies-a-lot-between-countries (Accessed: 11 March 2025).

Herrera, N. and Porch, D. 2008. 'Like going to a fiesta'–the role of female fighters in Colombia's FARC-EP', *Small Wars & Insurgencies*, 19(4), pp. 609–634.

Henig, J. (2008) 'Pigs and pit bulls', *FactCheck.org*, 10 September. Available at: https://www.factcheck.org/2008/09/pigs-and-pit-bulls/ (Accessed 11 March 2025).

Henry, M. (2021). 'On the necessity of critical race feminism for women, peace and security', *Critical Studies on Security*, 9(1), pp. 22–26.

Hobson, B. (1990) 'No Exit, No Voice: Women's Economic Dependency and the Welfare State', *Acta Sociologica*, 33(3), pp. 235–250. https://doi.org/10.1177/000169939003300305

Hochschild, A. and Machung, A. (2012) *The Second Shift: Working Families and the Revolution at Home*. New York, NY: Penguin Books.

Hoff, J. (2019) 'American women and the lingering implications of coverture', *The Social Science Journal*, 44(1), 41–55. https://doi.org/10.1016/j.soscij.2006.12.004

hooks, b. (2003) *The Will to Change: Men, Masculinity, and Love*. Washington, D.C.: Washington Square Press.

hooks, b. (2000) *Feminist Theory: from Margin to Center*. New York; London: Routledge.

Hoover-Green. (2018) *The Commander's Dilemma: Violence and Restraint in Wartime*. Cornell University Press. https://doi.org/10.7591/cornell/9781501726477.001.0001

Hudson, V., Bowen, D. L. and Nielsen, P. L. (2020). *The First Political Order: How Sex Shapes Governance and National Security Worldwide.* Columbia University Press. https://doi.org/10.7312/huds19466

Hudson, V. M. and Den Boer, A. (2004) *Bare branches: The security implications of Asia's surplus male population.* MIT Press.

Hudson, V. M. and Hodgson, K. B. (2020) 'Sex and Terror: Is the Subordination of Women Associated with the Use of Terror?', *Terrorism and Political Violence*, 34(3), pp. 605–632. https://doi.org/10.1080/09546553.2020.1724968

Hudson, V. M. and Matfess, H. (2017) 'In Plain Sight: The Neglected Linkage between Brideprice and Violent Conflict', *International* Security, 42(1), pp. 7–40. https://doi.org/10.1162/ISEC_a_00289

Human Rights Campaign (2023) 'Scott Lively report', *Human Rights Campaign Foundation.* Available at: https://assets2.hrc.org/files/assets/resources/Scott_Lively_Report.pdf (Accessed 11 March 2025)

Human Rights Watch (2022) 'Sweden's New Government Abandons Feminist Foreign Policy.' Available at: https://www.hrw.org/news/2022/10/31/swedens-new-government-abandons-feminist-foreign-policy (Accessed: 11 March 2025).

Hurl-Eamon, J. (2014) *Marriage and the British Army in the Long Eighteenth Century: 'The Girl I Left Behind Me'.* Oxford University Press.

International Food Policy Research Institute (2002) *Green Revolution: Curse or Blessing?* Available at: https://ebrary.ifpri.org/digital/collection/p15738coll2/id/64639/ (Accessed: 11 March 2025).

International Institute for Democracy and Electoral Assistance (n.d.) 'Gender quotas database', *International IDEA.* Available at: https://www.idea.int/data-tools/data/gender-quotas-database/quotas (Accessed 11 March 2025).

International Labour Organization (2020) *Global Wage Report 2020–21.* Available at: https://www.ilo.org/sites/default/files/wcmsp5/groups/public/@dgreports/@dcomm/@publ/documents/publication/wcms_762534.pdf (Accessed: 11 March 2025).

Inter-Parliamentary Union (2016), 'Sexism, harassment and violence against women parliamentarians', Issue Briefs. Available at: https://www.ipu.org/resources/publications/issue-briefs/2016-10/sexism-harassment-and-violence-against-women-parliamentarians (Accessed: 11 March 2025).

Inter-Parliamentary Union (n.d.) 'Data on Women in Parliament: Uganda', *IPU.* Available at: https://data.ipu.org/parliament/UG/UG-LC01/data-on-women/ (Accessed: 11 March 2025).

Iversen, T. and Rosenbluth, F. (2010) *Women, Work, and Politics.* New Haven, CT: Yale University Press.

Jeater, D. (2006) 'The British Empire and African Women in the Twentieth Century', in P. D. Morgan and S. Hawkins (eds.), *Black Experience and the Empire.* Oxford: Oxford University Press. https://doi.org/10.1093/acprof:oso/9780199290673.003.0009

Jenkins, S. (2013) 'Margaret Thatcher's Falklands gamble', *The Guardian*, 9 April. Available at: https://www.theguardian.com/politics/2013/apr/09/margaret-thatcher-falklands-gamble (Accessed: 11 March 2025).

Jenkins, S. (2012) 'Falklands war: Thatcher's 30-year legacy', *The Guardian*, 1 April. Available at: https://www.theguardian.com/uk/2012/apr/01/falklands-war-thatcher-30-years. (Accessed 11 March 2025)

Jester, N. (2019) 'Army recruitment video advertisements in the US and UK since 2002: Challenging ideals of hegemonic military masculinity?', *Media, War & Conflict*, 14(1), pp. 65 – 66. https://doi.org/10.1177/1750635219859488.

Jester, Natalie. "Army recruitment video advertisements in the US and UK since 2002: Challenging ideals of hegemonic military masculinity?." Media, War & Conflict 14, no. 1 (2021): 57 – 74.

Jin, X., Liu, L., Li, Y., Feldman, M. W. and Li, S. (2013) '"Bare branches" and the marriage market in rural China: Preliminary evidence from a village-level survey', *Chinese Sociological Review*, 46(1), pp. 83 – 104. Available at: https://www.ncbi.nlm.nih.gov/pmc/articles/PMC4512178/ (Accessed: 11 March 2025).

Johnson, P. M. (1994) 'A Glossary of Political Economy Terms.' Available at: https://webhome.au burn.edu/~johnspm/gloss/comparative_advantage.phtml (Accessed: 2 February 2025).

Johnson, A. (n.d.) 'Phyllis Schlafly. National Women's History Museum.' Available at: https://www.womenshistory.org/education-resources/biographies/phyllis-schlafly (Accessed: 11 March 2025).

Jones, A. (2021) 'Be a man: Why some men respond aggressively to threats to manhood', *Duke Today*, 28 January. Available at: https://today.duke.edu/2021/01/be-man-why-some-men-respond-aggressively-threats-manhood (Accessed: 11 March 2025).

Jozuka, E. (2016) 'Study finds millions of China's "missing girls" actually exist', *CNN*, 1 December. Available at: https://www.cnn.com/2016/12/01/asia/china-missing-girls/index.html (Accessed: 11 March 2025).

Juhn, C., Ujhelyi, G. and Villegas-Sanchez, C. (2014) 'Men, women, and machines: How trade impacts gender inequality', *Journal of Development Economics*, 106, pp. 179 – 193.

Kandiyoti, D. (1988) 'Bargaining with patriarchy', *Gender & Society*, 2(3), pp. 274 – 290.

Karam, F. and Zaki, C. (2024) 'When trade agreements are gender-friendly: Impact on women empowerment using firm data', *Journal of Economic Integration*, 39(4), pp. 875 – 898. Available at: https://www.jstor.org/stable/27343220 (Accessed: 12 March 2025).

Kareko, R. T. (2019) 'Female Engagement Teams', *Army University Press*, 25 October. Available at: https://www.armyupress.army.mil/Journals/NCO-Journal/Archives/2019/October/Female-Engagement-Teams/ (Accessed: 11 March 2025).

Keck, M. E. and Sikkink, K. A. (2014) *Activists beyond borders: Advocacy networks in international politics.* Cornell University Press.

Kennedy, L. (2019) 'How the Falklands War Cemented Margaret Thatcher's Reputation as the 'Iron Lady'', *HISTORY*, 3 May. Available at: https://www.history.com/news/margaret-thatcher-falklands-war (Accessed: 11 March 2025).

Kern, A., Reinsberg, B. and Lee, C., (2024) 'The unintended consequences of IMF programs: Women left behind in the labor market', *The Review of International Organizations*, 8(3), pp. 1 – 27. https://doi.org/10.1007/s11558-024-09542-7

Khan, S. (2019) 'Making Democracy Work for Women: Essays on Women's Political Participation in Pakistan' (Doctoral dissertation, Columbia University). https://doi.org/10.7916/d8-tj97-6064

Khan, S. (2017) 'Count me out: Gendered preference expression in Pakistan', Matt Golder Research Newsletter, Spring. Available at: https://mattgolder.com/files/research/newsletter_spring2017.pdf# (Accessed: 11 March 2025).

Khan, Sarah. "Making Democracy Work for Women: Essays on Women's Political Participation in Pakistan." PhD diss., Columbia University, 2020.

Khan, A., Tant, E. and Harper, C. (2023) 'Framing paper: The backlash against gender equality and women's rights', *ALIGN*, July. Available at: https://www.alignplatform.org/sites/default/files/2024-03/align-framingpaper-backlash-mar24-es.pdf (Accessed: 11 March 2025).

Kiefer, M. (2022) 'Of predators and new men: how ideology matters in constructing military masculinities', *Zeitschrift für Friedensund Konfliktforschung*, 11(1), pp. 41–63. https://doi.org/10. 1007/s4259702100068y.

Kilman, C. (2013) 'The Gender Spectrum', *Learning for Justice*, 14 May. Available at: https://www. learningforjustice.org/magazine/summer-2013/the-gender-spectrum (Accessed: 11 March 2025).

King, A. (2016) 'The female combat soldier', *European Journal of International Relations*, 22(1), pp. 122–143. https://doi.org/10.1177/1354066115581909

King, A. (2015) 'Women warriors: Female accession to ground combat', *Armed Forces & Society*, 41, pp. 379–387. https://doi.org/10.1177/0095327X14532913

Kleykamp, M., Wenger, J. B., Roer, E. H., Kubasak, M., Hubble, T., Skrabala, L., Rinderknecht, R. G., Saba, S. K., Verástegui, J. V. and Williams, K. M. (2024) 'Federal and Nonprofit Support for Veterans Transitioning to the Civilian Workforce', *Rand.org*, 24 October. Available at: https:// www.rand.org/pubs/research_briefs/RBA1363-3.html (Accessed: 11 March 2025).

Klugman, J. (2024) 'The Gender Dimensions of Forced Displacement: A Synthesis of New Research', *World Bank*, p. 1–47 Available at: https://documents.worldbank.org/en/publication/documents-reports/documentdetail/895601643214591612/the-gender-dimensions-of-forced-displacement-a-synthesis-of-new-research (Accessed: 11 March 2025).

Knowyourmeme (n.d.) 'Make Me a Sandwich.' Available at: https://knowyourmeme.com/memes/ make-me-a-sandwich (Accessed: 11 March 2025).

Korkman, Z. K. and Aciksoz, C. 'Erdogan's Masculinity and the Language of the Gezi Resistance', *Jadaliyya* (2013).

Kouchaki, M., Leavitt, K., Zhu, L. and Klotz, A. C. (2023) 'Research: What Fragile Masculinity Looks Like at Work', *Harvard Business Review*, 26 January. Available at: https://hbr.org/2023/01/ research-what-fragile-masculinity-looks-like-at-work (Accessed: 11 March 2025).

Kratochvíl, P. and O'Sullivan, M. (2023) 'A war like no other: Russia's invasion of Ukraine as a war on gender order', *European Security*, 32(3), pp. 347–366. https://doi.org/10.1080/09662839. 2023.2236951

Krook, M. L. and O'Brien, D. Z. (2012) 'All the president's men? The appointment of female cabinet ministers worldwide', *The Journal of Politics*, 74(3), pp. 840–855. https://doi.org/10.1017/ S0022381612000382

Krook, M. L. and Restrepo Sanín, J. R. (2020) 'The cost of doing politics? Analyzing violence and harassment against female politicians', *Perspectives on Politics*, 18(3), pp. 740–755. https://doi. org/10.1017/S1537592719001397

Kurtzleben, D. (2017) 'Female retired Marine with viral campaign ad hopes to bridge gap in Democratic Party', *NPR*, 3 August. Available at: https://www.npr.org/2017/08/03/541223715/ female-retired-marine-with-viral-campaign-ad-hopes-to-bridge-gap-in-democratic-p (Accessed: 11 March 2025).

Kwan, J., Sparrow, K., Facer-Irwin, E., Thandi, G., Fear, N. T. and MacManus, D. (2020) 'Prevalence of intimate partner violence perpetration among military populations: A systematic review and meta-analysis', *Aggression and Violent Behavior*, 53, 101419. https://doi.org/10.1016/j.avb. 2020.101419.

Ladbury, S. (2009) 'Testing Hypotheses on Radicalisation in Afghanistan', Open Library, Kabul: Independent Report for the Department of International Development (DFID). Available at: https://openlibrary.org/books/OL31074516M/Testing_hypotheses_on_radicalisation_in_Afghani stan (Accessed 4 February 2025).

Lahey, K. A. and de Villota, P. (2013) 'Economic Crisis, Gender Equality, and Policy Responses in Spain and Canada', *Feminist Economics*, 19(3), pp. 82–107. Available at: https://doi.org/10.1080/13545701.2013.812267 (Accessed: 11 March 2025).

LaMantia, B. (2024) 'Why Olympian Ilona Maher Wears Lipstick While Playing Rugby', *The Cut*, 26 August. Available at: https://www.thecut.com/article/why-olympian-ilona-maher-wears-lipstick-while-playing-rugby.html (Accessed: 11 March 2025).

Langdon, G. (2019) 'Why Are Feminist Theorists in International Relations so Critical of UNSCR 1325?', *E-International Relations*, 11 February. Available at: https://www.e-ir.info/2019/02/11/why-are-feminist-theorists-in-international-relations-so-critical-of-unscr-1325/ (Accessed: 11 March 2025).

Latella, L. (2023) 'The Pressure on Feminist Foreign Policy', *American-German Institute*. Available at: https://americangerman.institute/2023/12/the-pressure-on-feminist-foreign-policy/_(Accessed: 11 March 2025).

Learning for Justice Staff. (2017) 'Madres de Plaza de Mayo', *Learning for Justice*. Available at: https://www.learningforjustice.org/classroom-resources/texts/madres-de-plaza-de-mayo (Accessed 11 March 2025).

Leuven, V., Mazurana, D. and Gordon, R. (2016) 'Analysing the Recruitment and Use of Foreign Men and Women in ISIL through a Gender Perspective', in *Foreign Fighters under International Law and Beyond*, pp. 97–120. https://doi.org/10.1007/9789462650992_7

Little, B. (2021) 'Kennedy and Khrushchev: The showdown at the Vienna summit', *HISTORY*, 13 July. Available at: https://www.history.com/news/kennedy-krushchev-vienna-summit-meeting-1961 (Accessed: 11 March 2025).

Litvinova, D. (2024) 'Putin's crackdown casts a wide net, ensnaring the LGBTQ+ community, lawyers and many others', *AP News*, 6 March. Available at: https://apnews.com/article/russia-putin-crackdown-opposition-lgbtq-election-d9c96f550e6c0cb61363003c735fabec (Accessed: 11 March 2025).

Liu, S. J. S. (2022) 'Gender gaps in political participation in Asia', *International Political Science Review*, 43(2), pp. 209–225. https://doi.org/10.1177/0192512120935517

Loken, M. and Matfess, H. (2023) 'Introducing the Women's Activities in Armed Rebellion (WAAR) project, 1946–2015', *Journal of Peace Research*, 61(3), pp. 489–499. https://doi.org/10.1177/00223433221128340

Luciak, I. A. (2003). After the revolution: Gender and democracy in El Salvador, Nicaragua, and Guatemala. JHU Press.

Mackenzie, J. (2024) 'South Korea politician blames women for rising male suicides', *BBC News*, 9 July. Available at: https://www.bbc.com/news/articles/cml2kvd2dvno (Accessed: 11 March 2025).

Mama, A. (1995) 'Feminism or femocracy? State feminism and democratisation in Nigeria', *Africa Development: A Quarterly Journal of CODESRIA*, 20, pp. 37–58.

Manekin, D. and Wood, R. M. (2020) 'Framing the narrative: Female fighters, external audience attitudes, and transnational support for armed rebellions', *Journal of conflict resolution*, 64(9), pp. 1638–1665. https://doi.org/10.1177/0022002720912823

Mansell, J., Harell, A., Thomas, M. and Gosselin, T. (2022) 'Competitive loss, gendered backlash, and sexism in politics', *Political Behavior*, 44(1), pp. 455–476. https://doi.org/10.1007/s11109-021-09724-8

Mansilla-Domínguez, J. M., Recio-Vivas, A. M., Lorenzo-Allegue, L., Cachón-Pérez, J. M., Esteban-Gonzalo, L. and Palacios-Ceña, D. (2024) 'The role of duty, gender and intergenerational care in grandmothers' parenting of grandchildren: a phenomenological qualitative study', *BMC Nursing*, 23(477), pp. 1–10. https://doi.org/10.1186/s12912-024-02151-0

Marcos, M. A. T. (2023) 'Three-Generation Households Can Boost Female Employment', *Inter-American Development Bank*.

Maringira, G. (2021) 'Soldiers, Masculinities, and Violence', *Current Anthropology*, 62(S23), pp. S103–S111. https://doi.org/10.1086/711687.

Martin, P. (1944) 'Tonight at the Beachhead Bijou', *The Saturday Evening Post*, 12 August. Available at: https://www.columbia.edu/cu/lweb/digital/collections/rbml/lehman/pdfs/0103/ldpd_leh_0103_0030.pdf (Accessed 3 February 2025).

Martuscelli, C. (2023) 'EU populist right want you to make more babies – Viktor Orbán's policy', *Politico*, 11 September. Available at: https://www.politico.eu/article/eu-populist-right-want-you-make-more-babies-viktor-orban (Accessed: 11 March 2025).

Masters, J. (2024) 'What Are Economic Sanctions?' *Council on Foreign Relations*, 24 June. Available at: https://www.cfr.org/backgrounder/what-are-economic-sanctions#:~:text=Economic%20sanctions%20are%20defined%20as,aid%20reductions%2C%20and%20trade%20restrictions (Accessed: 11 March 2025).

Matfess, H. (2023) 'New frontiers in rebel socialisation: considering care and marriage', *Civil Wars*, 25(2–3), pp. 472–491.

Maynes, C. (2021) 'Russia Lifts Soviet-Era Rules On What Jobs Women Can Do', *National Public Radio*, 24 March. Available at: https://www.npr.org/2021/03/24/980638866/russia-lifts-soviet-era-rules-on-what-jobs-women-could-do (Accessed: 11 March 2025).

Mbah, N. L. (2019). *Emergent Masculinities: Gendered Power and Social Change in the Biafran Atlantic Age*. Ohio University Press.

Mean Girls (2004) Mark Waters (dir.) [film]. Paramount Pictures. 00 h 33 m 55s.

Meger, S. (2016) *Rape Loot Pillage: The Political Economy of Sexual Violence in Armed Conflict*. Oxford University Press. https://doi.org/10.1093/acprof:oso/9780190277666.001.0001

Messerschmidt, J. W. (2007) 'On Whiteness, Masculinities, And Lynching: Race, gender, and punishment: From colonialism to the war on terror.'

Messman-Rucker, A. (2025) 'Tariffs will put hair on your chest! Fox News' 'manly' defense of the Trump policy is bizarre', *Pride*. Available at: https://www.yahoo.com/news/tariffs-put-hair-chest-fox-233236384.html (Accessed: 11 March 2025).

Meyer-Parlapanis, D., Weierstall, R., Nandi, C., Bambonyé, M., Elbert, T. and Crombach, A. (2016) 'Appetitive Aggression in Women: Comparing Male and Female War Combatants', *Frontiers in Psychology*, 6, 26779084. https://doi.org/10.3389/fpsyg.2015.01972

Moghadam, V. M. (2024) 'The gendered politics of Iran-US relations: sanctions, the JCPOA and women's security', *Third World Quarterly*, 45(7), pp. 1199–1218. https://doi.org/10.1080/01436597.2024.2314005

Moloney, A. and Iricibar, V. (2024) 'Argentina's austerity measures under Javier Milei put women at risk, say activists', *The Irish Times*, 5 August 2024. Available at: https://www.irishtimes.com/world/americas/2024/08/05/argentinas-austerity-measures-under-javier-milei-put-women-at-risk-say-activists/ (Accessed: 11 March 2025).

Moncrief, S. (2017) 'Military socialization, disciplinary culture, and sexual violence in UN peacekeeping operations', *Journal of Peace Research*, 54(5), p. 715–730. https://doi.org/10.1177/0022343317716784.

Mongilio, H. (2022) 'Latest Military Sexual Assault Report Shows 'Tragic' Rise in Cases, Pentagon Officials Say', *USNI News*, 1 September. Available at: https://news.usni.org/2022/09/01/latest-military-sexual-assault-report-shows-tragic-rise-in-cases-pentagon-officials-say (Accessed: 11 March 2025).

Morgan, W. M. (2023) 'The Cuban Missile Crisis at 60', *Marine Corps History*. Available at: https://www.usmcu.edu/Outreach/Marine-Corps-University-Press/MCH/Marine-Corps-History-Summer-2023/The-Cuban-Missile-Crisis-at-60 (Accessed: 11 March 2025).

Moss, S. M. (2020) 'An introduction to Swedish feminist foreign policy', *Nordics.Info* and *Aarhus University*. Available at: https://nordics.info/show/artikel/swedish-feminist-foreign-policy (Accessed: 11 March 2025).

Mukhtarova, T., Baig, F. A. and Hasnain, Z. (2021) 'Five facts on gender equity in the public sector', *World Bank Blogs*, 27 September. Available at: https://blogs.worldbank.org/en/governance/five-facts-gender-equity-public-sector (Accessed: 11 March 2025).

Murray, R. (2024) 'The substantive representation of men: Intersectionality, masculinities, and men's interests', *European Journal of Political Research.* https://doi.org/10.1111/1475-6765.12684

Mutie, S. M. (2018) 'Self-mythologization in East African Political Writings: Kenyatta, Nyerere and Museveni', *Eastern African Literary and Cultural Studies*, 4(1), pp. 1–34. https://doi.org/10.1080/23277408.2017.1413828

Myrttinen, H. (2018) 'Stabilizing or Challenging Patriarchy? Sketches of Selected 'New' Political Masculinities', *Men and Masculinities*, 22(3), pp. 563–581. https://doi.org/10.1177/1097184X18769137

National Veteran Suicide Prevention Annual Report (2022) *VA Suicide Prevention Office of Mental Health and Suicide Prevention.*

National Women's History Museum (2012) *Coverture: The Word You Probably Don't Know But Should.* Available at: https://www.womenshistory.org/articles/coverture-word-you-probably-dont-know-should (Accessed: 20 February 2025).

NBC News (2024) 'Killing of Brazilian politician Marielle Franco exposes alleged ties between police and politicians', *NBC News*, 1 April. Available at: https://www.nbcnews.com/news/latino/killing-brazilian-politician-marielle-franco-exposes-alleged-ties-poli-rcna145876 (Accessed: 11 March 2025).

Neville-Shepard, R. and Kelly, C. R. (2020) 'Whipping it out: Guns, campaign advertising, and the White masculine spectacle', *Critical Studies in Media Communication*, 37(5), pp. 466–479. https://doi.org/10.1080/15295036.2020.1813902 (Accessed: 11 March 2025).

New York Civil Liberties Union (NYCLU) (2024) 'United States v. Windsor: Challenging the Federal Defense of Marriage Act.' Available at: https://www.nyclu.org/court-cases/united-states-v-windsor-challenging-federal-defense-marriage-act (Accessed: 11 March 2025).

Nicholson, L. (2017) 'Pity China's "bare branches": unmarried men stuck between tradition and capitalism', *Reuters*, 27 January. Available at: https://theconversation.com/pity-chinas-bare-branches-unmarried-men-stuck-between-tradition-and-capitalism-68592 (Accessed: 11 March 2025).

Nickerson, M. M. (2014) *Mothers of conservatism: Women and the postwar right.* Princeton: Princeton University Press.

Norwegian Labour and Welfare Administration (n.d.) *Unemployment benefit (dagpenger).* Available at: https://www.nav.no/dagpenger/en#what (Accessed: 22 February 2025).

Novelly, T. (2025) 'Air Force Officer Who Advocated for Women in Leadership Roles Removed from Command', *Military.com,* 4 February. Available at: https://www.military.com/daily-news/2025/01/23/air-force-officer-who-advocated-women-leadership-roles-removed-command.html (Accessed 4 February 2025).

O'Brien, D. Z. (2019) 'Female leaders and citizens' perceptions of political parties', *Journal of Elections, Public Opinion and Parties*, 29(4), pp. 465–489. https://doi.org/10.1080/17457289.2019.1669612

O'Connell, A. B. and Roberts, M. L. (2016) 'Reviewed Work: *What Soldiers Do: Sex and the American G.I. in World War II France* by Mary Louise Roberts', *The Journal of American History*, 103(1), pp. 152–154. Available at: https://www.jstor.org/stable/48560060 (Accessed: 4 March 2025).

Office of the Assistant Chief of Staff for Installation Management (2019) 'Soldier and Family Readiness Groups', *STAND-TO!*, 16 August. Available at: https://www.army.mil/standto/archive/2019/08/16/ (Accessed: 11 March 2025).

Okereke, C. (2023) 'How evangelical Christians in Africa are fueling homophobia and Uganda's anti-gay bill', *Foreign Policy*, 19 March. Available at: https://foreignpolicy.com/2023/03/19/africa-uganda-evangelicals-homophobia-antigay-bill/ (Accessed: 11 March 2025).

Okun, R. (2023) 'Father's Day activism: Dads fight for change on gun violence, climate crisis and more', *Ms. Magazine*, 18 June. Available at: https://msmagazine.com/2023/06/18/fathers-day-activism-gun-violence-climate-change/ (Accessed: 11 March 2025).

Olken, B. A. (2010) 'Direct democracy and local public goods: Evidence from a field experiment in Indonesia', *American political science review*, 104(2), pp. 243–267. https://doi.org/10.1017/S0003055410000079

Olya, G. (2023) 'Women Spend Nearly $1K on Their Appearance Each Year: See How Their Spending Compares to Men's', *Yahoo Finance*, 8 March. Available at: https://finance.yahoo.com/news/women-spend-nearly-1k-appearance-200011279.html (Accessed: 11 March 2025).

Ormhaug, C., Meier, P. and Hernes, H. (2009) 'Armed Conflict Deaths Disaggregated by Gender', p. 11–26. Available at: https://cdn.cloud.prio.org/files/57e53f14-19b1-42bb-9540-f5b4cbfe2dba/Armed%20Conflict%20Deaths%20Disaggregated%20by%20Gender.pdf?inline=true (Accessed: 11 March 2025).

OXFAM International (n.d.) 'Not all gaps are created equal: the true value of care work'. Available at: https://www.oxfam.org/en/not-all-gaps-are-created-equal-true-value-care-work#:~:text=Women%20and%20girls%20undertake%20more,unpaid%20care%20work%20every%20day (Accessed: 18 February 2025)

Oyěwùmí, O. (1997) *Making an African Sense of Western Gender Discourses*. NED – New edition ed. [online], University of Minnesota Press. Available at: http://www.jstor.org/stable/10.5749/j.ctttt0vh (Accessed: 31 January 2025).

Padilla, M. (2024) 'Trump rally protector for women', *19th News*, 30 October. Available at: https://19thnews.org/2024/10/trump-rally-protector-women/ (Accessed: 31 January 2025).

Paechter, C. (2018) 'Rethinking the possibilities for hegemonic femininity: Exploring a Gramscian framework', *Women's Studies International Forum*, 68, pp. 121–128. https://doi.org/10.1016/j.wsif.2018.03.005

Paling, E. (2016) 'Justin Trudeau ushers in new political masculinity: Study', *The Huffington Post*, 29 May. Available at: https://www.huffpost.com/archive/ca/entry/justin-trudeau-ushers-in-new-political-masculinity-study_n_10199328 (Accessed: 31 January 2025).

Parmanand, S. (2020) 'Duterte as the macho messiah: Chauvinist populism and the feminisation of human rights in the Philippines', *Review of Women's Studies*, 29(2), pp. 1–30.

Parker, K. (2017) 'Americans see different expectations for men and women', *Pew Research Center*. Available at: https://www.pewresearch.org/social-trends/2017/12/05/americans-see-different-expectations-for-men-and-women (Accessed: 31 January 2025).

Parker, K., Horowitz, J. M. and Stepler, R. (2017) On gender differences, no consensus on nature vs. nurture', *Pew Research Center*, December 5. Available at: https://www.pewresearch.org/social-trends/2017/12/05/on-gender-differences-no-consensus-on-nature-vs-nurture/ (Accessed: 31 January 2025).

Parkinson, S. E. (2021) 'Practical ideology in militant organizations', *World Politics*, 73(1), 52–81.

Parliament of Rwanda (2024) *Women Representation*. Available at: https://www.parliament.gov.rw/women-representation (Accessed: 31 January 2025).

PeaceWomen (n.d.a) 'The resolutions.' Available at: https://www.peacewomen.org/why-WPS/solutions/resolutions (Accessed: 31 January 2025).

PeaceWomen (n.d.b) 'National Action Plans at a Glance.' Available at: https://1325naps.peacewomen.org/#:~:text=NATIONAL%20ACTION%20PLANS:%20AT%20A,are%20on%20their%20fifth%20NAP (Accessed: 31 January 2025).

Perrin, A. (2018) '5 facts about Americans and video games', *Pew Research Center*, September 17. Available at: https://www.pewresearch.org/short-reads/2018/09/17/5-facts-about-americans-and-video-games/ (Accessed: 7 March 2025).

Perry, K. (2022) 'Better for whom? Sanction type and the gendered consequences for women', *International Relations*, 36(2), pp. 151–175. https://doi.org/10.1177/00471178211018843.

Peteet, Julie. *Gender in crisis: Women and the Palestinian resistance movement*. Columbia University Press, 1992.

Peterson, V. S., ed. (1992) *Gendered states: Feminist (re) visions of international relations theory*. Lynne Rienner Publishers.

Pettman, J.J. (1996) *Worlding Women: A Feminist International Politics*. London: Routledge. Available at: https://doi.org/10.4324/9780203991442 (Accessed: 4 February 2025).

Pew Research Center (2013) 'Broad Support for Combat Roles for Women', *Pew Research Center*, 29 January. Available at: https://www.pewresearch.org/politics/2013/01/29/broad-support-for-combat-roles-for-women/ (Accessed: 4 February 2025).

Pingali, P. L. (2012) 'Green Revolution: Impacts, limits, and the path ahead', *Proceedings of the National Academy of Sciences of the United States of America*, 109(31), pp. 12302–12308. Available at: https://doi.org/10.1073/pnas.0912953109 (Accessed: 16 July 2025).

Pletcher, K. (2025) 'Consequences of China's one-child policy', *Encyclopaedia Britannica*. Available at: https://www.britannica.com/topic/one-child-policy/Consequences-of-Chinas-one-child-policy (Accessed: 16 July 2025).

Population Matters (2024) 'Welcome to Gilead Report', *Population Matters*. Available at: https://populationmatters.org/resources/welcome-to-gilead-report/ (Accessed: 16 July 2025).

Population Matters (2021) 'Disturbing rise in countries coercing women into having more children, report finds', *Population Matters*. Available at: https://populationmatters.org/disturbing-rise-in-countries-coercing-women-into-having-more-children-report-finds/ (Accessed: 16 July 2025).

Porter, H. and Davidson, A., (2009) 'Qaddafi: The Vanity Fair photo album', *Vanity Fair*, 12 August. Available at: https://www.vanityfair.com/news/photos/2009/08/qaddafi-slideshow200908 (Accessed: 16 July 2025).

Post, A. S. and Sen, P. (2020) 'Why can't a woman be more like a man? Female leaders in crisis bargaining', *International Interactions*, 46(1), pp. 1–27. https://doi.org/10.1080/03050629.2019.1683008

Pratt, N. and Richter-Devroe, S., 2011. 'Critically examining UNSCR 1325 on women, peace and security', *International Feminist Journal of Politics*, 13(4), pp. 489–503.

Prillaman, S. A. (2023) *The Patriarchal Political Order: The Making and Unraveling of the Gendered Participation Gap in India.* Cambridge University Press.

Proceedings of the National Academy of Sciences (PNAS) (2024) 'Children perceive gendered division of household work', PNAS Podcast/Post. Available at: https://www.pnas.org/post/podcast/children-perceive-gendered-division-household-work (Accessed: 16 July 2025).

Purba, J. N. (2024) 'Defying Patriarchy: South Korea's 4B Movement and Women's Rejection of 'Future-Maker' Role', *Modern Diplomacy*, 12 September. Available at: https://moderndiplomacy.eu/2024/09/12/defying-patriarchy-south-koreas-4b-movement-and-womens-rejection-of-future-maker-role/#:~:text=Through%20various%20strategies%20and%20tactics,does%20not%20consider%20women%27s%20perspectives (Accessed: 19 February 2025).

r/navy (2025) 'Website Filtered', Reddit. Available at: https://www.reddit.com/r/navy/comments/1gjgvtj/i_get_the_weirdest_targeted_ads/?rdt=40404 (Accessed: 3 February 2025).

r/Navy (n.d.) 'I get the weirdest targeted ads.' Available at: https://www.reddit.com/r/navy/comments/1gjgvtj/i_get_the_weirdest_targeted_ads/ (Accessed: 19 February 2025).

Radio Free Europe/ Radio Liberty (2024) 'Wives, Mothers Of Mobilized Russian Troops In Rare Protest At Defense Ministry In Moscow', June 3. Available at: https://www.rferl.org/a/russia-moscow-wives-mothers-mobilized-soldiers-ukraine/32977644.html (Accessed: 3 February 2025).

Raley, S. and Bianchi, S. (2006) 'Sons, daughters, and family processes: Does gender of children matter?', *Annual Review of Sociology*, 32(1), pp. 401–421. https://doi.org/10.1146/annurev.soc.32.061604.123106

Ramdas, K. (2015) 'Beyond 'backwater' island to global city vision? Rethinking feminist geographies for Singapore after Lee Kuan Yew', *Geoforum*, 65, pp. 108–111.

Ramesh, R. (2005) 'Kissinger sorry for deriding Mrs Gandhi', *The Guardian*, 1 July. Available at: https://www.theguardian.com/world/2005/jul/02/india.randeepramesh2 (Accessed: 3 February 2025).

Rana, S. (2020) 'The Populist Backlash to Gender Equality in International Fora: Analyzing Resistance and Response at the United Nations', *Maryland Journal of International Law*, 35, pp. 156–171. Available at: https://ssrn.com/abstract=3769714 (Accessed: 3 February 2025).

Ray, R. and Enloe, C. (2002) 'Maneuvers: the international politics of militarizing women's lives', *Contemporary Sociology*, 31(2), pp. 187–189. https://doi.org/10.2307/3089511

Remedios, M. (2024) 'Afghanistan Under the Taliban: The social and economic costs of gender apartheid', *Future for Advanced Research and Studies*, 15 April. Available at: https://futureuae.com/en-US/Mainpage/Item/9158/afghanistan-under-the-taliban-the-social-and-economic-costs-of-gender-apartheid (Accessed: July 16, 2025).

Rennebohm, M. (2009) 'Icelandic women strike for economic and social equality, 1975.' Available at: https://nvdatabase.swarthmore.edu/content/icelandic-women-strike-economic-and-social-equality-1975 (Accessed: 19 February 2025).

Restrepo Sanín, J. (2020) 'Violence against women in politics: Latin America in an era of backlash', *Signs: Journal of Women in Culture and Society*, 45(2), pp. 302–310. https://doi.org/10.1086/704954

Reuss, A. and Titeca, K. (2017) 'When revolutionaries grow old: the Museveni babies and the slow death of the liberation', *Third World Quarterly*, 38(10), pp. 2347–2366. https://doi.org/10.1080/01436597.2017.1350101

Reuters (2020) 'Trump steel tariffs raised prices, shriveled up demand, led to job losses, some Michigan workers say', October 9. Available at: https://www.nbcnews.com/business/economy/

trump-steel-tariffs-raised-prices-shriveled-demand-led-job-losses-n1242695 (Accessed: 19 February 2025).

Revkin, M. R. and Wood, E. J. (2021) 'The Islamic State's Pattern of Sexual Violence: Ideology and Institutions, Policies and Practices', *Journal of Global Security Studies*, 6(2). https://doi.org/10. 1093/jogss/ogaa038.

Rich, A. (2021) *Of Woman Born: Motherhood as experience and institution*. WW Norton & Company.

Rice, J. K. (2002) 'Poverty, Welfare, and Patriarchy: How Macro-Level Changes in Social Policy Can Help Low-Income Women', *Journal of Social Issues*, 57(2), pp. 355–374. https://doi.org/10.1111/ 0022-4537.00218.

Riley, H. (2021) *Rethinking masculinities: Ideology, identity and change in the people's war in Nepal and its aftermath*. Rowman & Littlefield.

Robinson, A. L. and Gottlieb, J., (2021) 'How to close the gender gap in political participation: Lessons from matrilineal societies in Africa', *British Journal of Political Science*, 51(1), pp. 68–92. https://doi.org/10.1017/S0007123418000650

Rodríguez, F. (2024) 'The human consequences of economic sanctions', *Journal of Economic Studies*, 51(4), pp. 942–963. https://doi.org/10.1108/JES-06-2023-0299

Ross, K. (2024) 'The Minimum Wage is a Poverty Wage', *Center for American Progress*, 24 July. Available at: https://www.americanprogress.org/article/the-minimum-wage-is-a-poverty-wage/ (Accessed: 11 March 2025).

Roth, K. (2015) 'Slavery: The ISIS Rules', *Human Rights Watch*, 5 September. Available at: https:// www.hrw.org/news/2015/09/05/slavery-isis-rules (Accessed: 11 March 2025).

Rubin, A. (2025) 'Trump starts military overhaul by ousting first female Coast Guard commandant', *Axios*, 21 January. Available at: https://www.axios.com/2025/01/21/trump-military-coast-guard-commandant (Accessed: 4 February 2025).

Rudd, K. (2022) 'The Return of Red China', *Foreign Affairs*, 9 November. Available at: https://www. foreignaffairs.com/china/return-red-china (Accessed: 4 February 2025).

Ruiz, F., Burgo-Black, L., Hunt, S. C., Miller, M. and Spelman, J. F. (2022) 'A Practical Review of Suicide Among Veterans: Preventive and Proactive Measures for Health Care Institutions and Providers', *Public Health Reports*, 138(2), 003335492210852. https://doi.org/10.1177/ 00333549221085240.

RuPaul, C. (2014) *Born Naked*. RuCo Inc.: Luciane Piane.

Sack, E. J. (2010) 'Is Domestic Violence a Crime?: Intimate Partner Rape as Allegory', *Journal of Civil Rights and Economic Development*, 24(3), pp. 535–566.

Sainsbury, D. (2025) 'Gender, Policy Regimes, and Politics', in D. Sainsbury (ed.), *Gender and Welfare State Regimes*. Oxford: Oxford University Press, pp. 245–276.

Sánchez, R., Finot, J., and Villena, M. G. (2020) 'Gender Wage Gap and Firm Market Power: Evidence from Chile', IZA Discussion Papers, No. 13856, Institute of Labor Economics (IZA), Bonn.

Sandberg, S. (2013) *Lean in: Women, Work, and the Will to Lead*. New York: Alfred A. Knopf.

Sanders, L. (2024) 'Election: Harris, Trump, women, Latinos, Black voters', *AP News*, 7 November. Available at: https://apnews.com/article/election-harris-trump-women-latinos-black-voters-0f3fbda3362f3dcfe41aa6b858f22d12 (Accessed: 11 March 2025).

Sanderson, E. (2023) 'The unholy relationship between Uganda's anti-LGBTQ law and the US', *Global Affairs*, 8 June. Available at: http://globalaffairs.org/commentary-and-analysis/blogs/ unholy-relationship-between-ugandas-anti-lgbtq-law-and-us (Accessed: 11 March 2025).

Santos, A.P. (2018) 'The Price of 'Machismo Populism' in the Philippines', *The Atlantic*. Available at: https://www.theatlantic.com/international/archive/2018/06/duterte-kiss-philippines/562265/?gift=YoX4fGH-gweEGNihinvmRsPWfUmGtRcoecOxwcCjdv0&utm_source=copy-link&utm_medium=social&utm_campaign=share_(Accessed: 11 March 2025).

Schippers, M. (2007) 'Recovering the feminine other: masculinity, femininity, and gender hegemony', *Theory and Society*, 36(1), pp. 85–102. https://doi.org/10.1007/s11186-007-9022-4.

Schneider, S. H., Gödderz, A., Zille, H. and Sassenhagen, N. (2024) 'Who supports feminist development policy? Evidence from Germany', *European Journal of Politics and Gender*, 7(2), pp. 291–295.

Schramm, M. and Stark, A. (2020) 'Peacemakers or iron ladies? A cross-national study of gender and international conflict', *Security Studies*, 29(3), pp. 515–548. https://doi.org/10.1080/09636412.2020.1763450

Schwartz, D. (2022) 'Does testicle tanning work—and is it safe? A doctor explains', *VICE*, 20 April. Available at: https://www.vice.com/en/article/does-testicle-tanning-work-is-it-safe-according-to-a-doctor-tucker-carlson-testosterone/ (Accessed: 11 March 2025).

Searcey, D. and Boushnak, L. (2020) 'They Ordered Her to Be a Suicide Bomber. She Had Another Idea', *The New York Times*, 23 July. Available at: https://www.nytimes.com/2020/03/13/world/africa/Nigeria-Boko-Haram-bomber.html (Accessed: 11 March 2025).

Seguino, S. (2020) 'Industrial Policy and Gender Inclusivity', in A. Oqubay, C. Cramer, H. Chang, and R. Kozul-Wright (eds.), *The Oxford Handbook of Industrial Policy*. Oxford, UK, pp. 429–450.

Semu-Banda, P. (2008) 'Politics-Malawi: Elections Get Ugly for Women', *IPS News*, November 24. Available at: http://www.ipsnews.net/2008/11/politics-malawi-elections-get-ugly-for-women/ (Accessed: 11 March 2025).

Shannon, G., Minckas, N., Tan, D., Haghparast-Bidgoli, H., Batura, N. and Mannell, J. (2019) 'Feminisation of the health workforce and wage conditions of health professions: an exploratory analysis', *Human resources for health*, 17, pp. 1–16.

Sharrow, E. A., Rhodes, J. H., Nteta, T. M. and Greenlee, J. S. (2018) 'The first-daughter effect: The impact of fathering daughters on men's preferences for gender-equality policies', *Public Opinion Quarterly*, 82(3), pp. 493–523.

Shekhawat, S. (2015) 'Conflict Peace and Patriarchy: Female Combatants in Africa and Elsewhere', *African center for the Constructive Resolution of Disputes, Conflict Trends*, Issue 4, p. 1–56. Available at: https://www.files.ethz.ch/isn/196205/ct4-2015.pdf (Accessed: 11 March 2025).

Shepherd, L. J. (2016) 'Making war safe for women? National Action Plans and the militarisation of the Women, Peace and Security agenda', *International Political Science Review*, 37(3), pp. 324–335.

Sherman, C. (2024) 'Tradwives, TikTok, and women's gender roles', *The Guardian*, 24 July. Available at: https://www.theguardian.com/lifeandstyle/nginteractive/2024/jul/24/tradwives-tiktok-women-gender-roles (Accessed: 11 March 2025).

Shine, I. (2023) 'These countries have the highest childcare costs in the world', *World Economic Forum*, 19 July. Available at: https://www.weforum.org/stories/2023/07/highest-childcare-costs-by-country/ (Accessed: 11 March 2025).

Sikkink, K. A. and Clapp, H. (2024) 'How Feminist Foreign Policies Work to Enhance Gender Justice', *Georgetown Journal of International Affairs*. Available at: https://gjia.georgetown.edu/2024/02/18/how-feminist-foreign-policies-work-to-enhance-gender-justice/ (Accessed: 11 March 2025).

Singal, J. (2017) 'Having a daughter makes dads more politically polarized', *The Cut*, 13 December. Available at: https://www.thecut.com/2017/12/having-a-daughter-makes-dads-more-politically-polarized.html (Accessed: 11 March 2025).

Sjoberg, L. (2016) 'Witnessing the protection racket: Rethinking justice in/of wars through gender lenses', *International Politics*, 53(3), pp. 361–384. https://doi.org/10.1057/ip.2016.5

Sjoberg, L. (2013) *Toward a Feminist Theory of War*. Columbia University Press. Available at: http://www.jstor.org/stable/10.7312/sjob14860 (Accessed: 4 February 2025).

Sjoberg, L. (2010) 'Women fighters and the 'beautiful soul' narrative', *International Review of the Red Cross*, 92(877), pp. 53–68. https://doi.org/10.1017/s181638311000010x

Sjoberg, L. and Gentry, C.E. (2007) *Mothers, monsters, whores: women's violence in global politics*. Zed Books.

Sjoberg, L. and Peet, J. (2011) 'A(nother) Dark Side of the Protection Racket: Targeting Women in Wars', *International Feminist Journal of Politics*, 13(2), pp. 163–182. https://doi.org/10.1080/14616742.2011.560751.

Sjoberg, L. and Tickner, J. A. 'Introduction: International Relations through feminist lenses', in *Feminism and international relations*. Routledge, 2013.

Sjoberg, L., Via, S. E. and Enloe, C. H. (2010) *Gender, war, and militarism: feminist perspectives*. Available at: https://api.semanticscholar.org/CorpusID:141516070 (Accessed: 11 March 2025).

Skewes, L., Fine, C. and Haslam, N., (2018) 'Beyond Mars and Venus: The role of gender essentialism in support for gender inequality and backlash', *Plos one*, 13(7), 0200921.

Skujins, A. and AP (2024) 'We never let them in: Hungary's PM Viktor Orbán demands new laws tackling migration', *Euronews*, 6 September. Available at: https://www.euronews.com/my-europe/2024/09/06/we-never-let-them-in-hungarys-pm-viktor-orban-demands-new-laws-tackling-migration (Accessed: 11 March 2025).

Smith, J. C. (2021) 'Bulldozing Brexit: The role of masculinity in UK party leaders' campaign imagery in 2019 UK general election', *Journal of Elections, Public Opinion and Parties*, 31(4), pp. 450–469. https://doi.org/10.1080/17457289.2021.1968414

Smith, D. J. (2017) *To be a man is not a one-day job: Masculinity, money, and intimacy in Nigeria*. Chicago: University of Chicago Press.

Smithsonian National Portrait Gallery (2024) 'Lyndon Johnson and the Johnson Treatment'. Available at: https://npg.si.edu/blog/lyndon-johnson-and-johnson-treatment (Accessed: 11 March 2025).

Smith, A. (2014) 'Nigeria's Boko Haram Islamists Mock #BringBackOurGirls Effort', *NBC News*, 14 July. Available at: https://www.nbcnews.com/storyline/missing-nigeria-schoolgirls/nigerias-boko-haram-islamists-mock-bringbackourgirls-effort-n155091 (Accessed: 7 May 2024).

Sommers, M. and Schwartz, S. (2011) *Dowry and Division*. US Institute of Peace.

Sophie's Choice (1982) Pakula, A. J. (dir.) [film]. Universal Pictures.

Southern Poverty Law Center Learning for Justice (n.d.) 'Madres de Plaza de Mayo.' Available at: https://www.learningforjustice.org/classroom-resources/texts/madres-de-plaza-de-mayo (Accessed: 11 March 2025).

Speckhard, A. and Ellenberg, M. (2021) 'ISIS and the Allure of Traditional Gender Roles', *Women & Criminal Justice*, 33(2), pp. 150–170. https://doi.org/10.1080/08974454.2021.1962478.

Spencer, A. N. (2016) 'An Analysis of the Women in Islamic State', *Journal of Strategic Security*, 9(3), pp. 74–98. Available at: http://www.jstor.org/stable/26473339 (Accessed: 17 February 2025).

Spivak, G. C. (1988) *Can the subaltern speak?: Reflections on the History of an Idea*. Columbia University Press.

Spriggs, A. S. (2021) 'Discover Mitch Marner's pregame routines and superstitions', *Red Bull*. Available at: https://www.redbull.com/ca-en/pregame-rituals-mitch-marner (Accessed: 11 March 2025).

Stacey, D. (2024) 'Femonationalism in Europe: How the far right disguises xenophobia as freedom.' *El Pais*. Available at: https://english.elpais.com/international/2024-08-09/femonationalism-in-europe-how-the-far-right-disguises-xenophobia-as-freedom.html (Accessed: 11 March 2025).

Stein, J. (2006) 'Warriors and Wusses', *Los Angeles Times*, 24 January. Available: https://www.latimes.com/archives/la-xpm-2006-jan-24-oe-stein24-story.html (Accessed: 11 March 2025).

Stellenbosch Business School (2022) 'Equal pay but unequal taxes – SA women carry a greater tax burden.'

Stern, M. and Strand, S. (2022) 'Periods, Pregnancy, and Peeing: Leaky Feminine Bodies in Swedish Military Marketing', *International Political Sociology*, 16(1). https://doi.org/10.1093/ips/olab025.

Steyerl, H. (2017) 'The Color of Women: An Interview with YPJ Commanders Dilovan Kobani, Nirvana, Ruken, and Zerin – Journal #86', *E-flux.com*. Available at: https://www.e-flux.com/journal/86/160968/the-color-of-women-an-interview-with-ypj-commanders-dilovan-kobani-nirvana-ruken-and-zerin (Accessed: 4 February 2025).

Stryżyńska, W. (2023) 'Men want to increase care work at home but social structures block it, report says', *The Guardian*, 18 July. Available at: https://www.theguardian.com/global-development/2023/jul/18/men-want-to-care-but-social-structures-prevent-them-doing-more-at-home-report-finds (Accessed: 4 February 2025).

Strzyżyńska, W., and Kumar, R. (2023) "Gut-churning': anger as Hungarian president addresses major women's rights conference', *The Guardian*, July 19. Available at: https://www.theguardian.com/global-development/2023/jul/19/gut-churning-anger-as-hungarian-president-addresses-major-womens-rights-conference (Accessed: 4 February 2025).

Suleiman, O. (2021) 'Disentangling the nexus between gender inequality and political instability', *Bush School of Government & Public Service*. Available at: https://bush.tamu.edu/wp-content/uploads/2021/07/Suleiman-Paper-No.-20.pdf (Accessed: 4 February 2025).

Swift, J. A. (2018) 'Meet Dr. Sharrelle Barber: The social epidemiologist who met Afro-Brazilian activist Marielle Franco on the day of her assassination', *Black Women Radicals*. Available at: https://www.blackwomenradicals.com/blog-feed/meet-dr-sharrelle-barber-the-social-epidemiologist-who-met-afro-brazilian-activist-marielle-franco-on-the-day-of-her-assassination (Accessed: 4 February 2025).

Synenko, A. (2024) 'Opinion | Sexual Violence in War Is Not Inevitable', *The New York Times*, 2 December. Available at: https://www.nytimes.com/2024/12/02/opinion/sexual-violence-war.html (Accessed: 4 February 2025).

Tanyag, M. (2018) 'Duterte, Hypermasculinity and the Key to Populism', *Australian Institute of International Affairs*. Available at: https://lens.monash.edu/2018/03/07/1327081/duterte-hypermasculinity-and-the-key-to-populism (Accessed: 4 February 2025).

Taub, A. (2014) 'How Australia's twisted racial politics created horrific detention camps for immigrants', *Vox*, 4 November. Available at: https://www.vox.com/2014/11/4/7138391/australia-racism-immigration-asylum (Accessed: 4 February 2025).

Tebaldi, C. (2023) 'Tradwives and truth warriors', *Gender and Language*, 17(1), pp. 14–38. https://doi.org/10.1558/genl.18551

Teele, D. L., Kalla, J. and Rosenbluth, F. (2018) 'The ties that double bind: social roles and women's underrepresentation in politics', *American Political Science Review*, 112(3), pp. 525–541. https://doi.org/10.1017/S0003055418000217

Tekna (2022) *Social welfare in Norway: The nuts and bolts.* Available at: https://www.tekna.no/en/career/a-career-in-norway/social-welfare-in-norway-the-nuts-and-bolts/ (Accessed: 11 March 2025).

Textor, C. (2025) 'Sex ratio in China 1953–2024', *Statista*, 17 January. Available at: https://www.statista.com/statistics/251102/sex-ratio-in-china/ (Accessed: 11 March 2025).

The Bridge (2019) 'Factsheet: Operation Sovereign Borders.' Available at: https://bridge.georgetown.edu/research/factsheet-operation-sovereign-borders/ (Accessed: 11 March 2025).

The Clayman Institute for Gender Research (2014) *Male 'identity threat' can disadvantage women in high-status professions.* Available at: https://gender.stanford.edu/news/male-identity-threat-can-disadvantage-women-high-status-professions (Accessed: 11 March 2025).

The Donor Committee for Enterprise Development (n.d.) *Industrial Policy.* Available at: https://www.enterprise-development.org/implementing-psd/industrial-policy/ (Accessed: 11 March 2025).

The Economist (2023) 'The age of the grandparent has arrived', 12 January. Available at: https://www.economist.com/international/2023/01/12/the-age-of-the-grandparent-has-arrived (Accessed: 22 February 2025).

The Economist (2004) 'Nudity, drinking, smoking: Winston Churchill's unusual diplomacy', 27 August. Available at: https://www.economist.com/culture/2024/08/27/nudity-drinking-smoking-winston-churchills-unusual-diplomacy (Accessed: 22 February 2025).

The Guardian (2015) 'Lee Kuan Yew – the best quotes from Singapore's founding father', 22 March. Available at: https://www.theguardian.com/world/2015/mar/23/lee-kuan-yew-the-best-quotes-from-singapores-founding-father (Accessed: 22 February 2025).

The Harris Poll (2023) *Are grandmothers who provide childcare key in driving the US economy?* Available at: https://theharrispoll.com/briefs/are-grandmothers-who-provide-childcare-key-in-driving-the-us-economy/ (Accessed: 22 February 2025).

The White House (2025) 'Fact Sheet: President Donald J. Trump Declares National Emergency to Increase our Competitive Edge, Protect our Sovereignty, and Strengthen our National and Economic Security.' Available: https://www.whitehouse.gov/fact-sheets/2025/04/fact-sheet-president-donald-j-trump-declares-national-emergency-to-increase-our-competitive-edge-protect-our-sovereignty-and-strengthen-our-national-and-economic-security/ (Accessed: 11 March 2025).

The White House. (2001) 'Radio Address by Mrs. Bush.' Available at: https://georgewbush-whitehouse.archives.gov/news/releases/2001/11/20011117.html (Accessed: 22 February 2025).

The World Bank (n.d.) 'The World Bank in Singapore'. Available: https://www.worldbank.org/en/country/singapore/overview (Accessed: 22 February 2025).

Tickner, J. A. and Sjoberg, L. (2013) *Feminism and International Relations: Conversations about the Past, Present and Future.* Routledge. https://doi.org/10.4324/9780203816813

Tilly, L.A. (1994) 'Women, Women's History, and the Industrial Revolution', *Social Research*, 61(1), pp. 115–137. Available at: https://www.jstor.org/stable/40971024 (Accessed: 25 February 2025).

True, J. (2009) 'Trading-off gender equality for global Europe? The European Union and free trade agreements', *European foreign affairs review*, 14(5), pp. 723–742. Available at: https://research.monash.edu/en/publications/trading-off-gender-equality-for-global-europe-the-european-union- (Accessed: 4 February 2025).

Tucker, C. J., McHale, S. M. and Crouter, A. C. (2003) 'Dimensions of mothers' and fathers' differential treatment of siblings: Links with adolescents' sex-typed personal qualities', *Family Relations*, 52(1), pp. 82–89. https://doi.org/10.1111/j.1741-3729.2003.00082.x

Twaij, A. (2016) '"I hate this beard, by God": Iraqi men celebrate freedom in Mosul by shaving', *The Guardian*, 8 November. Available at: https://www.theguardian.com/global/2016/nov/08/i-hate-this-beard-by-god-iraqi-mosul-men-celebrate-freedom-by-shaving (Accessed: 7 March 2025).

UNICEF Data (2023) 'Gender norms and unpaid work.' Available at: https://data.unicef.org/topic/gender/gender-norms-and-unpaid-work/ (Accessed: 19 February 2025).

United Nations Trade and Development (2024) 'Global Trade Update (July 2024).' Available at: https://unctad.org/publication/global-trade-update-july-2024#:~:text=Global%20forecasts%20for%20GDP%20growth,record%20level%20seen%20in%202022 (Accessed: 7 March 2025).

United Nations and She Stands for Peace (n.d.) 'The Four Pillars of United Nations Security Council Resolution 1325.' Available at: https://www.un.org/shestandsforpeace/content/four-pillars-united-nations-security-council-resolution-1325 (Accessed: 10 February 2025).

UN Women (2024) 'In the biggest electoral year in history, 113 countries have never had a woman head of state, new UN Women data shows', *UN Women*, 24 June. Available at: https://www.unwomen.org/en/news-stories/press-release/2024/06/in-the-biggest-electoral-year-in-history-113-countries-have-never-had-a-woman-head-of-state-new-un-women-data-shows (Accessed: 10 February 2025).

UN Women (2022) *Feminist Foreign Policies: An Introduction*. Available at: https://www.unwomen.org/en/digital-library/publications/2022/09/brief-feminist-foreign-policies (Accessed: 10 February 2025).

UN Women (2020) 'Democratic backsliding and the backlash against women's rights.' Available at: https://www.unwomen.org/en/digital-library/publications/2020/06/discussion-paper-democratic-backsliding-and-the-backlash-against-womens-rights (Accessed: 10 February 2025).

Urban Dictionary (2009) 'Sophie's Choice.' Available at: https://www.urbandictionary.com/define.php?term=Sophie%27s%20choice (Accessed: 2 February 2025).

Urban Dictionary (2007a) 'ring by spring.' Available at: https://www.urbandictionary.com/define.php?term=ring%20by%20spring (Accessed: 19 February 2025).

Urban Dictionary (2007b) 'MRS Degree.' Available at: https://www.urbandictionary.com/define.php?term=MRS%20Degree (Accessed: 19 February 2025).

U.S. Bureau of Labor Statistics (2024) 'American Time Use Summary.' Available at: https://www.bls.gov/news.release/atus.nr0.htm#:~:text=%2D%2DOn%20the%20days%20they,with%2022%20percent%20of%20men (Accessed: 10 February 2025).

U.S. Department of Veteran Affairs (2021) 'Common Challenges During Re-adjustment to Civilian Life – Veterans Employment Toolkit', *www.va.gov*. Available at: https://www.va.gov/vetsinworkplace/docs/em_challengesReadjust.asp (Accessed: 10 February 2025).

U.S. House of Representatives (2017) 'Biography of Tim Walz, 115th Congress, House of Representatives, Committee on House Administration' (HHRG-115-HA00-Bio-WalzT-20170215). Available at: https://www.congress.gov/115/meeting/house/105558/witnesses/HHRG-115-HA00-Bio-WalzT-20170215.pdf (Accessed: 10 February 2025).

Upton, R. E. 2018. "It Gives Us a Power and Strength which We Do Not Possess': Martiality, manliness, and India's Great War enlistment drive', *Modern Asian Studies*, 52(6), pp. 1977–2012.

Uwen, G. S. O. and Eyang, A. E. (2023) 'Officers and men, and fallen heroes: The discursive construction of regimented masculinity in the Nigerian Army', in *Forum for Linguistic Studies* (Vol. 5, No. 3), p. 1–14.

Valdini, M. E. (2019) *The inclusion calculation: Why men appropriate women's representation.* Oxford University Press.

Van der Gaag, N., Gupta, T., Heilman, B., Barker, G. and van den Berg, W. (2023) 'State of the World's Fathers 2023 Centering Care in a World in Crisis', *equimundo.org, diakses pada* 3.

Van Hooker, B. (2024) 'Lyndon B. Johnson's obsession with his penis, explained', *MEL Magazine.* Available at: https://melmagazine.com/en-us/story/lyndon-b-johnson-penis (Accessed: 11 March 2025).

Van Hooker, Brian (2022) 'An Exceedingly Historical Account of 'Jumbo,' LBJ's Very Large Penis', *Mel Magazine*, 12 May.

Van Veen, S., Verkade, A., Ukwuagu, C. and Muthoni, M. (2018) 'Breaking a culture of silence: Social norms that perpetuate violence against women and girls in Nigeria', *Oxfam.* Available at: https://policy-practice.oxfam.org/resources/breaking-a-culture-of-silence-social-norms-that-perpetuate-violence-against-wom-620458/ (Accessed: 11 March 2025).

Vescio, T. K., Schermerhorn, N. E., Gallegos, J. M. and Laubach, M. L. (2021) 'The affective consequences of threats to masculinity', *Journal of Experimental Social Psychology*, 97, 104195. https://doi.org/10.1016/j.jesp.2021.104195

Volman, D. (2024) 'Why African homophobia is still the real Western import', *Foreign Policy in Focus*, 6 May. Available at: https://fpif.org/why-african-homophobia-is-still-the-real-western-import/ (Accessed: 11 March 2025).

Walsh, J. (2025) 'Trump's Tariff Pause Sets Back the "Make Men Manly Again" Movement', *The Nation.* Available at: https://www.thenation.com/article/politics/trump-tariff-manliness/ (Accessed: 11 March 2025).

Wang, S. (2023) 'Do women always represent women? The effects of gender quotas on substantive representation', *Political Behavior*, 45(4), pp. 1979–1999. https://doi.org/10.1007/s11109-022-09808-z

Watson Institute for International and Public Affairs (2001) 'Human and Budgetary Costs to Date of the U.S. War in Afghanistan, 2001-2022.' Available at: https://watson.brown.edu/costsofwar/figures/2021/human-and-budgetary-costs-date-us-war-afghanistan-2001-2022 (Accessed: 11 March 2025).

Webster, K., Chen, C. and Beardsley, K. (2019) 'Conflict, peace, and the evolution of women's empowerment', *International Organization* [online], 73, pp. 255–289. Available at: https://api.semanticscholar.org/CorpusID:159366084 (Accessed: 11 March 2025).

Weichselbaumer, D. and Winter-Ebmer, R. (2007) 'The effects of competition and equal treatment laws on gender wage differentials', *Economic Policy*, 22(50), pp. 236–287.

White, M., Salas, C. and Gammage, S. (2003) 'Trade impact review: Mexico case study NAFTA and the FTAA: a gender analysis of employment and poverty impacts in agriculture', *Women's Edge Coalition*, 1, p. 1–48. Available at: https://www.iatp.org/sites/default/files/NAFTA_and_the_FTAA_A_Gender_Analysis_of_Employ.pdf (Accessed: 11 March 2025).

Wilén, N. and Heinecken, L. (2018) 'Regendering the South African army: Inclusion, reversal and displacement', *Gender, Work & Organization*, 25(6), pp. 670–686. https://doi.org/10.1111/gwao.12257

Wilkinson, C. (2018) 'Mother Russia in queer peril: the gender logic of the hypermasculine state', in *Revisiting Gendered States: Feminist Imaginings of the State in International Relations.* Oxford: Oxford University Press.

Windsor, R. (2025) '4B movement: what is it and how did it start?', *The Week*, 11 January. Available at: https://theweek.com/culture-life/what-is-south-korea-4b-movement (Accessed: 19 February 2025).

Wittlin, N. M., LaFrance, M., Dovidio, J. F. and Richeson, J. A. (2024) 'US cisgender women's psychological responses to physical femininity threats: Increased anxiety, reduced self-esteem', *Journal of Experimental Social Psychology*, 110(104547), pp. 104547–104547. https://doi.org/10.1016/j.jesp.2023.104547

Women and Gender Equality Canada (n.d.) 'What is Gender-based Analysis Plus (GBA+)?', *Government of Canada*. Available at: https://www.canada.ca/en/women-gender-equality/gender-based-analysis-plus/what-gender-based-analysis-plus.html (Accessed: 11 March 2025).

Wood, E. J. and Toppelberg, N. (2017) 'The persistence of sexual assault within the US military', *Journal of Peace Research*, 54, pp. 620–633. Available at: https://api.semanticscholar.org/CorpusID:149272262 (Accessed: 11 March 2025).

World Bank Group (2019) 'Women in Half the World Still Denied Land, Property Rights Despite Laws', 25 May. Available at: https://www.worldbank.org/en/news/press-release/2019/03/25/women-in-half-the-world-still-denied-land-property-rights-despite-laws (Accessed: 20 February 2025).

World Economic Forum (2019) *Global Gender Gap Report 2020*. Available at: https://www3.weforum.org/docs/WEF_GGGR_2020.pdf (Accessed: 20 February 2025).

World Food Program USA (n.d.) 'Women Are Hungrier.' Available at: https://www.wfpusa.org/drivers-of-hunger/women/ (Accessed: 7 February 2025).

Wright, K. A. and Rosamond, A. B. (2024) 'Sweden, NATO and the gendered silencing of feminist foreign policy', *International Affairs*, 100(2), pp. 589–607.

www.todaysmilitary.com. (n.d.) 'Infantry — Today's Military'. Available at: https://www.todaysmilitary.com/careers-benefits/careers/infantry (Accessed: 7 February 2025).

Wyrod, R. (2008) 'Between women's rights and men's authority: masculinity and shifting discourses of gender difference in urban Uganda', *Gender & Society*, 22(6), pp. 799–823. https://doi.org/10.1177/0891243208325888

Yang, K. (2025) 'Accommodating Veterans in China', *China Review*, 25(1), pp. 107–139.

Yazdi-Feyzabadi, V., Zolfagharnasab, A., Naghavi, S., Behzadi, A., Yousefi, M. and Bazyar, M. (2024) 'Direct and indirect effects of economic sanctions on health: a systematic narrative literature review', *BMC Public Health*, 24(1), p. 2242. https://doi.org/10.1186/s12889-024-19750-w

Yeoh, B., Huang, S. and Willis, K. (2000) 'Global cities, transnational flows and gender dimensions: the view from Singapore', *Tijdschrift voor economische en sociale geografie*, 91(2), pp. 147–158.

Yeung, J., Stambaugh, A. and Seo, Y. (2024) 'South Korea government struggles to reverse declining birth rate', *CNN*, 9 May. Available at: https://www.cnn.com/2024/05/09/asia/south-korea-government-population-birth-rate-intl-hnk/index.html (Accessed: 11 March 2025).

You Yenn, T. (2007) 'Inequality for the greater good: Gendered state rule in Singapore', *Critical Asian Studies*, 39(3), pp. 423–445.

Young, I. M. (2003) 'Feminist Reactions to the Contemporary Security Regime', *Hypatia*, 18(1), pp. 223–231. https://doi.org/10.1111/j.1527-2001.2003.tb00792.x.

Young, M. B. and Buzzanco, R. (eds.) (2008) *A Companion to the Vietnam War*. Oxford: Blackwell Publishing. Available at: https://www.google.com/books/edition/A_Companion_to_the_Vietnam_War/WsULqb6k0BoC (Accessed: 12 March 2025).

Yuccas, J. and Novak, A. (2024) 'Rugby Olympian Ilona Maher Is Breaking Stereotypes and Empowering Women through Social Media', *CBS News*, July 29. https://www.cbsnews.com/

news/olympian-ilona-maher-rugby-breaking-stereotypes-empowering-women-through-social-media/ (Accessed: 12 March 2025).

Zahay, M. L. (2022) 'What "Real" Women Want: Alt-Right Femininity Vlogs as an Anti-Feminist Populist Aesthetic', *Media and Communication*, 10(4), pp. 170–179. https://doi.org/10.17645/mac.v10i4.5726

Zaremberg, G., Tabbush, C. and Friedman, E. J. (2021) 'Feminism (s) and anti-gender backlash: lessons from Latin America', *International Feminist Journal of Politics*, 23(4), pp. 527–534. https://doi.org/10.1080/14616742.2021.1956093

Index

Note: Page numbers in references following "n" refer notes.

Abbott, T.   152
Abdi, A.   103
Aciksoz, C. S.   49
Action on Armed Violence (AOAV)   131
Agarwal, B.   69
Agius, C.   148, 152
agricultural revolution
– in Rwanda   73–74, 89–90
Ahmed, S.   179
Alesina, A.   63
Alter, K. J.   159
Angelou, M.   25
appetitive aggression
– male and female combatants   124
armed groups
– femininity and recruitment   113–120
– Islamic State recruitment   112–113
– militarized masculinity   108–111
– participation in war   108–109
– political violence and promise of equality
    114–116
– socialization   122–130
Ashwin, S.   47
Assad, B.   112, 148
Atwood, M.   33, 180
– *The Handmaid's Tale*   33
austerity programs   81
– and liberalization   97–99

Babül, E. M.   150
backlash   159–160
– anticipating   171
– bargaining with patriarchy   160, 162
– domestic   164–169
– fertility-focused   166
– against gender equality   157–160
– at individual level   169–170
– international   163–164
– and intimate partner violence (IPV)   169
– precarious masculinity   160–161
Backlash (Faludi)   159

Balboa, R.   181
Bannon, I.   112, 134
Barnett, K.   81
Barrera, J.   28
Becker, G.   58–59, 61
bell hooks   180
Berry, M.   9, 169
Bianchi, S.   26
Biden, J.   95, 175
Billström, T.   145
birth rates
– in China   33–34
– in Hungary   32–33
Boko Haram   19
– female suicide bombers in   133–134
– Safe House   34
Bowen, D. L.   142
Brewster, R.   94, 95
#BringBackOurGirls campaign   133–134
Bringe, K.   66
British Army
– recruitment ads and gender equality   115–
    116
Brown, K. E.   149
Bush, L.   140

Calarco, J.   62
campaign trail design
– female political elite behavior   40–42
– male political elite behavior   45–47
Campbell, H.   98, 99
Captain America   108
Carlson, T.   170
Castro, F.   50
Checkel, J. T.   26, 123
Chibok abductions   133–134
childcare programs
– and grandparental support   85–86
– in United States   84–86, 86n4
– variation among countries'   84–86
Childs, S.   45, 52

China
- One-Child Policy   33 – 34
Churchill, W.   48
Cohen, D. K.   127 – 128, 130 – 131
collective action
- Icelandic women's strike   69 – 70
comparative advantage
- household economy/economics   58
- international trade   92 – 93
Corbin, J.   46
Correia, M. C.   112, 134
Council on Foreign Relations   99
coverture   75 – 76
- and male guardianship system   76
- and women's physical security   77
- on women's property rights   76
Creed, A.   181
Cupac, J.   9

Davidson-Schmich, L. K.   23, 37
DDR programs   135 – 136
"Dead Aim" (America campaign ads)   46
demobilization process   134
descriptive representation
- female political elite behavior   44 – 45
- male political elite behavior   51 – 52
Dietrich Ortega, L. M.   126
DiMuccio, S.   8
division of labor   19 – 20, 59, 63 – 64
domestic economy
- government spending   82 – 88
- policy   74
- property laws and women's participation in
    78
- see also economics
domestic politics   20 – 21
domestic violence   136
- see also violence
Drury, A. C.   102
Duriesmith, D.   148 – 149, 152
Duterte, R.   41, 152 – 153

Ebetürk, I.   9
economics   74 – 82
- governments' economic policies   74, 88 – 89
- see also government spending; household
    economy/economics

economic sanctions
- Council on Foreign Relations   99
- Cuba   101
- drug shortages   100 – 101
- effect on civil society   101
- government cuts to public education   101
- Iran   100 – 103
- Pompeo's model of policy change   100
- public health effects   100 – 101
- societal-wide economic insecurity   102
- on women's labor force participation   102
- Yugoslavia   100 – 101
egalitarianism   72, 125
- backlash against   163, 170
- economic development   89
Eichler, M.   108
Eisenhower, D. D.   50
Eisenstein, Z.   148
Eksi, B.   48
Elshtain, J. B.   109
Eltahawy, M.   167
emasculation   9
Empowerment, Knowledge and Transformative
    Action (EKATA)   91
Engelbrecht, M.   50
Enloe, C.   20, 132, 138
Equal Pay for Equal Work Law (2009)   79
Erdogan, T.   48 – 49
export processing zones (EPZs)   99
Eyang, A. E.   126

Fagan, L.   120
Faludi, S.   159 – 160
- Backlash   159
Family and Medical Leave Act (FMLA)   84
Farabundo Martí National Liberation Front
    (FMLN)   126 – 127
FARC see Revolutionary Armed Forces of Colom-
    bia (FARC)
Farris, S. R.   12
fatherhood   30 – 31
Female Engagement Teams (FET)   140
female political elite behavior   40 – 45
- on campaign trail   40 – 42
- counterparts during crisis bargaining   43
- in office   42 – 43
- quota vs. non-quota   45

– substantive and descriptive representation
44 – 45
femininity   7
– under gender hierarchy   9 – 11
– hegemonic   11, 12
– and military recruitment   113 – 120
– performance   11
– in public   179 – 180
feminist foreign policy (FFP)   144
– Canada   96
– Germany   145
– Sweden   144 – 145
femocracies   45
fertility-focused backlash politics   166
Field, E.   78
Folbre, N.   62, 66, 69
"4B movement," South Korea   69 – 71
fragile masculinity   8 – 9
– see also masculinity
Franco, M.   168
fratriarchy   124 – 125
Fridkin, K. L.   41
Fry, R.   66

Gaddafi, M.   36
Gammage, S.   94
Gandhi, I.   36, 40, 52 – 53
Gao, M.   70
Gay, R.   179
gender apartheid   79
gender-based analysis plus (GBA+)   96
gender budgeting   89
gender discrimination   79, 88, 116
gender equality   89, 96
– backlash against   157 – 160
– limits to militarism for   116 – 118
– political violence   114 – 116
– in Rwanda   161
– Sweden's feminist foreign policy   144 – 145
gender essentialism   5, 7, 40 – 41
gender gap in politics   22 – 25, 35
– see also participation in politics; political preference gap
gender hierarchy   4 – 5, 7 – 8, 13, 173
– as analytical framework   13
– and expectations   20
– femininity under   9 – 11

– and government spending   82 – 88
– international system   178 – 179
– intersectionality   11 – 13
– masculinity under   8 – 9
– in national politics   175 – 178
– on personal lives   174 – 175
– see also economics; political elite behavior
gender inequality   9, 15, 22, 62 – 64
gender norms   5 – 7, 21, 39
– household economy/economics   64 – 67
gender quotas 38 – 39, 45
gender stereotypes   40 – 41
Gentry, C. E.   114
Geva, D.   40
Gezi Park Protests   48
Gill, L.   111, 126
Giovarelli, R.   77
Giuliano, P.   63
Goldin, C.   62
government economic regulations   74 – 75,
88 – 89
– labor conditions   78 – 80
– property   75 – 78
– taxation   80 – 82
government spending   82 – 88
– childcare programs   84 – 86
– development and industrial policies   86 – 88
– welfare programs   82 – 83
green revolution   73
– government regulations   74 – 82
– governments' economic policies   74, 88 – 89
Grossman, D.   123
Grown, C.   81

The Handmaid's Tale (Atwood)   33
hegemonic femininity   11, 12
hegemonic masculinity   8, 11, 12
Hegseth, P.   120, 145 – 146
Heinecken, L.   129
Herrera, N.   117
Hobson, B.   62
home
– as apolitical space   20
– gendered socialization in   25 – 26, 35
– women's responsibilities in   23
household economy/economics   57
– altruism in   59

– bargaining   58, 62, 67 – 71
– comparative advantage   58
– division of labor   19 – 20, 59, 63 – 64
– feminist interrogation   62
– foundational studies   61
– gendered consequences of   59 – 63
– gender norms and   64 – 67
– rationality   58
– specialization   58, 59, 61 – 62
– unpaid care work   60 – 61
Huang, S.   86
Hudson, V.   113, 142
Hughes, M.   52
Hurl-Eamon, J.   111
hypermasculinity   46, 47, 129
– *see also* masculinity

Iceland   69 – 70
industrial policy   87 – 88
international economy   91 – 92
– austerity programs and liberalization   97 – 99
– economic sanctions   99 – 103
– trade agreements   92 – 97
– Trump's gendered protectionism   94 – 96
international financial institutions (IFIs)   97 – 99
International Monetary Fund (IMF)   89, 98 – 99
International Parliamentary Union (IPU)   167
international politics   20 – 21, 25
– backlash in   163 – 164
international security   107, 141
international trade   92 – 97
– Canada's feminist foreign policy   96
– comparative advantage   92 – 93
– countries winners and losers   93
– gender provisions   96 – 97
– gender-sensitive trade policies   96
– Mexico   93 – 94
– specialization   93
– Trump's gendered protectionism   94 – 96
intersectionality   4 – 5, 11 – 13
intimate partner violence (IPV)   136, 169
– *see also* violence
Iraq Body Count   131
Iversen, T.   21, 64, 65, 67 – 68

Johnson, B.   46
Johnson, L. B.   50 – 51

Kandiyoti, D.   11, 162
Kelly, C. R.   46n3
Kemper, B.   95
Kennedy, J. F.   50 – 51
Kenney, P. J.   41
Khan, S.   22, 23
Khrushchev, N.   50
Kim Jong-il   149
Kim Jung-un   149
King, A.   128, 130
Kishi, R.   9, 169
Kissinger, H.   36
Knowles, E.   8
Korkman, Z. K.   49
Kristersson, U.   144
Krook, M. L.   43, 168

labor conditions, government regulations   78 – 80
land tenure systems
– in India   77
– in Uganda   77
– women's property rights and security   77 – 78
land titling program   78
– *Lean In* (Sandberg)   4
– Lee Kwan Yew   87
– Le Pen, M.   40
– Lima, L. de   153

Madame la Présidente   42
Magufuli, J.   165
Maher, I.   7
male political elite behavior   45 – 52
– on campaign trail   45 – 47
– in office   48 – 51
– substantive and descriptive representation   51 – 52
Mama, A.   44
Manchin, J.   46
Maringira, G.   126
Marner, M.   6
marriage   31 – 35, 59, 81
masculinist/masculine protection   109 – 110, 146, 147n2
– Australia's immigration policy   151 – 152

– civilians and combatants in war zones   131–
   132
– colonization and imperial expansion   148
– Duriesmith's narratives   148–149, 152
– Duterte's   152–153
– Iraqi women's critique   150
– Islamic State   149
– logic of   141
– norms   131, 148
– state as   147–153
– Sweden as humanitarian superpower   148
– Wilkinson's narrative   151
masculinity   8–9
– election performances   46
– hegemonic   8, 11, 12
– in hockey   6–7
– intra-male competition   47
– Johnson and Corbyn's campaign   46–47
– Johnson's Vietnam war performance   50–51
– Kennedy's Cold War performances   50–51
– male candidates performing   45
– Murray's cultures   52
– Museveni's performance   49–50
– policing in boys   8
– precarity of   160–161
– psychological studies   10
– Putin's public persona   47
– social media era and   170
– street   47
– in Turkish politics   48–49
– and warfare   22
– warfighting and   107–111
– Xi Jinping's public persona   47
– see also hypermasculinity; militarized masculinity
matrescence   28
matrilineality   23–24
Mean Girls movie   11
Messman-Rucker, A.   95
militarized masculinity   108
– femininity and recruitment   113–120
– Islamic State recruitment   112–113
– just warriors and beautiful souls   109–110
– participation in war   108–109
– peacekeeping operations   125
– recruitment ads   110–111
– see also masculinity; socialization

military recruitment see recruitment
Moncrief, S.   125
Monet, C.   13
motherhood
– and gendered political socialization   28–30
– as patriarchal institution   28
– as political identity   29–30
Mothers of Plaza de Mayo   29
Murray, R.   51, 52
Museveni, Y.   49
Sowing the Mustard Seed   49
Myrttinen, H.   124, 125

National Action Plans (NAPs)   143, 146
national economies see economics
Nehru, J.   52–53
Neville-Shepard, R.   46n3
Nielsen, P. L.   142
9/11 (September 11) attacks   140
non-lethal violence   131, 137
North American Free Treaty Agreement (NAFTA)
   93–94
Novák, K.   166
Nunn, N.   63

O'Brien, D. Z.   43
Okereke, C.   164
Okun, R.   31
One-Child Policy (China)   33–34
Operation Sovereign Borders (OSB)   151–152
Orbán, V.   32, 166
Oyewùmí, O.   13n1

Palin, S.   40
Parmanand, S.   153
participation in politics   22–25
– collective organizing   23
– cross-national studies   23
– patrilineal vs. matrilineal communities   24
– structural marginalization   39
– see also political preference gap
patriarchal bargain   11, 160, 162
patriarchy   7–8, 11, 33
– feminist curiosity and   174
– industrial and postindustrial societies   64
pay gap   78–79
peacekeeping operations   125

Peet, J. 133
Peksen, D. 102
Perry, K. 101
Person Other than Grunt (POG) 123
Peteet, J. 127
Peterson, J. 62, 170
Pingali, P. L. 73
"pink ghetto" 43, 88
political elite behavior 36 – 37, 40 – 52
– on campaign trail 40 – 42, 45 – 47
– female 40 – 45
– male 45 – 52
– in office 42 – 43, 48 – 51
– substantive and descriptive representation 44 – 45, 51 – 52
political party 37 – 40
– candidates winnowing and selection process 37 – 38
– decision-making processes 38
– gender quotas 38 – 39
political preference gap 20
– matrilineal societies 23 – 24
– men's 22
– women's 21 – 22
political socialization 27 – 31
– fatherhood 30 – 31
– motherhood 28 – 30
– see also socialization
political violence 114 – 116
– see also violence
Pompeo, M. 100
Pope Francis 153
Porch, D. 117
Prillaman, S. A. 22, 23
property
– government economic regulations 75 – 78
Purba, J. N. 70
Putin, V. 47

Raley, S. 26
Ramdas, K. 87
Rana, S. 163
rational actor/rationality 58, 97
Reagan, R. 82
recruitment 113 – 120
– American military 116
– British military 115 – 116
– Islamic State masculinity 112 – 113
– Swedish military 116
Restrepo Sanín, J. R. 168
Revolutionary Armed Forces of Colombia (FARC) 115, 117
Revolutionary United Front (RUF) 127
Rice, J. K. 83
Rich, A. 28 – 29
Riley, H. 125, 134
Rodríguez, F. 100
Roosevelt, F. D. 48
Rosamond, A. B. 145
Rosenbluth, F. 21, 64, 65, 67 – 68
Royal African Company (RAC) 75
Rudd, K. 47
RuPaul 5, 6
Ruto, W. 167

Salas, C. 94
Samba-Panza, C. 40
Sandberg, S. 4, 6
– Lean In 4
Sandinista National Liberation Front (FSLN) 119
Schippers, M. 11
Schlafly, P. 44
Seguino, S. 87, 88
sexual violence 132 – 133, 132n4
– see also violence
Shekhawat, S. 135
Sherman, C. 158
Sjoberg, L. 109, 114, 133, 147
slut-shaming 41
Smith, J. C. 45, 47
social dominance orientation 22
socialization 26 – 31, 130 – 134
– in armed groups 122 – 130
– civilians in war zones 137 – 138
– under gender hierarchy 24, 35
– in home 25 – 26, 35
– horizontal 122 – 123
– men's 124 – 127
– peacekeeping forces 125
– vertical 122 – 123, 127
– wartime 134 – 137
– women's 127 – 130
Sophie's Choice movie 57, 62, 71

South African National Defense Forces (SANDF)
129–130
Sowing the Mustard Seed (Museveni)   49
specialization
– household economy/economics   58, 59,
61–62
– international trade   93
Spivak, G. C.   12
Steenkamp, L.-A.   80
Streep, M.   57
street masculinity   47
– *see also* masculinity
structural adjustment programs (SAPs)   97–99,
101
substantive representation
– female political elite behavior   44–45
– male political elite behavior   51–52
Sweden
– feminist foreign policy   144–145
– as humanitarian superpower   148
– military recruitment   116

Tanyag, M.   153
taxation   80–82
– balanced budgets and sacrificed women
81–82
– explicit and implicit gender bias   80–81
– marriage penalty   81
Tebaldi, C.   158
Thatcherism   43
Thatcher, M.   43, 152
"the personal is political"   20, 34, 174
Tigray People's Liberation Front (TPLF)   10, 66,
114, 117
Tilly, L. A.   63–64
TradWife   7, 157–158, 169
Trudeau, J.   36
True, J.   96
Trump, D.   36, 70, 120
– gendered protectionism   94–96

unitary model
– household economy/economics   61–62
United Nations Security Council Resolution 1325
(UNSCR 1325)   142–143
Upton, R. E.   111

U.S. Marine Corps   117
US Navy advertisement   107, 110–111
Utrata, J.   47
Uwen, G. S. O.   126

Valdini, M.   38
violence   130–134
– non-lethal   131, 137
– perpetration of   124
– sexual   132–133, 132n4
– *see also* intimate partner violence (IPV)
violence against women in politics (VAWIP)
167
Volman, D.   166

wage gap   78–79
Wallström, M.   144
Wamalwa, B.   77
Watts, S.   29
White, M.   94
Wilén, N.   129
Wilkinson, C.   151
Willis, K.   86
Women, Peace and Security (WPS) agenda
142
– feminist foreign policy   144–145
– participation   143
– protection   143
– relief and recovery   143
– Trump Administration pushback   145–146
Women's Activities in Armed Rebellion (WAAR)
project   119
Wood, E. A.   48
World Food Programme (WFP)   62
Wright, K. A.   145

Xi Jinping   47

Yang, K.   136
Yeoh, B.   86
Yoon Suk Yeol   165
Young, I. M.   109, 141n1, 150
You Yenn, T.   87

Zahay, M. L.   157
Zürn, M.   159

www.ingramcontent.com/pod-product-compliance
Lightning Source LLC
Chambersburg PA
CBHW030320270326
41926CB00010B/1441